English
Français
Deutsche
Italiano
Español
Português

www.forgottenbooks.com

Mythology Photography **Fiction**
Fishing Christianity **Art** Cooking
Essays Buddhism Freemasonry
Medicine **Biology** Music **Ancient
Egypt** Evolution Carpentry Physics
Dance Geology **Mathematics** Fitness
Shakespeare **Folklore** Yoga Marketing
Confidence Immortality Biographies
Poetry **Psychology** Witchcraft
Electronics Chemistry History **Law**
Accounting **Philosophy** Anthropology
Alchemy Drama Quantum Mechanics
Atheism Sexual Health **Ancient History**
Entrepreneurship Languages Sport
Paleontology Needlework Islam
Metaphysics Investment Archaeology
Parenting Statistics Criminology
Motivational

THE

LIFE AND TIMES

OF

James Catnach

"Death made no conquest of this man,
For now he lives in fame, though not in life."

280
WOOD-CUTS,
OF WHICH
42
ARE BY
BEWICK.

THE
Cries of London.

Cherries.

Here's round and sound,
Black and white heart cherries,
Two-pence a pound.

Milk below.

Rain, frost, or snow, or hot
   cold,
  I travel up and down,
The cream and milk you buy
   me
  Is best in all the town.
For custards, puddings, or for t
  There's none like those y
   buy of me.

Oranges.

Here's oranges nice !
  At a very small price,
I sell them all two for a penny.
Ripe, juicy, and sweet,
  Just fit for to eat,
So customers buy a good many.

Crumpling Codlings.

Come, buy my Crumpling C(
  lings,
  Buy all my Crumplings
Some of them you may eat ra
  Of the rest make dumpling:
Or pies, or puddings, which y
  please.

The dog he cut capers, and turned out his toes;
'Twill soon cure the vapours, he such attitude shows.
The dame made a curtsey, the dog made a bow,
The dame said, "your servant," the dog said, "bow wow."

Now, my friends, you have here just printed and pub—lish—ed, the Full, True, and Particular account of the Life, Trial, Character, Confession, Condemnation, and Behaviour, together with an authentic copy of the last **Will and Testament;** or, DYING SPEECH, of that eccentric individual "Old Jemmy Catnach," late of the *Seven Dials,* printer, publisher, toy-book manufacturer, dying-speech merchant, and ballad-monger. Here, you may read how he was bred and born the son of a printer, in the ancient Borough of Alnwick, which is in Northumberlandshire. How he came to London to seek his fortune. How he obtained it by printing and publishing children's books, the chronicling of doubtful scandals, fabulous duels between ladies of fashion, "cooked" assassinations, and sudden deaths of eminent individuals, apocryphal elopements, real or catch-penny accounts of murders, impossible robberies, delusive suicides, dark deeds and public executions, to which was usually attached the all-important and necessary "Sorrowful Lamentations," or, "Copy of Affectionate Verses," which, according to the established custom, the criminal composed, in the condemned cell, the night before his execution.

Yes, my customers, in this book you'll read how Jemmy Catnach made his fortune in Monmouth Court, which is to this day in the Seven Dials, which is in London. Not only will you read how he did make his fortune, but also what he did and what he didn't do with it after he had made it. You will also read how "Old Jemmy" set himself up as a fine gentleman :—

JAMES CATNACH, ESQUIRE,

Dancer's Hill,

South Mimms,

Middlesex.

And how he didn't like it when he had done it. And how he went back again to dear old Monmouth Court, which is in the Seven Dials aforesaid. And how he languished, and languishing, did die—leaving all his old mouldy coppers behind him—and how, being dead, he was buried in

HIGHGATE CEMETERY.

THE

LIFE AND TIMES

OF

JAMES CATNACH,

(LATE OF SEVEN DIALS),

BALLAD MONGER.

BY

CHARLES HINDLEY,

*Editor of "The Old Book Collector's Miscellany; or, a Collection of
Readable Reprints of Literary Rarities," "Works of John Taylor—
the Water Poet," "The Roxburghe Ballads," "The Catnach
Press," "The Curiosities of Street Literature," "The Book
of Ready-Made Speeches," "Life and Adventures of a
Cheap Jack," "Tavern Anecdotes & Sayings," etc.*

LONDON:

REEVES AND TURNER,

196, STRAND, W.C.

1878.

TO

Mr. GEORGE SKELLY,

OF

THE MARKET PLACE,

AND

Mr. GEORGE II. THOMPSON,

OF

BAILIFFGATE,

ALNWICK,

In the County of

NORTHUMBERLAND,

THE

LIFE AND TIMES

OF

JAMES CATNACH

Is most Respectfully

DEDICATED,

As a slight acknowledgement of the several favours
granted and assistance rendered to the

AUTHOR,

during the progress of the Work
through the Press.

CHARLES HINDLEY.

ROSE HILL TERRACE,
BRIGHTON,
January, 1878.

INTRODUCTION.

"THE LIFE AND TIMES OF JAMES CATNACH," owes its origin to the circumstance that, in 1869, the compiler of the present work published "The Catnach Press," and guaranteed only "TWO HUNDRED AND FIFTY COPIES PRINTED—namely: 175 on Fine and 75 on Extra-thick paper. *Each copy numbered.*" The outer and descriptive title set forth that the work contained :—

> "A COLLECTION of Books and Wood-cuts of James Catnach, late of Seven Dials, Printer, consisting of Twenty Books of the Cock Robin Class, from 'This is the House that Jack Built,' to 'Old Mother Hubbard' (printed with great care) *spécialité* at THE CATNACH PRESS, from the old plates and wood-cuts, prior to their final destruction, to which is added a selection of Catnachian wood-cuts, many by Bewick, and many of the most anti-Bewickian character it is possible to conceive."

The announcement of the publication of the work was first made known through the medium of the metropolitan press, some few days prior to the copies being delivered by the bookbinders, and so great was the demand of the London and American trade, that every copy was disposed of on the day of issue. By many, the notice of publication was allowed to go unheeded, thinking, as it often occurs, that such advertisement was only a *ruse*, but they were doomed to disappointment, the publisher and editor rigidly

adhered to their announced number of copies, and Mr. G.
Rutland, the well known and extensive bookseller of
Newcastle-upon-Tyne, is of opinion that not one reached
the North of England, the cradle and birthplace of the two
Catnachs, and the brothers Bewick. The work is now
eagerly sought after by book-collectors, who indulge in
literary rarities.

While engaged in collecting information for "The Catnach
Press," and interviewing the producers of ballads, broadsides
and chap-books, we met with a vast assemblage of street-
papers and of a very varied character, which were
afterwards published in 4to. form, and a limited number of
copies under the title of :—

> "CURIOSITIES OF STREET LITERATURE : Comprising 'Cocks,'
> or 'Catchpennies,' a large and curious assortment of Street-
> Drolleries, Squibs, Histories, Comic Tales, in Prose and Verse,
> Broadsides on the Royal Family, Political Litanies, Dialogues,
> Catechisms, Acts of Parliament and Street Political Papers. A
> variety of 'Ballads on a Subject,' Dying Speeches and Confes-
> sions, to which is attached the all-important and necessary
> Affectionate Copy of Verses.".

The work was published in 1871, and is now out of print.
In the meanwhile we have been collecting additional facts
and scraps in respect to James Catnach's manners and
customs, his birth, parentage, and education. In the
early part of last year, we had the good fortune to get
acquainted with Mr. George Skelly, of Alnwick—who, like
ourselves, is possessed of the *cacoethes scribendi*, and was at
the time supplying, *con amore*, an article to a local journal,
entitled "John and James Catnach," which we found to
contain certain information relative to the elder Catnach,
and also of the earlier portion of the life of James, of which
we had no previous knowledge. At our solicitation to be
allowed to make a selection from the same, we received a
most courteous and gentlemanly letter, which, in addition to

containing several pieces of information and answers to
many queries we had put to Mr. Skelly, he wound up by
saying : " You have full liberty to make use of anything
that I have written, and it will afford me much pleasure if I
can further your intentions in any way."

From that date Mr. George Skelly continued to corres-
pond with us on the subject of the " Two Catnachs," nearly
up to the last moment of our going to press with our own
" Life and Times of James Catnach," and to him we are
greatly indebted for much of the information therein
contained.

Mr. Skelly is fortunate, by his residence in Alnwick, in
having the acquaintance and friendship of Mr. Mark Smith
—James Catnach's fellow apprentice, Mr. Thomas Robertson,
Mr. Tate, the local historian, and several other *Alnwick-
Folk*. And he has made the best possible use of the
circumstances, as our own pages fully testify.

To Mr. George H. Thompson, also of Alnwick, our
thanks being due are hereby given, for the kind and ready
manner in which he volunteered his services to aid and
assist, to the best of his time and ability, in supplying all the
information he possessd or could glean from his friends and
acquaintauces in the good old borough of Alnwick, or the
county at large.

James Catnach, on his arrival in London, seems to have
just fitted to the stirring times. The Peninsular wars had
concluded, politics and party strife ran high, squibs and
lampoons were the order of the day. The battle of
Waterloo immediately followed, "and there was mounting
in hot haste," and a great scrambling for place and power,
by all shades of politicians. In 1816, Princess Charlotte
Augusta, daughter of George, Prince Regent, afterwards
George IV., married Prince Leopold of Saxe Coburg, and
died in childbirth, in 1817. In Spa Fields, London, about
0,000 persons assembled to vote an address from the

distressed manufacturers to the Prince Regent, on the
15th of November, 1816. A second meeting took place on
December 2nd following, and terminated in an alarming
riot; the shops of several gunsmiths were attacked for arms
by the rioters, and in the shop of Mr. Beckwith, on
Snow Hill, Mr. Platt was wounded, and much injury was done
before the tumult was suppressed. For this riot, John
Cashman, the seaman, was hanged in Skinner Street, 12th
March, 1817. Watson, the ringleader, escaped to America.
The Green Bag inquiry took its name from a *Green Bag*, full
of documents of alleged seditions, laid before Parliament by
Lord Sidmouth, February, 1817. Secret committees
presented their reports on the 19th of the month, and bills
were brought in on the 21st to suspend the Habeas Corpus
Act, and prohibit seditious meetings then frequent. Mr.
Henry Hunt, well known as the " Radical Reformer," was
looked up to by many of his party as the fearless champion
of their cause, and consequently kept the country in an
unsettled state, particularly so in connection with the
Manchester reform meeting, called the "Peterloo Massacre,"
which caused many political papers and virulent lampoons
to be, from time to time, published for street sale. 1820
opened with the death of the Duke of Kent and King
George III., and accession of George IV., followed by the
Cato Street Conspiracy, winding up with the memorable
trial of Queen Caroline; all these circumstances, following
as they did in such quick succession, tended very materially
to cause fly-sheets and broadsides to be issued from the
Seven Dials presses in general, and the " Catnach Press "
in particular, in enormous quantities.

Many other circumstances—now matters of history,
caused Catnach to succeed in the peculiar line of business
he had marked out for himself, and as his stock of presses,
type, woodcuts, &c., continued to increase his ways and
means became more and more easy and lucrative, until he

ultimately retired from the business in favour of his sister, in 1838, when he purchased a house and grounds at Dancer's Hill, South Mimms, in the county of Middlesex; but this secluded retreat was not the means of filling the glass of contentment in Jemmy's case; nay, we now know to the contrary, and that he preferred more eagerly the active turmoil of business life and the streets of London, even though—

"God made the country, and man made the town."

Old Jemmy Catnach signally failed to find tongues in trees, books in running brooks, sermons in stones, or good in *anything*—"exempt from public haunt."

During the progress of our work through the press we had, by special appointment, several interviews with, also letters from, Mr. John Morgan, a street author, and who may be said to be the oldest of his peculiar class. "I'm the last one left of our old crew, Sir," he observed, during our conversation. He is now upwards of 70 years of age, and formerly wrote for "Old Jemmy" Catnach, with whose personal history he is well acquainted, and still continues to write for the "Seven Dials Press." In allusion to the Poet !— Mr. John Morgan, the following article entitled "The Bards of the Seven Dials and their Effusions," was published in "THE TOWN," 1839, a weekly journal, conducted by the late Mr. Renton Nicholson, better known as "Baron Nicholson," of Judge and Jury notoriety :—

The Life and Death of John William Marchant, who suffered the extreme penalty of the law, in front of the Debtor's door, Newgate, on Monday, July 8th, 1839, for the murder of Elizabeth Paynton, his fellow servant, on the Seventeenth of May last, in Cadogan Place, Chelsea. By John Morgan. London : J. Catnach, 2 and 3, Monmouth Court, 7 Dials.

The work is a quarto page, surrounded with a handsome black border, "Take no thought for to-morrow, what thou shalt eat, or what thou shalt put on," says a certain writer, whose wisdom we all reverence, and then he adds "Sufficient unto the day is the evil thereof"—a remark particularly applicable to the bards of Seven Dials, whose pens are kept in constant employment by the fires, rapes, robberies, and murders, which, from one year's end to the other, present them with a daily allowance of evil sufficient for their subsistence. But, at present, it is only one of these poets, "John Morgan," as he modestly signs himself, whom we are about to notice ; and as some of our readers may be curious to see a specimen of the poetry of Seven Dials, we shall lay certain portions of John Morgan's last effusion before them, pointing out the beauties and peculiarities of the compositions as we go along. After almost lawyer-like particularity as to dates and places, the poem begins with an invocation from the murderer in *propria persona*.

> " Oh ! give attention awhile to me,
> All you good people of each degree ;
> In Newgate's dismal and dreary cell,
> I bid all people on earth farewell."

Heaven forbid, say we, that *all* the people on earth should ever get in Newgate, to receive the farewell of such a blood-thirsty miscreant.

> " John William Marchant is my name,
> I do confess I have *been to blame.*"

And here we must observe that the poet makes his hero speak of his offence rather too lightly, as if, indeed, it had been nothing more than a common misdemeanour.

> " I little thought, my dear parents kind,
> I should leave this earth with a troubled mind."

Now this *is* modest ; he is actually surprised that his parents are at all grieved at the idea of getting rid of such a scoundrel, and well he might be.

> " I lived as servant in Cadogan Place,
> And never thought this would be my case,
> To end my days on the fatal tree :
> Good people, pray drop a tear for me."

There is a playfulness about the word " drop," introduced just here, after "the fatal tree," which, in our mind, somewhat diminishes the plaintiveness of the entreaty ; but we must not be hypocritical.

> "Upon a Friday, in the afternoon."

There ! it was on that cursed unlucky day, Friday, on which the song tells us never to cut our nails, doubtless for fear we should meddle with a razor :—

> " I filled the neighbourhood around with gloom ;
> It was the fatal seventeenth of May
> I took my fellow-servants life away.
>
> Elizabeth Paynton, the servant maid,
> Of me was never in the least afraid :
> She never thought, with a deadly knife,"

Now, reader, mark the exquisite pathos of the concluding line :

> "John Marchant would take her life."

" If that isn't cutting," as the calf said to the butcher, " Blow me ! "

*   *   *   *   *   *   *

> " Towards this maiden, I do declare,
> No malice ever I once did bear ;
> The servants they all were gone from home,
> And me and *Betsy was left alone.*"

Now this is another little bit of playfulness ; for in the next verse we are told that Betsy was not " left alone," for that it was the unfortunate youth's romping rudeness which made her threaten to report his behaviour to her master " when he came home," upon which says the convict :—

> " In rage and frenzy, away I flew
> And fetched the razor, as I tell you,
> And momently did commit the deed,
> For which I die, as you plainly read.
>
> That the deed was done then I did not know
> Till her crimson blood did in torrents flow ;
> My eyes I cast on her crimson gore
> That in streams was flowing upon the floor."

Upon which the criminal rushes off in a fright to Hammersmith, and from thence to Windsor, accompanied all the way by Betsy's ghost, who seems to have been quite as good a walker as he was himself.

> " Now every hour, as you shall hear,
> Appeared before me this maiden fair ;
> She would not leave me by night or day—
> Then to justice I gave myself straightway."

Which seems to us, by-the-by, to have been getting out of the frying-pan into the fire ; but there is no telling what rashness a man in a panic will not be guilty of. Then comes his trial and condemnation, the account of which is most remarkably precise and pithy.

> " At the Old Bailey I was tried and cast,
> And the dreadful sentence on me was past
> On a Monday morning, alas ! to die,
> And on the eighth of this month of July."

A marvellous particularity as to dates, intended, doubtless, to show the convicts anxiety that, although he died young, his name should live long in the minds of posterity. Then follows his farewell to father and mother, and an impudent expression of confidence that his crime will be forgiven in heaven, an idea, by-the-by, which is reported to have been confirmed by the Ordinary of Newgate, who told him that the angels would receive him with great affection ; and this it was, perhaps, which induced our bard of Seven Dials to represent his hero as coolly writing poetry up to the very last moment of his existence ; taking his farewell of the public in these words :—

> " Adieu, good people of each degree,
> And take a warning, I pray, by me ;
> The bell is tolling, and I must go,
> And leave this world of misery and woe."

But we cannot exactly see what business the fellow—" a pampered menial," had to speak ill of the world, when he was very comfortably off in it, and might have lived long and happily if it had not been for his own wickedness ; a hint which we throw out for the benefit of Mr. John Morgan, in his future effusions, trusting he will not make his hero die grumly, when poetic justice does not require it.

But we must now take our leave, with a hearty wish to the whole fraternity of Seven Dials bards, that they may never go without a dinner for want of the means of earning it, or that, in other words, though they seem somewhat contradictory, " Sufficient unto the day may the evil thereof."

Again, the writer of an article on " Street Ballads," in the " National Review," for October, 1861, makes the following remarks :—

" This Ballad—' Little Lord John out of Service '—is one of the few which bear a signature—it is signed ' John Morgan ' in the copy which we possess. For a long time we believed this name to be a mere *nom de-plume ;* but the other day, when making a small purchase Monmouth Court, we were informed, in answer to a casual question that this is the real name of the author of some of the best comic ballads. Our informant added that he is an elderly, we may say old, gentleman, living somewhere in Westminster ; but the exact whereabouts we could not discover. Mr. Morgan followed no particular visible calling, so far as our informant knew, except writing ballads, by which he could not earn much of a livelihood, as the price of an original ballad, in these buying-cheap days, has been screwed down by publishers to somewhere about a shilling, sterling. Something more like bread-and-butter might be made, perhaps, by poets who were in the habit of singing their own ballads, as some of them do, but not Mr. Morgan. Should this ever meet the eye of that gentleman (a not very probable event, we fear), we beg to apologise for the liberty we have taken in using the verses and name, and hope he will excuse us, having regard to the subject in which we are his humble fellow-labourers. We could scarcely avoid naming him, the fact being that he is the only living author of street-ballads whose name we know. That self-denying mind, indifferent to worldly fame, which characterised the architects of our cathedrals and abbeys, would seem to have descended on our ballad-writers ; and we must be thankful, therefore, to be able to embalm and hand down to posterity a name here and there, such as William of Wykeham, and John Morgan. In answer to our inquiries in this matter, generally, we have been told, ' Oh, anybody writes them,' and with that answer we have had to rest satisfied. But in presence of that answer, we walk about the streets with a new sense of wonder, peering into the faces of those of our fellow-lieges who do not carry about with them the external evidence of overflowing exchequers, and saying to ourselves, 'That man may be a writer of ballads.'"

We cannot close our self-imposed labour without remarking the many changes that have taken place during the time that our work has been going through the press, the most notable of which is the somewhat sudden and unexpected death, on the last day of 1876, of the Rev. Thomas Hugo, Rector of West Hackney, and author of the "Bewick Collector." His remarkable collection of wood-blocks and books, illustrated by the Brothers Bewick, was by far the largest ever formed, and contained some of the choicest proofs, in various states and on a variety of papers, and in many instances acquired with great difficulty and at large cost, and at a time and with opportunities that will never occur again. Mr. Hugo

directed by his will that his entire collection should be
offered to the British Museum, and this proposition was
accordingly made, but declined on the ground that the
national collection was already so well provided with
" Bewicks," and would only be inconvenienced by acquiring
so large a number of duplicates. Under these circumstances
the whole of the choice and valuable collection was sub-
mitted to public sale by those eminent and old-established
auctioneers of literary property and works illustrative of the
fine arts—Messrs. Sotheby, Wilkinson, and Hodge, of
Wellington Street, Strand, London, on Wednesday, 8th of
August, 1877, and following day, included 674, lots and
realized £1,124 1s. 0d.

At the sale of Mr. Hugo's literary property, we purchased
several of the lots containing Bewick's wood-blocks, many
of which we have made use of in this work. Had Mr.
Hugo lived we should have had the benefit of his experience
and the absolute use of his memoranda on the subject of
street literature.

THE

LIFE AND TIMES

OF

James Catnach

> " Death made no conquest of this man,
> For now he lives in fame, though not in life."

———

JAMES—or as he was popularly called, " *Jemmy*," or,
" *Old Jemmy* " Catnach, late of the Seven Dials,
London, printer and publisher of ballads, battledores,
lotteries, primers, &c., and whose name is ever associated
with the literature of the streets, was the son of John Catnach,
a printer, of Alnwick, an ancient borough, market town, and
parish of Northumberland, where he was born August 18th,
1792. The elder Catnach by himself, and afterwards in
conjunction with his partner and subsequent successor,
William Davison, employed Thomas Bewick, an English
artist, who imparted the first impulse to the art of wood-
engraving, for several of his publications.

Of the early life of John Catnach, the father, we have
little information. He was born in 1769, at Burnt Island, a

royal burgh and parish of Fifeshire, Scotland, where his
father was possessed of some powder-mills. The family
afterwards removed to Edinburgh, when their son James
was bound apprentice to his uncle, Sandy Robinson, the
printer. After having duly served out his indentures, he
worked for some short time in Edinburgh, as a journeyman,
then started in a small business of his own in Berwick-upon-
Tweed, where he married Mary Hutchinson, who was a
native of Dundee, a seaport-town in Scotland. While at
Berwick a son and heir, John, was born. In 1790 they
removed their business to Alnwick, and during their residence there seven children were born to them : and from
the Register of Baptisms in St. Michael's Church we glean
that four of them were baptised at one time, viz., September
24, 1797, and there described as " of John Catnach, printer,
and Mary his wife : Dissenter. " [?] John Catnach had been
brought up in the Roman Catholic faith, and his wife as a
Presbyterian. The following is taken *verbatim* from the
Parish Register :—

Sep^{t.} 24, 1797.

Margaret, Daug^{r.} of John Catnach, printer, and Mary
his Wife, Born Decr. 26th 1790. Dissenter.

James, son of John Catnach, printer, and Mary his Wife.
Born August 18th 1792. Dissenter.

Mary, Daug^{r.} of John Catnach, printer, and Mary, his
Wife. Born February 26th 1794. Dissenter.

Nancy, Daug^{r.} of John Catnach, printer, and Mary his
Wife. Born Sepr. 2nd 1795. Dissenter.

May 23, 1798.

Elizabeth Catnach. Born March 21, 1797, 4th Daughter
of John Catnach, printer, native of Burnt Island, Shire of
Fife, by his wife Mary Hutchinson, Native of Dundee,
Angus Shire, Scotland.

Decr. 14, 1798.

Isabella Catnach, Born Novr. 2, 1798. 5th Daughter of

Jn⁰· Catnach, Stationer, Nat. of Scotland, by his wife, Mary Hutchinson, Nat. of Dundee, Angus Shire, Scotland.

March 28, 1800.

Jane Catnach, 6th Daughter of John Catnach, printer, Native of Edinburgh *(sic)* by his wife Mary Hutchinson, Native of Dundee, Scotland.

To the above we have to add that there were two sons— John, born to John and Mary Catnach. John I. who was born at Berwick-upon-Tweed, died August 27, 1794, aged 5 years and seven months, and we find him duly recorded in the Register òf Deaths. John II., whose name appears at the end of the inscription on a tombstone in Alnwick churchyard, and of which further mention will be made in another portion of our work, died, presumably unbaptized, March 5, 1803, aged 4 months.

Alnwick, towards the close of the last century, had made little or no progress in sanitary reforms. The Castle, the ancient seat of the Percies, had but just been restored by the first Duke of Northumberland, according to the prevailing style of the times. The streets offered but few attractions; they were badly paved, and the flagging of the footpaths was in a wretched condition ; they were lighted at nights by a few lamps of an antiquated description. At this time many of the feudal customs, which have since disappeared, were in great repute. The stocks, bull-baiting, cock-fighting, the kicking of football in the open streets, were always sure to draw together a gazing throng. At nights the streets were considerably enlivened by the strains of the borough waits.*

---

* WAITS, according to Dr. Busby, is a corruption of *Wayghtes* (hautboys), a word which has no singular number. The word, he says, has been transferred from the instruments to the performers, who are in the habit of parading our streets by night, at Christmas time.

There is scarce a young man of any fashion, who does not make love with the town music. The *waits* often help him through his courtship. —*Tatler*, No. 222.

Hautboys were anciently their musical instruments, but afterwards fiddles, with which they nightly serenaded the inhabitants between Martinmas and the end of January. Their ordinary dress consisted of blue coats, yellow breeches and vests, and their hats were usually decorated with a profusion of lace. From 1770 to 1823 the family of Coward acted as waits, of whom Thomas Coward was the last of his race. Mr. Tate, the Alnwick historian, declared that although he had listened to Paganini, and other celebrated performers on the violin, none of their strains had such charms for him as the Border Airs when played by Thomas Coward.

John Catnach was not long a resident before he became acquainted with many of the principal tradesmen in the place. Naturally he was of a free-and-easy disposition, and, like many of his kinsmen on the Borders, was particularly fond of the social glass. The latter practice he allowed to grow upon him in such a way that it ultimately interfered very much with his business, and hastened his death.

The shop that he commenced business in, was situated in Narrowgate Street, and adjoining the old Half-Moon hostelry. In gaining access to the place you had to ascend a flight of steps. Whilst in this shop he secured a fair amount of patronage, and the specimens of printing that emanated from his press are of such a character as to testify to his qualifications and abilities in the trade which he adopted as his calling. He possessed a fond regard for the traditions and customs which for centuries had been so closely associated with the Border country.

When the printing press was first introduced into Alnwick is not exactly known ; but that it was considerably before the time of Catnach and Davison is certain. John Vint, the bookseller, and author of the "Burradon Ghost," for several years used a press for printing purposes in the town, and Thomas Lindsay carried on a similar business at a still earlier period.

Although Alnwick has not very greatly extended during
the present century, yet the condition of its buildings and
the general aspect of the town have undergone considerable
changes. On the east side of the gate now entering into the
Column field, stood the parish pound, and near to it the
pump ; the former since removed to the Green Bat, and the
latter down Denwick Lane. On the south side of the street,
on the site of a portion of Dr. Easton's premises, stood John
Weatherburn's thatched house, and behind was the large
barn, occasionally used as a theatre, where the celebrated
Stephen Kemble frequently appeared in the character of
Falstaff before large and fashionable audiences, and the
Duchess of Northumberland occasionally honoured the
theatre with her presence. The barn was two stories
high, the upper part being used as a hay loft ; the
theatre beneath occasionally went by the name of "The
Hay Market." . Behind the barn, which stood in the stack-
yard, was a footway leading from the Green Bat into Love
Lane. It was frequently so deep and miry as to be of little
use to the public. Some distance farther down, lived a noted
character called Billy Bone, whose house was the great
rendezvous for that wandering tribe who had no settled resi-
deuces of their own. Mr. Bone, who, in the early period
of his life, was a member of that community himself, was
well acquainted with their habits, and his house was
consequently the most popular of its class. It was
capable of accommodating upwards of twenty guests, the
uniform charge for each being threepence per night. As
Mr. Bone was a noted player on the violin, the evening's
amusements occasionally concluded with a dance, which was
kept up with more vigour than elegance to a later hour than
was consistent with the comforts of his neighbours.

John Catnach had a great relish for printing such works
as would admit of expensive embellishments, which, at the
time he commenced business, were exceedingly rare. The

taste he displayed in the execution of his work will be best
exemplified in examining some of the printed editions of the
standard works which emanated from his press ; and in no
instance is this more characteristically set forth than in those
finely printed books which are so beautifully illustrated by
the masterly hand of Thomas Bewick and his accomplished
and talented pupil, Luke Clennell.   Notably among which
are :—

1.—" The Beauties of Natural ,History.   Selected from
Buffon's History of Quadrupeds, &c.   Alnwick : J. Catnach,
[n. d.]   *Circa* 1795,   12mo., pp. 92.   With 67 cuts by
Bewick."

1*a*.—Another edition.   Published and Sold by the Booksellers.   By Wilson and Spence, York, and J. Catnach,
printer, Alnwick.   (Price 1*s*. 6*d*. sewed, or 2*s*. half-bound.)
1805.

The embellishments of "The Beauties of Natural History" form an unique and valuable collection. They are very small and were done at an exceedingly low price, yet every bird and animal is exquisitely brought out in its minutest detail; whilst many of the illustrations which served as "tail pieces" are gems of art.

2.—"Poems by Percival Stockdale. With cuts by Thomas Bewick. Alnwick: Printed by J. Catnach. 1806."

3.—" The Hermit of Warkworth. A Northumberland Ballad. In three Fits. By Dr. Thos. Percy, Bishop of Dromore. With Designs by Mr. Craig; and Engraved on Wood by Mr. Bewick. Alnwick: Printed and Sold by J. Catnach. Sold by Lackington, Allan, and Co., London; Constable and Co., Edinburgh; and Hodgson, Newcastle. 1806." The Arms of the Duke of Northumberland precedes the Dedication, thus:—

TO HER GRACE
FRANCES JULIA,
DUCHESS OF NORTHUMBERLAND,
This Edition of
THE HERMIT OF WARKWORTH,
Is respectfully Inscribed
By Her Grace's Obliged and Humble Servant,

J. CATNACH.

ALNWICK, *October*, 1805.

The illustrations of "The Hermit of Warkworth" are, upon the whole, very creditable, and are well calculated to enhance the value of the book, but as works of art some few of them fall far short of many of Craig or Bewick's other productions. The Northumberland Arms above, and all the following original woodcuts, have been kindly lent by the Rev. Thomas Hugo, M.A., F.R.S.L., F.S.A., &c., the author of "The Bewick Collector," and possessor of the largest and most perfect collection of works illustrated by Thomas and John Bewick, together with the original wood blocks thereof, ever formed.

THE HERMIT OF WARKWORTH.

"And now, attended by their host,
The hermitage they view'd."

DARK was the night, and wild the storm,
   And loud the torrent's roar ;
And loud the sea was heard to dash
   Against the distant shore.

Musing on man's weak hapless state,
  The lonely hermit lay ;
When, lo ! he heard a female voice
  Lament in sore dismay.

With hospitable haste he rose,
  And wak'd his sleeping fire :
And snatching up a lighted brand,
  ' Forth hied the reverend sire.

    *   *   *

With nothing but his hunting spear,
  And dagger in his hand,
He sprung like lightning on my foes,
  And caus'd them soon to stand.

He fought till more assistance came;
  The Scots were overthrown;
Thus freed me, captive, from their bands,
  To make me more his own.

4.—"The Minstrel; or, The Progress of Genius. In
Two Parts. With some other Poems. By James Beattie,
LL.D. With sixteen cuts from Designs by Mr. Thurston;
and engraved on Wood by Mr. Clennell, Alnwick. Printed
by Catnach and Davison. Sold by the Booksellers in England and Scotland. 1807. 12mo. and Royal 8vo., pp. 142."

"The Minstrel, by Beattie," is enriched by the masterly
engravings of Clennell, and nothing can be finer than some
of the productions of this far-famed artist.   The general
portraiture of each picture is characterised by a great amount
of taste.   Mr. Hugo, who possesses a very fine copy in half-
morocco, says: " This is one of the most ambitious productions of the Alnwick press," also adding, "It is asserted, and
can hardly be denied, that Thomas Bewick had a hand in
some of the cuts."

   5.—" The Grave.   A Poem.   By Robert Blair.   To
which is added Gray's Elegy.   In a Country Church Yard..
With Notes Moral and Explanatory.   Alnwick: Printed by
Catnach and Davison.   Sold by the Booksellers in England,
Scotland, and Ireland.   1808.   12mo., pp. xiv., 72.   With a
frontispiece and other cuts by Thomas Bewick."

"Of joys departed,
Not to return, how painful the remembrance!"

6.—"The Poetical Works of Robert Burns. With his Life. Engravings on Wood by Bewick, from designs by Thurston. In two volumes. Alnwick : Printed by Catnach and Davison. Sold by the Booksellers in England, Scotland, and Ireland. 1808."

Many of the engravings produced for Burns' Poems, are of a very superior class, and cannot be too highly commended.

WILLIE BREW'D A PECK O' MAUT.

THE POOR AND HONEST SODGER.

"Sae wistfully she gaz'd on me."

John Catnach also printed and published a series of Juvenile Works, as The Royal Play Book: or, Children's Friend. A Present for Little Masters and Misses. The Death and Burial of Cock Robin, &c. ADORNED with CUTS.—Which in many cases were the early productions of Thomas Bewick.—Alnwick: Sold Wholesale and Retail by J. Catnach, at his Toy-Book Manufactory.

After commencing business, John Catnach was very diligent in trying to establish a trade. That he succeeded in the enterprise there can be little doubt, but it is equally certain that he was never able to save anything from his labours. His ideas were considerably in advance of his means, and as his business began to increase, so in like manner he became more tenaciously wedded to his dissipated habits.

In the year 1807, John Catnach took an apprentice—a lad named Mark Smith, of whom more anon; a few months afterwards he entered into partnership with Mr. William Davison. The latter was a native of Newcastle-upon-Tyne, and in the place of his birth he duly served his apprenticeship as a chemist and druggist to Mr. Hind, and for whom he ever cherished a fond regard. The union was not of long duration—certainly under two years—but it is very remarkable that two such men should have been brought together, for experience has shown that they were both of a speculative mind, although in most other respects, morally and socially, the very opposite of each other.

During the partnership of these two men, the respective trades of chemist and bookseller were carried on by them; and when Mr. Davison was left to himself he still prosecuted with vigour these two departments; for, although reared to the prescribing of physics, he had a fine taste and relish for the book trade, and the short time that he was in partnership with Catnach enabled him to acquire a good amount of valuable information on this subject. Be this as it may, he soon laid the basis of a large and lucrative business. He certainly was no niggard in worldly matters, and when twitted, as he often was, about his new-fangled ideas, he would quaintly reply "that he had more pleasure in spending money than any in hoarding it up."

It was about this same period that Mr. Davison published The Repository of Select Literature; being an Elegant Assemblage of Curious, Scarce, Entertaining and Instructive Pieces in Prose and Verse. Adorned with beautiful Engravings by Bewick, &c. Alnwick: Printed by W. Davison. Sold by the Booksellers in England and Scotland. 1808. This small work is a fine specimen of book making; its pages are adorned with some of Bewick's and Clennell's best impressions. In many of his small books the illustrations are admirably carried out. You will often find some of his fly sheets adorned by the productions of some great master. There is one that we would particularly refer to, and that is "Shepherd Lubin." In size it is very small, but, like most of Bewick's pieces, sufficiently large to show the inimitable skill of the artist. The picture tells its own tale :—

> " Young Lubin was a shepherd's boy,
>   Who watched a rigid master's sheep,
> And many a night was heard to sigh,
>   And many a day was seen to weep."

Lubin, a shepherd boy, was sent adrift on a cold winter's night in search of a missing sheep. The storm was raging fast and furious. In the foreground of the picture is seen the lifeless body of the youth, lying upon the driven snow ; the trusty collie dog with his forepaw resting upon the head of his young master, and not far from them is also the dead object of their search. The storm has abated, but the ground is thickly covered with snow, and in the distance is seen an aged tree. The manipulation of the several figures is so forcibly portrayed, that it is impossible to look upon this small vignette without pleasure and admiration.

The chemistry department in Mr. Davison's establishment was noted in the North of England. As a school for the study of medicine, it was remarkable for the many eminent men that emanated from it ; and it is pleasing to look back upon the names of not a few who in after life became distinguished in the various walks of science. Amongst the most celebrated may be instanced Dr. John Davison, Dr. William Davison, the late lamented Mr. Duncan Ferguson, Professor Thomas Strangeways, Dr. William Brown, Dr. Thomas Call, Dr. William Armstrong, Mr. Robert Dunn, Mr. Philip Thornton, Mr. Hopper, Dr. Robert Heatley, Mr. Henry Hunter, &c. Messrs. Dunn and Thornton were with Mr. Davison about 1812, and both of them went to

London, where they not only acquired eminence, but also amassed considerable fortunes.

Mr. Davison was a man of quick discernment, and not ignorant of the wants and drawbacks which the sons of toil had to contend against. In those days it was only the few who could command an access to the treasured stores of literature, and even to them this was only accomplished with a great amount of labour and expense. Having all this in view, he was not slow in giving effect to ideas long matured; and we find amongst some of his earliest works that he published a revised edition of "Hutton's Arithmetic." The work necessary in carrying it out in its full entirety was entrusted to the late Mr. James Ferguson, who for thirty-five years was the esteemed master of the Corporation Schools under the old *régime*. The author introduced into the work many considerable additions, and perhaps so signal a success never attended the publishing of any local work before. It soon established itself as a standard and household work in the district, and almost countless were the editions that it passed through.

One of the greatest undertakings of his life in the book trade was the issuing of a large Family Bible. Over this work he spent a great amount of money, and perhaps no other book that he was ever engaged in occupied so much of his time, but in a pecuniary point of view he must have been a heavy loser by the enterprise. A great amount of money was spent in getting up the plates, and the book failed in securing that success commensurate with the expense that had been lavished upon it. He also published a very finely illustrated Book of Common Prayer.

In politics Mr. Davison was what is now termed a Liberal ; he had strong leanings to what was then known as the Progressive School. He took a great interest in the several contests in the county that occurred during his lifetime ; 1826, 1841, 1847, and 1852 were memorable epochs in his

life, and with the exception of '41 and '52 he published Poll
Books of the whole of the proceedings connected with the
others. He was the means of bringing out many works of
a local character, and one of the most remarkable was " The
Life of Jamie Allen, the Northumbrian Piper." The only
illustration in the book is a portrait of Allen. The principal
part of the work was arranged by Mr. Andrew Wright, and
contains many traits of the peculiar modes of the gipsy life.
There are several amusing stories told about the manner in
which the chief, incidents contained in the work were
collected. Many of the scenes, plots, and adventures, were
obtained from the itinerant tribes of muggers, tinkers, and
such like. It is now getting scarce, and as years roll on it
will undoubtedly increase in value. In style it is inferior to
that published a few years later by McKenzie and Dent;
but few works of a similar kind possess the quaint and rich
peculiarities of a race that is fast disappearing from amongst
us.

There were few men who took more pride than Mr.
Davison did in bringing out young and unknown authors.
During the fifty years that he was in business, he was instru-
mental in inducing many to "write a book." He also
assisted many others in bringing their labours before the
public.

THE REPOSITORY OF SELECT LITERATURE.

THE POETICAL WORKS OF ROBERT FERGUSON.

The following may be adduced as some of the local works which he printed for their authors : " Poems, chiefly in the Scottish dialect," by Thomas Donaldson (this book is best known by the appellation of "Tam O' Glanton"); " The Cave of Hoonga," and other poems by the late Miss Hindmarsh ; " The Metrical Legends of Northumberland," by James Service ; " The Pleasures of Sight," and " Miscellaneous Poems," by John Lamb Luckley ; and " Wilkes' Newspaper Extracts." The whole of these are adorned with vignettes from the masterly hand of Bewick and others. But independent of these he printed many hundreds of pieces of a minor character, a great portion of which has now disappeared.

THE LITERARY MISCELLANY : BY VARIOUS AUTHORS.

"The morning wakes, the huntsman sounds,
At once rush forth the joyful hounds.
They seek the wood with eager pace,
Through bush, through brier, explore the chase." —*Somerville.*

During a great many years of his life he took a special interest in trying to cultivate a taste for the drama; not many knew more than he did of the numerous vicissitudes that accompany an itinerant life. Miller, in his "Life of a Showman," furnishes us with many instances of the sufferings, hardships, and wants, which the strolling player is ever heir to. Mr. Davison's frank and genial disposition was the means of bringing him into contact with many of this order,—Old Wright, William Palmer, Billy Purvis, and George Fisher, together with others, always found ready access to him; so that his house and shop at all times were very similar to what Willie Creech's was in Auld Reekie during the last century.

Northumbrians have always taken a great interest in the fine arts, but their choice of subjects is very questionable. Mr. Davison possessed many blocks of a curious description. They are remarkable at this day in showing the class of pictures that were wont to adorn the walls of many of the peasantry in this county at the commencement of the present century. Amongst some of the ludicrous pieces are to be found, "The Curate going out on Duty," "The Vicar's Return from Duty," "The Countryman in London," "Out of Place and Unpensioned," "The Stage Doctor," "Love in a Village," "Troubled with Gout," "Let us all be Unhappy together," "The Frenchman in Billingsgate." These productions were chiefly vended by chapmen, who attended fairs and markets.

Mr. Davison possessed a very excellent impression of the engraving of the Chillingham Wild Bull. This has been generally admitted to be Bewick's masterpiece, and large sums have been paid for copies. For a very elaborate, exhaustive, and descriptive history of this Engraving, see Hugo, pp. 430—41. He had also a fine collection, comprising brilliant impressions of the Lion, Tiger, and Elephant, of Bewick's, over which he was very choice.

" I dream'd I lay where flowers were springing.—*Burns' Poems*.

. GIN AND BITTERS.

Mr. Davison continued in business at Alnwick up to the time of his death, in 1858, at the ripe age of 77. He was by far the most enterprising printer that had settled in the North of England. His collection of wood blocks was very large, and it is hardly possible to form an adequate conception of the many hundred of beautiful specimens which he possessed. He stated that he had paid Thomas Bewick upwards of five hundred pounds for various wood-cut blocks. With a view of disposing of some of his surplus stock, he printed and published in 4to., a catalogue.—"NEW SPECIMENS OF CAST-METAL ORNAMENTS AND WOOD TYPES, SOLD BY W. DAVISON. ALNWICK. With impressions of 1,100 Cast Ornaments and Wood Blocks, many of the latter executed by Thomas Bewick." This catalogue—now exceedingly rare—is of the greatest interest and utility, as it embraces a series of cuts dispersed, as Mr. Hugo plainly shows, among a considerable number of publications, and enables those who collect Bewick's pieces to detect the hand of the Artist in many of his less elaborated productions.

CRAZY JANE.

Those of our readers who desire more information as to the many books printed by W. Davison, the Alnwick publisher, are referred to "The Bewick Collector," and the Supplement thereto by the Rev. Thomas Hugo, M.A., &c. London, 1866—68. These volumes, illustrated by upwards of two hundred and ninety cuts, comprise an elaborate descriptive list of the most complete collection yet formed of the works of the renowned wood engravers of Newcastle-upon-Tyne. Not only to Bewick collectors, but to all persons interested in the progress of Art, and especially of wood engraving, these volumes, exhibiting chronologically the works of the Fathers of that Art in England, cannot fail to be of the highest interest.

WAITING FOR DEATH.

"At length, old and feeble, trudging early and late,
Bow'd down by diseases, he bends to his fate;
Blind, old, lean, and feeble, he tugs round a mill,
Or draws sand, till the sand of his hour-glass stands still."

Charles Dibdin.

THE POOR OLD HORSE.—In the morning of his days he was handsome, sleek as a raven, sprightly and spirited, and was then much caressed and happy. When he grew to perfection, in his performances, even on the turf, and afterwards in the chase, and in the field, he was equalled by few of his kind; after which he fell into the hands of different masters, but from none of them did he ever eat the bread of idleness, and, as he grew in years, his cup of misery was still augmented with bitterness—he became the property of a general, a gentleman, a farmer, a miller, a butcher, a higgler, and a maker of brooms. A hard winter coming on, a want of money obliged his poor owner to turn him out to shift for himself, his former fame and great value are now, to him, not worth a handful of oats. But his days and nights of misery are now drawing to an end. So that, after having faithfully dedicated the whole of his powers and his time to the service of unfeeling man, he is at last turned out, unsheltered and unprotected, to starve of hunger and of cold.—*Thomas Bewick.*

In or about the latter part of the year 1808, John Catnach, with his wife and family, left Alnwick for Newcastle-upon-Tyne, and commenced business in a small shop in Newgate Street, and among other Works which he printed there, mention may be made of "The Battle of Chevy Chase," a selection from the works of "Dr. Samuel Johnson, in two volumes," and "The Life of John Thompson, Mariner. Written by Himself: Also, his Divine Selections, in Prose and Verse. From esteemed Authors. Embellished with Engravings. Newcastle : Printed for the Author. By J. Catnach, Newgate Street. 1810. 12mo., pp. lxxvi., 214. With two tail-pieces by Thomas Bewick."

John Thompson was a British seaman who lost a leg and endured many hardships at the Battle of Trafalgar, and afterwards made a living out of his misfortunes and assumed piety. Catnach was induced, by specious reasoning, to undertake the printing of the book, but the eleemosynary author dying just as it was all worked off but not bound, he had the whole of the stock thrown on his hands.

John Catnach, at Newcastle, worked ardently and attentively for awhile, but without finding his expectations realised. Alas! time and the change of scene and companions had not improved the man. He contrived to get into a great amount of debt, without the least possible chance, from his irregular mode of living, of being able to pay it off. Evidently, he made up his mind for the worst, and the downward course would seem to have been the only way open to him. From bad to worse, and from one extreme to the other, he rapidly drifted. The loose and irregular manner in which he had existed was beginning to tell upon his constitution. His business had been neglected, and his adventures were nearly at a climax. Everything around him betokened gloom and despair. The tiny craft, which had been tossed to-and-fro in the raging ocean of life, was soon to disappear among its surging billows. The wreck came, with a terrific blow; but it was not unlooked for. Poor Catnach was a bankrupt, and as such sent to the debtor's gaol. But just before the climax he had managed to send his wife and daughters to London, together with a wooden printing press, some small quantity of type, and other articles of his trade that could be hurriedly and clandestinely got together.

During the five years' residence of John and Mary Catnach in Newcastle, they had one child, Isabella, burned to death, and another born to them, Julia Dalton.

Mr. Mark Smith, who had been bound apprentice to John Catnach, but by reason of whose removal from the Borough of Alnwick, the indentures had been rendered void, was then in London, serving out his time as a turnover and improver with Mr. John Walker, of Paternoster Row, and on being made acquainted with the arrival of Mrs. Catnach and her family, paid them a visit at their lodgings in a court leading off Drury Lane, and assisted in putting up the press and arranging the other few matters and utensils in connection with their tiny printing office, there to await John Catnach's release from prison and arrival in the metropolis.

London life to John Catnach proved very disastrous, matters never went smoothly with him. It was evident to all his friends that he had made a great mistake in leaving the North of England. Mr. Mark Smith continued to visit the family as opportunities presented themselves. On one occasion he found them in extremely distressed circumstances, so much so, that he had to afford them some temporary relief from his slender earnings and then left the northern sojourners for the night, promising that he would return to see them at an early date. Anxious to learn how they were succeeding in the crowded metropolis, it was not many days before he again visited them, but this time he found them in a sorry plight; the landlady had distrained upon their all for arrears of rent. This was an awkward predicament; but the indomitable young Northumbrian, like the more burly Doctor Johnson of old, when his friend Goldsmith was similarly situated, resolved to do all he could to rescue him from the peril in which he was placed. Not being prepared for a case of such pressing emergency, the full debt and costs being demanded, he was compelled to borrow the required amount of Mr. Matthew Willoughby, a native and freeman of the Borough of Alnwick,* then residing in London, and once more his old master was free.

Catnach then removed his business to a front shop in Wardour Street, Soho, and took apartments for his wife and family in Charlotte Street, Fitzroy Square. Again he shortly removed his business to Gerrard Street, where he had hardly got his plant into working order, when on returning home on the evening of the 29th of August, 1813, he had the misfortune to fall down and injure his leg. He was immediately taken to St. George's Hospital, Hyde Park Corner, when rheumatic fever supervened, and although

---

* The Willoughby family have long resided in Alnwick. Over the entrance of the Plough Inn, in Bondgate, there is the following inscription :—

"That which your Father
    Hath purchased, and left you to possess,
Do you dearly hold
    To show his worthiness."
                        M. W.
                        1714.

The initials "M. W." are those of Matthew Willoughby.

Few parts of Alnwick have undergone greater improvements during the last half century than Bondgate, not only as regards the state of the streets but also the character of the houses, and perhaps the greatest of all the improvements has been effected with that portion of ground which commonly passes by the name of "the hill." This was formerly a piece of waste ground, one portion of which was a sand-bank and the other overgrown with grass, which served as a pasture for that class of animals whose owners were unable to provide them with a better.

placed under the skilful treatment of Dr. Young, he never rallied, his constitution being completely broken, but by means of superior medical treatment he lingered until the 4th of December in the same year, on which day he died.

A day was appointed for the funeral, and Mr. Mark Smith and one of the daughters of the deceased, went to the hospital for the purpose of following the remains to the grave, but when they arrived there some accident, it was said, had befallen the horse that was to have drawn the hearse, hence the obsequies were postponed till the following day, but Mr. Mark Smith was unable to be there, owing to business engagements elsewhere. Thus we are unable to state where John Catnach lies buried. We have made inquiries of the officials of St. George's Hospital, but their records afford us no further information on the subject than we have given above. But Mr. Mark Smith maintains an opinion to this day, that the postponement of the funeral was but a *ruse* on the part of the hospital authorities, to enable them to use at least some portion of the corpse for dissecting and anatomical purposes.

Such is a brief *résumé* of the latter years of John Catnach's life. It is apparent that, by a little application and self-denial, this man might have made for himself a name and position in the world. He possessed all the necessary talents for bringing success within his reach. The ground which he took is the same which in after years proved to be of inestimable value to hundreds of publishers who never possessed half the amount of ability and good taste in printing and embellishing books that was centred in him.

After his death, and just at the time when his widow and daughters were sunk in the greatest poverty, his son James, who in after years became so noted in street literature publications, made his way to the metropolis. It appears that this extraordinary man at one time contemplated devoting his life to rural pursuits; in fact, when a youth he

served for some time as a shepherd boy, quite contrary to
the wish and desire of his parents.   Every opportunity he
could get he would run away, far across the moors and over
the Northumbrian mountains, and, always accompanied with
his favourite dog Venus, and a common-place book, in
which he jotted down in rhymes and chymes his notions of
a pastoral life.*   Thus he would stay away from home for
days and nights together.

  This project, however, was abandoned, and he commenced to serve as a printer in the employment of his
father.   It is rather remarkable that he and Mr. Mark Smith
were both bound on the same day as apprentices to Mr.
John Catnach, and that they afterwards worked together as
"improvers" in their trade with Mr. Joseph Graham, a
copy of whose "imprint" follows, of which Mr. Hugo, in
the Supplement to his "Bewick Collector," pp. 256 (5137),
says :—"This very beautiful Cut was done by Thomas Bewick,
sometime about the year 1794, for a well-known Alnwick
printer."

  * We have been very recently informed by Mrs. Benton, the only
survivor of the family of John and Mary Catnach, that the MS. book
alluded to above, remained in the family for many years, and was last
known to be in the possession of the sister Mary—Mrs. Haines, of
Gosport, to the date of about 1863.

THE HERMIT, ANGEL, AND GUIDE.—*Parnell's Hermit.*

Mr. Graham for several years kept a printing office in Fenkle Street, which branches from Narrowgate Street; he was succeeded by his son, at the sale of whose stock the Bewick-cut-block was purchased by Mr. Pike.

Previous to, and for some time after, the commencement of the present century, Fenkle Street contained the best houses and was undoubtedly the leading and most fashionable street in Alnwick. Here was the Angel Inn, the chief hostelry and posting house of that period, and further down were the Nag's Head, the Spread Eagle, and the Half Moon, all houses of considerable repute.

During the time Catnach the elder was laid up in St. George's Hospital, where, as we have previously shown, he remained for fourteen weeks, when death put an end to his mental and bodily sufferings, the family continued in very distressed circumstances, but were from time to time partially relieved by Mr. Mark Smith, who, on one or two evenings during the week, after he had finished his own day's work in the City, used to set up and work off any little printing jobs that had been obtained since his last visit. Temporary assistance was also given by Mr. Matthew Willoughby, and a few other Northern friends, who happened to be in London at the time. James Catnach, the son, did not arrive in town until after the father's death and burial. He was at the time working at Newcastle-upon-Tyne, which is thirty-six miles from Alnwick. Communications from, and transportation to, the metropolis in those days being long, tedious, and very costly.

Soon after the father's death, the family again removed, and when James Catnach, in 1813—14, being in his twenty-second year, commenced business in the little shop and parlour of No. 2, Monmouth Court, Seven Dials, his start in life may be said to have been a very humble one; he had only the old wooden press which his father had used at Alnwick and afterwards at Newcastle, together with such small assortments of type and woodcuts that had been sent off to London with the family at the approach of the father's bankruptcy. His mother and sisters were now entirely dependant upon him for their support, and knowing this, he undoubtedly threw more energy and perseverance into the matter than he would have done, for the least drawback might have been the means of frustrating his hopes and expectations. He resolved, by rigid application, to do all he could towards making his position tenable and secure, and the result was, that in a few years he laid the foundation of a peculiar, yet lucrative business.

A large part of the trade which James Catnach commenced to do in London, had for years previous to this been done in Scotland, as well as in several parts of the North of England. Books of small histories, ballad poetry, and legends of remarkable places which were frequented by ghosts, fairies, hobgoblins, and the like, and similar works were printed in many parts of Caledonia long before the time of Robert Burns. This poet, in one of his letters, says, " that it was through the kindness of one of his early schoolmistresses that he first became acquainted with this particular kind of literature ; " and there can be little doubt that he penned, when under the impulse of such imaginations, what Scott has styled, his " inimitable tale of Tam O'Shanter."

At the time when the broadsides, catch-pennies, and awfuls were in the ascendency, the whole of the United Kingdom was overrun with chapmen, ballad-singers, and itinerants of every grade and description. Whenever anything sensational was upon the *tapis*, these members of the wandering tribe would make their way to central or stated points, in order to be supplied with the requisite sheets on their earliest appearance. Before the time of stage-coaches, letters, and such like, on the king's service, were carried by men mounted on horses, and the danger attending the road was very great. From the days of Robin Hood, the hero of Sherwood Forest, down to those of Dick Turpin, Tom King, Claude Duval, the Ladies' Highwaymen, and Jerry Abershaw, the highways, the desolate heath, and the trackless moor were the rendezvous of robbery, bloodshed, and murder. When the stage-coach was introduced a better state of things began to show forth ; and when the distance, which lies between the metropolis of England and that of Scotland, could be traversed in a few days, the inhabitants of the two countries began to commune together more freely. The progress in intelligence, which the people had made by being allowed to follow their daily vocations without let or hindrance, or the constant fears and alarms caused by civil and internal commotions, tended in no small way to heal animosities, and bind more closely the feelings and affections of the inhabitants of the two realms. After the Union, feuds and Border warfares became things of the past, the chivalry and enterprise of the freebooter and the moss-trooper were no longer encouraged ; the slogan war cries of the north were set aside, but still kept sacred as rallying · standards, which for centuries had been upheld by the valiant arms of the greatest chieftains of the Borders ; the heroic deeds of the Percy and the Douglas were still sung, cherished, and admired, but not in the midst of war and sanguinary conflicts : a new epoch in society had arrived, of which history gives no better illustrations than the accomplishments of the past three centuries. During this space of time, ill-feeling and prejudice had gradually been uprooted, and in their place, good-will and social intercourse prevailed.

The late George Daniel, of Canonbury Square, Islington, near London, who formerly possessed the " Elizabethan Garland," which consists of Seventy Ballads, printed between the years 1559 and 1597,—at the sale of whose library it was purchased by the late Joseph Lilly for Henry Huth,

Esq., says in an article on "Old Ballads," in his "Love's Last Labour Not Lost:"—"If any portion of English literature be more generally interesting than another, it is ancient ballad lore. Battles have been fought and heroes immortalised in its inspiring strains. It has made us familiar with the manly virtues, sympathies, sports, pastimes, traditions, the very language of our forefathers, gentle and simple. We follow them to the tented field, the tournament, the border foray, the cottage ingle, and the public hostelrie. We glow with their martial spirit, and join in their rude festivities. Narrative and sentiment, reality and romance, the noblest patriotism and the tenderest love, the wildest mirth and the deepest melancholy, inform, delight, and subdue us by turns. The impulses of the heart, those gems of truth ! were the inspirations of the muse. Hence thoughts of rare pathos and beauty, and felicity of expression that no study could produce, no art could polish, find a response in every bosom. In peace, the ballad might be the 'woeful' one made to a 'mistress's eyebrow:' in war, it was the trumpet sounding 'to arms !' or the muffled drum rolling from the warrior's requiem.

"The merit of our old English Border Ballads was long ago acknowledged far beyond sea-girt land. Joseph Scaliger, when he visited England, in 1566, among many minute observations recorded in his entertaining 'Table Talk,' particularly notices the excellence of our Border Ballads, the beauty of Mary Stuart, and our burning coal instead of wood in the north.

"The tunes to which these ballads were sung are centuries older than the ballads themselves. Many of them are lost in antiquity. While most of the ballads quoted by Shakespeare, Beaumont and Fletcher, and Samuel Rowlands, extend not beyond a single verse, or even a single line ; yet how suggestive are they ! It was such penny broadsides that composed the 'bunch' of the military mason, Captain Cox, of Coventry, and that stocked the pedlar's pack of Autolycus ; and their power of fascination may be learnt from the varlet's own words, when he laughingly brags how nimbly he lightened the gaping villagers of their purses, while chanting to them his merry trol-my-dames.

"'What hast here'? Ballads? I love a ballad in print, a'-life, for then we are sure they are true.' 'Heres's one,' says the roguish Autolycus, 'set to a very doleful tune, how an usurer's wife was brought to bed with twenty money bags at a burden ; and how she longed to eat adder's heads, and toads carbonado'd; it is true, and but a month old. Here's the midwive's name to 't, one Mistress *Taleporter,* and five or six honest wives that were present ; why should I carry lies abroad? Here's another ballad, of a fish that appeared upon the coast, on *Wednesday* the fourscore of *April,* forty thousand fathom above water, and sung this ballad against the hard hearts of maids ; it was thought to be a woman, and was turned into a cold fish, for she would not exchange flesh with one that lov'd her. The ballad is very pitiful, and as true—five justices hands at it ; and witnesses, more than my pack will hold.'

"We delight in a Fiddler's Fling, full of mirth and pastime! We revel in the exhilarating perfume of those odoriferous chaplets gathered on sunshiny holidays and star-twinkling nights, bewailing how beautiful maidens meet with faithless wooers, and how fond shepherds are cruelly.jilted by deceitful damsels; how despairing Corydons hang, and how desponding Phillises drown themselves for love ; how disappointed lads go to sea, and how forlorn lasses follow them in jackets and trousers ! Sir George Etheridge, in his comedy of 'Love in a Tub,' says, 'Expect at night to see an old man with his paper lantern and crack'd spectacles, singing you woeful tragedies to kitchen maids and cobblers' apprentices.' Aubrey mentions that his nurse could repeat the history of England, from the Conquest to the time of

Charles I., in ballads. And Aubrey, himself a book-learned man, delighted in after years to recall them to his remembrance. In Walton's 'Angler,' Piscator, having caught a chub, conducts Venator to an 'honest ale house, where they would find a cleanly room, lavender in the windows, and *twenty ballads* stuck about the wall.' 'When I travelled,' says the Spectator, 'I took a particular delight in hearing the songs and fables that are come from father to son, and are most in vogue among the common people of the countries through which I passed.' The heart-music of the peasant was his native minstrelsy, his blithesome carol in the cottage and in the field."

"Two hundred years ago," wrote Douglas Jerrold,* "and the Street Ballad Singer was not only the poet and musician for the poor, but he was their newsmonger, their journalist, as then the morning and evening papers were not: the saints of Sunday showed not the spite of devils at Sunday prints conned over by the poor; historians, encyclo-pædists, and philosophers were not purchasable piecemeal by pennies; and though the Globe Theatre, on the Bankside, Southwark, had its gallery for two-pence, the works of a certain actor playing there, were not printed at the price. Hence, the ballad singer supplied music and reading to the poor: he brought enjoyment to their very doors. He sung to them the news, the Court gossip of the day, veiled perhaps in cunning allegory—for the Virgin Queen would snip off the ears of a ballad monger, as readily as her waiting-woman would snip a lace—throwing on a dark point, the light of a significant look, and giving to the general obscurity of the text explanatory gestures, nods, and winks, for the assistance of homespun understandings.

"It is upon record that the Ballad Singer must have acted no contemptible part in the civil wars. Have we not

---

* "Heads of the People; or, Portraits of the English."—1841.

evidence of his stirring, animating importance? Has the reader ever met with the 'Rump: or an Exact Collection of The Choycest Poems and Songs relating to the Late Times, and continued by the most Eminent Wits from *Anno* 1639, to *Anno* 1661?' If so, can he not figure to himself the English Ballad Singer, bawling, yelling the ditty to a grinning, rejoicing crowd, as party rose and fell? The very songs, at first written for a few, and sung in watchful secrecy in holes and corners, were, as the Commonwealth waned and died, roared, bellowed to the multitude. Hark, reader! what lungs of brass—now what a roar of voices! Look! the music issues from the metal throat of yonder dirty-faced Phœbus, in rags, and the shouts and laughter from the mob, frantic with joy at the burden of his lay—the downfall of Old Noll, and the coming of the King, that silken, sorry rascal, Charles the Second. How the ballad-singing rogue screams his joyful tidings! and how the simple, giddy-headed crowd, hungering for shows and holidays, toss up their arms and jump like satyrs! And there, darting, slinking by, passes the wincing Puritan, his face, ash-coloured with smothering anger at the profane tune. And now, a comely gentleman makes through the crowd, and with a patronising smile, and bestowing something more than the cost price—for he is marvellously tickled with the theme—secures a copy of the song. The reader may not at the instant recognise the buyer: he is, we can swear to him, one Mr. Samuel Pepys, afterwards secretary to the Admiralty; but what is more to his fame, the greatest ballad collector of the day: let his treasures, left to Cambridge, bear honourable witness for him. See, he walks down Charing Cross, carrying away the burden of the song, and with a light and loyal heart humming, 'The King enjoys his own again,' written by one Martin Parker, a verse maker, who informs us that—

'Whatever yet was published by me,
　　Was known by " Martin Parker," or M.P.' "

But, hark ! let us listen to the words of the ballad—

WHAT Booker doth prognosticate
　　Concerning Kings', or Kingdoms' fate?
I think myself to be as wise
As he that gazeth on the skies.
　　My skill goes beyond
　　The depth of a Pond,
Or Rivers in the greatest rain.
　　Thereby I can tell
　　All things will be well
When the King enjoys his own again.

There 's neither Swallow, Dove, nor Dade
Can soar more high, nor deeper wade ;
Nor show a reason from the stars
What causeth peace or civil wars :

The Man in the Moon
May wear out his shoon,
By running after Charles his wain,
But all 's to no end
For the times will not mend
Till the King enjoys his own again.

Though for a time we see Whitehall
With cobwebs hanging on the wall,
Instead of silk and silver brave,.
Which formerly it used to have,
With rich perfume
For every room,
Delightful to that princely train ;
Which again you shall see
When the time it shall ,be
That the King enjoys his own again.

Full forty years the royal crown
Hath been his father's and his own ;
And is there any one but he
That in the same should sharer be ?
For who better may
The sceptre sway
Than he that hath such right to reign ?
Then let 's hope for a peace,
For the wars will not cease
Till the King enjoys his own again.

Till then upon Ararat's hill
My hope shall cast her anchor still,
Until I see some peaceful dove
Bring home the branch I dearly love ;
Then will I wait
Till the waters abate,

Which now disturb my troubled brain,
    Else never rejoice
    Till I hear the voice
That the King enjoys his own again.

             Martin Parker.

Who shall say that our Ballad Singer has not shouted to crowds like these ; has not vended his small ware to men, aye, as illustrious as the immortal writer of that best of all history—history in undress—The Diary of Samuel Pepys?

Although the library of the British Museum contains a much larger number of broadside ballads than any other of the public libraries, yet the ROXBURGHE COLLECTION, taken alone, is but second in extent to the collection known by the name of Samuel Pepys, the diarist, which is in the library of Magdelene College, Cambridge. The latter is in five volumes, containing 1,800 ballads, of which 1,376 are in **Black Letter.** This famed collection was commenced by the learned Selden.

John Selden died 1654, and Pepys continued collecting till near the time of his death, in 1703, which fact he records on the title page of his volumes thus :—" My collection of Ballads " (following the words with an engraved portrait of himself) " Begun by Mr. Selden : Improved by ye addition of many Pieces elder thereto in Time, and the whole continued down to the year 1770, when the Form, till then peculiar thereto—viz., of the Black Letter with Pictures seems (for cheapness sake) wholly laid aside, for that of White Letter without Pictures."

Besides the ballads, Pepys left to the Magdelene College an invaluable collection of manuscript naval memoirs, of prints, ancient English poetry, and three volumes of " Penny Merriments." These amount in number to 112, and some of them are *Garlands,* that contain many ballads in each.

The Seven Dials!—Jemmy Catnach and Street-Literature are, as it were, so inseparably bound together that we now propose to give a short history of the former to enable us, to proceed uninterruptedly with the latter. Charles Dickens, as Boz, long since "sketched" the Seven Dials. Many other descriptive writers have trodden over the same ground, and Charles Knight, in his "London," writes thus :—

"Seven Dials! the region of song and poetry—first effusions, and last dying speeches. It was here—in Monmouth Court, a thoroughfare connecting Monmouth Street with Little Earl Street—that the late eminent Mr. Catnach developed the resources of his genius and trade. It was he who first availed himself of greater mechanical skill and a larger capital than had previously been employed in that department of THE TRADE, to substitute for the execrable tea-paper, blotched with lamp-black and oil, which characterised the old broadside and ballad printing, tolerably white paper and real printer's ink. But more than that, it was he who first conceived and carried into effect, the idea of publishing collections of songs by the yard, and giving to purchasers, for the small price of one penny (in former days the cost of a single ballad), strings of poetry, resembling in shape and length the list of Don Juan's mistresses, which Leporello unrolls on the stage before Donna Anna. He was no ordinary man, Catnach ; he patronised original talents in many a bard of St. Giles's, and is understood to have accumulated the largest store of broadsides, last dying speeches, ballads, and other stock-in-trade of the flying stationer's, upon record.

"The Seven Dials were built for wealthy tenants, and Evelyn, in his 'Diary,' notes, 1694, 'I went to see the building near St. Giles's, where Seven Dials make a star from a Doric pillar placed in the middle of a circular area, in imitation of Venice.' The attempt was not altogether in vain. This part of the parish has ever since 'worn its *dirt*

with a difference.' There is an air of shabby gentility
about it. The air of the footman or waiting-maid can be
recognised through the tatters, which are worn with more
assumption than those of their unsophisticated neighbours.

> " 'You may break, you may shatter the vase if you will ;
>   But the scent of the roses will hang round it still.'

"The Seven Dials are thus described in Gay's ' Trivia :'—

> " ' Where famed St. Giles's ancient limits spread,
>   An in-railed column rears its lofty head ;
>   Here to seven streets seven dials count their day,
>   And from each other catch the circling ray ;
>   Here oft the peasant, with inquiring face,
>   Bewildered, trudges on from place to place ;
>   He dwells on every sign with stupid gaze—
>   Enters the narrow alley's doubtful maze—
>   Tries every winding court and street in vain,
>   And doubles o'er his weary steps again.'

"This column was removed in July, 1773, on the sup-
position that a considerable sum of money was lodged at
the base ; but the search was ineffectual."

Seven Dials !—It is here that the literature of St. Giles's
has fixed its abode ; and a literature the parish has of its
own, and that, as times go, of a very respectable standing
in point of antiquity. In a letter from Letitia Pilkington,
to the demure author of "Sir Charles Grandison," and
published by the no less exemplary and irreproachable
Mrs. Barbauld, the lady informs her correspondent that
she has taken apartments in Great White Lion Street,
and stuck up a bill intimating that all who have not found
" reading and writing come by nature," and who had had
no teacher to make up the defect by art, might have
"letters written here." With the progress of education,
printing presses have found their way into St. Giles's, and

it is now no exaggeration to say that, compared with the rest of the metropolis, the streets radiating from Seven Dials display more than the average of booksellers and stationers' shops, circulating libraries, and the like.

The taste of Seven Dials and its immediate neighbourhood is more literary than scientific, and the modern seems preferred to ancient literature. Romantic series of the Thomas Prest school—he who *did* the novels for E. Lloyd—appear greatly in demand, such as " Ela, the Outcast," " Angelina," " Ernestine De Lacy," " Emily Fitzormond," " Death Grasp," " Mary Clifford," " Gertrude of the Rock," " Rosalie ; or, the Vagrant's Daughter," "Susan Hopley ; or, the Vicissitudes of a Servant Girl," " Kathleen," " Hebrew Maiden," " Vileroy ; or, the Horrors of Zindorf Castle," "The Penny Pickwick," " Gallant Tom," "The Maniac Father," "The Victim of Seduction," " Henrietta ; or, the Grave of the Forsaken," " The Wreck of the Heart," " The Miller's Maid," " Ada, the Betrayed ; or, the Murder at the Old Smithy," &c., &c., *ad infinitum.*

The fact of all the works we have enumerated belonging to the illustrated class, will have prepared the reader to expect other symptoms of a taste for art ; and accordingly, in Monmouth Street, we find one of the greatest ateliers from which the milk shops, ginger beer stalls, greengroceries, and pot houses of the suburbs are supplied with sign boards. Theatrical amateurs appear to abound ; at least the ample store of tin daggers, blunt cutlasses, banners, halberds, battle axes, &c., constantly exposed for sale at a cellar in Monmouth Street, indicate a steady demand. Nor is this all ; in no part of the town do we find singing birds in greater numbers and variety, and as most of the houses, being of an old fashion, have broad ledges of lead over the shop windows, these are frequently converted into hanging gardens, not so extensive as those of Babylon, but possibly yielding as much pleasure to their occupants. In short, what with literature and a taste for flowers and birds, there is much of the "sweet south" about the Seven Dials, harmonising with the out-of-door habits of its occupants.

Several years ago, Mr. Albert Smith, who lived at Chertsey, discovered in his neighbourhood part of the Seven Dials—the column doing duty as a monument to a Royal Duchess—when he described the circumstance in a pleasant paper, entitled "Some News of a famous Old Fellow," in his "Town and Country Magazine." The communication is as follows :—" Let us now quit the noisome mazes of St. Giles's and go out and away into the pure and leafy country. Seventeen or eighteen miles from town, in the county of Surrey, is the little village of Weybridge. Formerly, a couple of hours and more were passed pleasantly enough upon a coach through Kingston, the Moulseys, and Walton, to arrive there over a sunny, blowy common of pink heath and golden furze, within earshot, when the wind was favourable, of the old monastery bell, ringing out the curfew from Chertsey Church. Now the South-Western Railway trains tear and racket down in forty-five minutes, but do not interfere with the rural prospects, for their path lies in such a deep cutting that the very steam does not intrude upon the landscape.

" One of the lions to be seen at Weybridge is Oatlands, with its large artificial grotto and bath-room, which is said— but we cannot comprehend the statement—to have cost the Duke of Newcastle, who had it built, £40,000. The late Duchess of York died at Oatlands, and lies in a small vault under Weybridge Church, wherein there is a monument, by Chantrey, to her memory. She was an excellent lady, well-loved by all the country people about her, and when she died they were anxious to put up some sort of a tribute to her memory. But the village was not able to offer a large sum of money for this purpose. The good folks did their best, but the amount was still very humble, so they were obligated to dispense with the services of any eminent architect, and build up only such a monument as their means could compass. Somebody told them that there was a column to be sold cheap in a stonemason's yard, which might answer their purpose. It was accordingly purchased ; a coronet was placed upon its summit ; and the memorial was set up on Weybridge Green, in front of the Ship Inn, at the junction of the roads leading to Oatlands, to Shepperton Locks, and to Chertsey. This column turned out to be the original one from Seven Dials.

" The stone on which the dials were engraved or fixed, was sold with it. The poet Gay, however, was wrong when he spoke of its seven faces. It is hexagonal in its shape ; this is accounted for by the fact that two of the streets opened into one angle. It was not wanted to assist in forming the monument, but was turned into a stepping stone, near the adjoining inn, to assist the infirm in mounting their horses, and there it now lies, having sunk by degrees into the earth ; but its original form can still be easily surmised. It may be about three feet in diameter.

" The column itself is about thirty feet high and two feet in diameter, displaying no great architectural taste. It is surmounted by a coronet, and the base is enclosed by a light iron railing. An appropriate inscription on one side of the base indicates its erection in the year 1822, on the others are some lines to the memory of the Duchess.

" Relics undergo strange transpositions. The obelisk from the mystic solitudes of the Nile to the centre of the Place de la Concorde, in bustling Paris—the monuments of Nineveh to the regions of Great Russell Street—the frescoes from the long, dark, and silent Pompeii to the bright and noisy Naples—all these are odd changes. But, in proportion to their importance, not much behind them is that old column from the crowded dismal regions of St. Giles to the sunny tranquil Green of Weybridge."

At the time Jemmy Catnach commenced business in Seven Dials it took all the prudence and tact which he could command to maintain his position, as at that time " Johnny" Pitts,* of the Toy and Marble Warehouse, No. 6, Great St. Andrew Street, was the acknowledged and established printer of street literature for the " Dials " district ; therefore, as may be easily imagined, a powerful rivalry and vindictive jealousy soon arose between these " two of a trade"—most especially on the part of " Old Mother" Pitts, who is de-scribed as being a coarse and vulgar-minded personage, and as having originally followed the trade of a bumboat woman at Portsmouth : she " vowed vengeance against the young fellow in the court for daring to set up in their business, and also spoke of him as a young " Catsnatch," " Catblock," " Cut-throat," and many other opprobrious terms being freely given to the new comer. Pitts' staff of " bards" were duly cautioned of the consequences which would inevitably follow should they dare to write a line for Catnach—the new *cove* in the court. The injunction was for a time obeyed, but the " Seven Bards of the Seven Dials " soon found it not only convenient, but also more profitable to sell copies of their effusions to both sides at the same time, and by keeping their own council they avoided detection, as each printer accused the other of obtaining an early sold copy, and then reprinting it with the utmost speed, and which was in reality often the case, as " Both Houses " had emissaries on the constant look-out for any new production suitable for street-sale. Now, although this style of " double dealing " and competition tended much to lessen the cost price to the " middle-man," or vendor, the public in this case did not

---

*Pitts, a modern publisher of love garlands, merriments, penny ballads, '
" Who, ere he went to heaven,
Domiciled in Dials Seven !"—
G. DANIEL's "Democritus in London."

E

get any of the reduction, as a penny broadside was still a
penny, and a quarter ·sheet still a halfpenny to them, the
" street-patterer" obtaining the whole of the reduction as
extra profit.

The feud existing between these rival publishers, who
have been somewhat aptly designated as the Colburn and
Bentley of the " páper" trade, never abated, but, on the
contrary, increased in acrimony of temper until at last not
being content to vilify each other by words alone, they
resorted to printing off virulent lampoons, in which Catnach
never failed to let the world know that " Old Mother Pitts"
had been formerly a bumboat woman, while the Pitts' party
announced that—

> " All the boys and girls around,
>   Who go out prigging rags and phials,
>   Know Jemmy *Catsnatch* ! ! ! well,
>   Who lives iñ a back slum in the Dials.
>   He hangs out in Monmouth Court,
>   And wears a pair of blue-black breeches,
>   Where all the " Polly Cox's crew" do resort
>   To chop their swag for badly printed *Dying* Speeches."

Catnach's London contemporaries, in addition to Johnny
Pitts, of the Toy and Marble Warehouse, were Birt, 29,
Great St. Andrew Street ; T. Evans, 79, Long Lane ; Rocliff,
Old Gravel Lane ; Batchelor, Long Alley ; Marks, Brick
Lane, Spitalfields, and a little later on S. Hodges (from the
late J. Pitts), Wholesale Toy Warehouse, 13, Dudley Street,
Seven Dials, while the provincial districts were well re-
presented : Manchester had its Cadman, Bebbington, and
Jacques ; Birmingham, its W. Pratt and Russell ; Liverpool,
its McCall and Jones ; Durham, its Walker ; Newcastle and
Hull were supplied by W. and T. Fordyce ; Preston, by
John Harkness ; Dudley, by Cook ; Brighton, by J. Phillips,
of Meeting House Lane, commonly known as the " Lanes,"
and Sheffield, by Ford and Swindells, &c., &c.

In spite of all the opposition and trade rivalry, Catnach

persevered; he worked hard, and lived hard, and just fitted to the stirring times. The Peninsular wars had just concluded, politics and party strife ran high, squibs, lampoons, and political ballads were the order of the day, and he made money. But he had weighty pecuniary family matters to bear up with, as thus early in his career, his father's sister also joined them, and they all lived and huddled together in the shop and parlour of No. 2, Monmouth Court, doing a small and very humble trade as a jobbing master, printing and publishing penny histories, street-papers, and halfpenny songs, relying for their composition on one or two out of the "Seven Bards of the Seven Dials," and when they were on the drink, or otherwise not inclined to work, being driven to write and invent them himself.

The customers who frequented his place of business were of the lowest grades of society. Their modes of existing were very precarious; vagrants, miscreants, and the vilest outcasts of society were connected with the catchpenny trade. There are few who are conversant with Mayhew's "London" but know something of the many thousands of individuals who are living in the great metropolis of England without the means of earning an honest livelihood. We have many instances how the beggars and the itinerants spend their lives: during the day time they go about the streets and upon the highways as objects of charity, pity, and commiseration; at night they meet together in some well-known place, where the wallet containing the contents of the day's gathering is turned out, and, sitting down, they each divest themselves of the disguises of the day, and commence to spend the remainder of the night in feasting, revelry, and song. Burns, in his "Jolly Beggars," has furnished us with a fine illustration of these peculiar people. The begging trade had, like other professions, its given orders. Asking alms from house to house was the lowest. When anyone, after a few years' toil grew tired of the life, they invariably aspired to become vendors of small wares, ballads, and catch-pennies. Many of these things are now curiosities, and form mementos of a past state of things. No one was ever more fond of these small books, containing history, biography, ballad poetry, odd sayings and doings, than was the great author of "Waverley," and the matchless characters which run through the whole of his novels show how keenly he had cherished every passing event in his memory. In our own day we find the late Mr. Robert White, author of the "Battle of Bannockburn," pursuing a similar course. And one, whose memory as an author we shall always reverence, once told us that nothing gave him more pleasure than a friendly chat with a strolling player, a mountebank, or a proprietor of a Punch and Judy show. His conclusions about these men were that they always possessed a certain fund of amuse-ment and information. The persons mostly connected with the catchpenny trade were those who by folly, intemperance, and crime, had been reduced to the greatest penury. Any-one with a few coppers in his pockets could easily knock out an existence, especially when anything sensational was in the wind.

One class of literature which Jemmy Catnach made almost his own, was children's farthing and halfpenny books. Among the great many that he published we select, from our own private collection, the following as a fair sample :—" The Tragical Death of an Apple Pie," " The House that Jack Built," " Jumping Joan," " The Butterflys' Ball and Grass-hoppers' Feast," " Jerry Diddle and his Fiddle," " Nurse Love-Child's Gift," " The Death and Burial of Cock Robin," " The Cries of London," " Simple Simon," " Jacky Jingle and Suky Shingle," and—" Here you have just prin—ted and pub—lish—ed, and a—dor—ned with ten beau—ti—ful and ele—gantly engraved embellish—ments, and for the low charge of one *farden*—Yes ! one *farden* buys :—

NURSERY RHYMES.

See-saw, sacradown,
Which is the way to London
   town?
One foot up, and the other down,
And that is the way to London
   town.

Hey diddle, the cat and the fiddle,
   The cow jumped over the
      moon,
The little dog laughed to see the
      sport,
And the dish ran away with
      the spoon.

Ding, dong, bell !
Pussy's in the well.
Who put her in ?
Little Johnny Green.
Who pulled her out?
Little Johnny Snout.
What a naughty boy was that,
To drown poor pussy cat,
Who never did him any harm,
And kill'd the mice in his father's
      barn.

Jack and Jill went up the hill,
   To get a pail of water ;
Jack fell down and broke his crown,
   And Jill came tumbling after.

Cock a doodle do,
The dame has lost her shoe,
And master's lost his fiddle stick
And don't know what to do.

I had a little husband,
    No bigger than my thumb,
I put him in a quart pot,
    And there I bid him drum.

Who's there ?   A Grenadier !
What do you want? A pot of beer.
Where's your money? Oh, I forget.
Then get you gone, you drunken
    sot.

There was an old woman
    lived in a shoe,
She had so many children
    knew not what to do ;
She gave them some broth
    out any bread,
Then she beat them all well
    sent them to bed.

Hush-a-bye, baby, on the tree top,
When the wind blows the cradle
    will rock.
When the bough breaks the cra-
    dle will fall,
Down comes the baby, cradle and
    all.

Young lambs to sell,
Young lambs to sell,
If I'd as much money as I
    tell,
I wouldn't cry young lambs

Goosey, goosey, gander,
  Whither dost thou wander?
Up stairs and down stairs,
  And in my lady's chamber;
There you'll find a cup of sack,
And plenty of good ginger.

The cock doth crow
To let you know,
If you be wise
'Tis time to rise.

The lion and the unicorn fighting
  for the crown,
The lion beat the unicorn round
  about the town;
Some gave them white bread,
  some gave them brown, .
Some gave them plum cake, and
  sent them out of town.

My mother and your mother
  Went over the way;
Said my mother to your mother,
  It's chop-a-nose day!

J. Catnach, Printer, 2, Monmouth Court,
7 Dials.

The Cries of London have ever been very popular, whether as broadsides, or in book form. In the British Museum is a series of "Cries of London," about the oldest is a Black-Letter ballad, by W. Turner, called :—

> "The Common Cries of London Town,
>   Some go up street and some go down."

Under the title is a woodcut of a man with a basket on his head. The only known copy is dated 1662, but contains internal evidence, in the following stanza, that it was written in the reign of James I.

> "That 's the fat foole of the Curtin,
>   And the lean foole of the Bull :
> Since Shanke did leave to sing his rimes
>   He is counted but a gull.
> The Players on the Banckeside,
>   The round Globe and the Swan,
> Will teach you idle tricks of love,
>   But the Bull will play the man."

Shanke, the comic actor here mentioned, was one of Prince Henry's players, in 1603; and John Taylor the *Water-Poet*, informs us that the Swan Theatre, on the Bankside, in the liberty of Paris Gardens, had been abandoned by the players in 1613. The Curtain Theatre, in Holywell Street, Shoreditch Fields,* had also fallen into disuse before the reign of Charles I. The Globe and Bull were employed until after the Restoration.

---

* The Curtain Road, now notorious for cheap and shoddy furniture, still marks the site of the Curtain Theatre, at the same date there was another playhouse in the parish of St. Leonard, Shoreditch; distinguished as "The Theatre," where the Chamberlain's Company had settled, which J. Burbadge, who long resided in Holywell Street, Shoreditch, pulled down about 1595—6, and built the Globe.

Other London Cries are mentioned by different authors, and a long list of them, under the title of the " Cries of Rome," may be seen in Thomas Heywood's " Rape of Lucrece," 1608. In the old play of " The Three Lords and Three Ladies of London," 1590, it appears that wood-men went about with their beetles and wedges on their backs, crying " Have you any wood to cleave?" In " The Loyal Subject," by Beaumont and Fletcher, act 3, scene 5, we find that in the reign of James I. potatoes had become so common, that " Potatoes! ripe Potatoes!" were publicly hawked about the City. " The Cries of London" are enumerated in Brome's " Court Beggars," 1653. " The London Chanticleers, a witty Comedy full of Various and Delightfull Mirth," 1659. This piece is rather an interlude than a play, and is amusing and curious, the characters being, with two exceptions, all London criers. The allusions to old usages, with the mention of many well-known ballads, and some known no longer, contribute to give the piece an interest and a value of its own.

The principal *Dramatis Personæ* consists of :—

HEATH.—*A broom man.* " Brooms, maids, brooms! Come, buy my brooms, maids; 'Tis a new broom, and will sweep clean. Come, buy my broom, maids!"

BRISTLE.—*A brush man.* " Come, buy a save-all. Buy a comb-brush, or a pot-brush; buy a flint, or a steel, or a tinder-box."

DITTY.—*A ballad man.* " Come, new books, new books, newly printed and newly come forth! All sorts of ballads and pleasant books! *The Famous History of Tom Thumb* and *Unfortunate Jack*, *A Hundred Goodly Lessons* and *Alas, poor Scholar, whither wilt thou go? The second part of Mother Shipton's Prophecies, newly made by a gentleman of good quality*, foretelling what was done four hundred years ago, and *A Pleasant Ballad of a bloody fight seen i' th' air*, which, the astrologers say, portends scarcity of fowl this year. The

Ballad of the Unfortunate Lover. I have *George of Green,
Chivy Chase, Collins and the Devil; or, Room for Cuckolds,
The Ballad of the London 'Prentice, Guy of Warwick, The
Beggar of Bethnal Green, The Honest Milkmaid; or, I
must not wrong my Dame, The Honest Fresh Cheese and .
Cream Woman.* Then I have *The Seven Wise Men of
Gotham, A Hundred Merry Tales, Scoggin's Jests; or, A
Book of Prayers and Graces for Young Children.* I have
very strange news from beyond seas. The King of Morocco
has got the black jaundice, and the Duke of Westphalia is
sick of the swine-pox, with eating bacon ; the Moors increase
daily, and the King of Cyprus mourns for the Duke of
Saxony, that is dead of the stone ; and Presbyter John is
advanced to Zealand ; the sea ebbs and flows but twice in
four-and-twenty hours, and the moon has changed but once
the last month."

BUDGET.—*A Tinker.* " Have you any work for the tinker?
Old brass, old pots, old kettles. I'll mend them all with a
tara-tink, and never hurt your metal."

GUM.—*A Tooth drawer.* " Have you any corns upon
your feet or toes ? Any teeth to draw ? "

JENNETING.—*An Apple wench.* "Come, buy my pear-
mains, curious John Apples, dainty pippins ? Come, who
buy ? who buy ? "

CURDS.—*A fresh Cheese and Cream woman.* " I have
fresh cheese and cream ; I have fresh cheese and cream."

In the "Instructive Library," printed for the Man in the
Moon, 1710, we have the cries of " Knives to grind," " Old
chairs to mend," " Pears to bake," " Milk, a penny a quart,"
" Grey peas and bacon," " Fresh herrings," and "Shrews-
bury puddings."

The following is a fac-simile of a Catnachian edition of

THE
Cries 'of London.

Milk below.

Cherries.

Here's round and sound,
Black and white heart cherries,
Two-pence a pound.

Rain, frost, or snow, or hot or
    cold,
  I travel up and down,
The cream and milk you buy of
    me
  Is best in all the town.
For custards, puddings, or for tea,
  There's none like those you
    buy of me.

Oranges.

  Here's oranges nice!
  At a very small price,
I sell them all two for a penny.
  Ripe, juicy, and sweet,
  Just fit for to eat,
So customers buy a good many.

Crumpling Codlings.

Come, buy my Crumpling Cod-
  lings,
  Buy all my Crumplings.
Some of them you may eat raw,
  Of the rest make dumplings,
Or pies, or puddings, which you
  please.

Filberts.

Come, buy my filberts ripe and
    brown,
They are the best in all the town,
I sell them for a groat a pound,
And warrant them all good and
    sound,
You're welcome for to crack and
    try,
They are so good I'm sure you'll
    buy.

Sweep.

Sweep, chimney sweep,
Is the common cry I keep,
    If you rightly understand me;
With my brush, broom, and my
    rake,
Such cleanly work I make,
    There's few can go beyond me.

Clothes Pegs, Props, or Lines.

Come, maids, and buy my pegs
    and props,
    Or lines to dry your clothes,
And when they are dry they 'll
    smell as sweet
    As any damask rose,
Come buy and save your clothes
    from dirt,
They 'll save you washing many
    a shirt.

Peas and Beans.

Four pence a peck, green Hast-
    ings !
    And fine garden beans.
They are all morning gathered ;
    Come hither, my queens,
Come buy my Windsor beans
    and peas,
You'll see no more this year like
    these.

Strawberries.

Rare ripe strawberries and
Hautboys, sixpence a pottle.
Full to the bottom, hautboys.
Strawberries and Cream are
    charming and sweet,
Mix them and try how delightful
    they eat.

Hot Cross Buns,
One a penny, Buns,
Two a penny, Buns,
Hot Cross Buns.

LONDON :

Printed by J. Catnach, 2, Monmouth
Court, 7 Dials.

Nurse Love-Child's
NEW YEAR'S GIFT.

FOR

LITTLE MISSES AND MASTERS.

J. CATNACH, PRINTER,

2 & 3,

MONMOUTH-COURT, 7 DIALS.

Who killed Cock Robin?
I said the sparrow,
With my bow and arrow,
I killed Cock Robin.

Tell-Tale tit,
Your tongue shall be slit,
And all the dogs in the town
Shall have a little bit.

Pussy-Cat, pussy-cat, where have
you been?
I've been up to London, to look
at the Queen.
Pussy-cat, pussy-cat, what did you
do there!
I frightened a little mouse under
the chair.

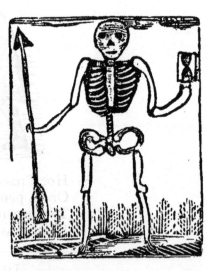

Life is a jest, and all things
show it ;
I thought so once, but now
I know it.

Johnny Armstrong kill'd a calf,
Peter Henderson got the half ;
Willie Wilkinson got the head,
Ring the bell, the calf is dead.

As I went to Bonner,
  I met a pig
  Without a wig,
Upon my word and honour.

All of a row,
Bend the bow,
Shot at a pigeon
And killed a crow.

Snail, snail, come
  out of your hole,
Or else I will beat
  you as black as a
  coal.

All the birds in the air fell
  to sighing and sobbing,
When they heard the bell toll
  for poor Cock Robin.

Bell horses, Bell horses,
  What time of day ?
One o'clock, two o'clock,
  Three and away.

One, two, three,
I love coffee,
And Billy loves tea.
How good you be,
One, two, three,
I love coffee,
And Billy loves tea.

JACK THE GIANT KILLER.

There was an old woman went up
 in a basket,
  Seventy times as high as the
  moon;
What she did there I could not
 but ask it,
For in her hand she carried a
 broom.
" Old woman, old woman, old
 woman," said I,
" Whither, oh whither, oh whither
 so high?"
" To sweep the cobwebs from the
 sky,
And I shall be back again, by-
 and-by."

Needles and pins,
 Needles and pins ;
When a man marries
 His trouble begins.

A MERMAID.

Hark ! Hark !
The dogs do bark,
Beggars are coming to tow
 Some in jags,
 Some in rags,
And some in velvet gowns

A CASTLE.

I 'll tell you a story
 About Jack-a-Nory,
And now my story 's begu
 I 'll tell you another
About Jack and his broth
And now my story 's do

Many other nursery books of a similar kind might be mentioned as some of the chief attractions that emanated from the "Catnach Press," and which, to the juvenile population, were more eagerly welcomed than the great sensational three-volume novels are by many in our day.

It is remarkable, that at a time when "Art" holds so high a place in popular education, and teaching by object-lessons is adopted as the best method of elementary teaching in infant schools, the books given to young children as rewards or inducements to them to exercise their memories should not be more carefully prepared. In spite of the great advances made in the art of illustration, we still meet with so-called "Toy-Books," the pictures in which are either contemptibly bad or repulsively ugly. It should not be forgotten, that, to young children, picture-books are the chief means of education, and that, to accustom them to look at badly-drawn and coarsely-executed pictures, is as undesirable as to permit them to hear wrongly-pronounced or vulgar words.

Catnach received a very indifferent education, and that little at the establishment of Mr. Goldie, in Alnwick, where his attendance was very irregular, and this drawback assisted very much in blunting his relish for the higher walks of literature. The father had not carried out the heavenly injunction so much practised in Scotland, by giving to his son the best of blessings—"a good education." A great fault he had, and a grevious one, and that was in allowing his own social pleasures to interfere with the mental training of his offspring.

Jemmy had a tenacious love for money, and this propensity he retained throughout life. As a man of business he was rough and brusque in his manners, but this mattered little, as his trade lay amongst a class who were low and insensitive in their habits and modes of living ; and

his many peculiarities, both in speech and dress, would be
little heeded by his mixed-medley customers.

It was hardly possible that anything creditable in good
printing could emanate from the establishment of Catnach;
his stock of type was miserably bad, whilst his wood blocks,
which we shall hereafter allude to, were of the rudest kind,
and it mattered little what was the quality of the paper so
long as the sheets met with a ready sale. The productions
issued at the "Catnach Press" were not destined to rank
high in the annals of literature; and they bear a sorry
appearance when placed alongside of several works of a
similar kind, which were printed at the same period in many
parts of the kingdom. In this respect Jemmy Catnach
was very unlike his father, for, whilst the former had a
niggardly turn in all his dealings, the latter was naturally
inclined to the reverse.

Another series of juvenile works of a larger size
and price, consists of "The adventurous exploits of
Robinson Crusoe," "The butchery and bloody deeds of
Jack the Giant Killer," "The treacherous and inveterate
hatred that lingered in the bosom of Blue Beard," "The
amusing story and career of Tom Hickathrift," "The
touching and heart-rending account as portrayed in the
story of the Babes in the Wood," "The adventures of Ali
Baba; or, the Forty Thieves," and many others, concluding
with the ever popular "Old Mother Hubbard and her
Wonderful Dog," a fac-similed copy of a true Catnachian
Edition here follows, and although the woodcuts in the body
of the work are of the most anti-Bewickian character, it is
possible to conceive; the piece at the end is very chaste,
and said to have been drawn by Thurston, and engraved by
Thomas Bewick, for the elder Catnach. The old block has
been very much worked, and is still with the others doing
duty in the office of the "Catnach Press," Monmouth Court.

OLD
MOTHER HUBBARD
AND HER
WONDERFUL DOG.

Old Mother Hubbard went to the cupboard
   To get the poor dog a bone ;
But when she came there the cupboard was bare,
   And so the poor dog had none.

She went to the baker's to buy him some bread,
When she came back the dog was dead.
Ah! my poor dog, she cried, oh, what shall I do?
You were always my pride—none equal to you.

She went to the undertaker's to buy him a coffin,
When she came back, the dog was laughing.
Now how this can be quite puzzles my brain,
I am much pleased to see you alive once again.

She went to the barber's to buy him a wig,
When she came back he was dancing a jig.
O, you dear merry grig, how nicely you 're prancing ;
Then she held up the wig, and he began dancing.

She went to the sempstress to buy him some linen,
When she came back the dog was spinning.
The reel, when 'twas done, was wove into a shirt,
Which served to protect him from weather and dirt.

To market she went, to buy him some tripe,
When she came back he was smoking his pipe.
Why, sure, cried the dame, you'd beat the great Jocko,
Who before ever saw a dog smoking tobacco?

She went to the alehouse to buy him some beer,
When she came back he sat on a chair.
Drink hearty, said Dame, there's nothing to pay,
'Twill banish your sorrow and moisten your clay.

She went to the tailor's to buy him a coat,
When she came back he was riding the goat.
What, you comical elf, the good dame cried,
Who would have thought a dog would so ride?

She went to the hatter's to buy him a hat,
When she came back he was feeding the cat.
The sight made her stare, as he did it so pat,
While puss sat on the chair, so she showed him the hat.

She went to the shop to buy him some shoes,
When she came back he was reading the news.
Sure none would believe (she laughed as she spoke),
That a dog could be found to drink ale and smoke.

She went to the hosier's, to buy him some hose,
When she came back he was drest in his clothes.
How now? cries the dame, with a look of surprise,
To see you thus drest, I scarce credit my eyes.

She went to the fruiterer's to buy him some fruit,
When she came back he was playing the flute.
Oh, you musical dog, you surely can speak :
Come, sing me a song, then he set up a squeak.

She went to the tavern for white wine and red,
When she came back he stood on his head.
This is odd, said the dame, for fun you seem bred,
One would almost believe you 'd wine in your head.

The dog he cut capers, and turned out his toes,
'Twill soon cure the vapours, he such attitude shows.
The dame made a curtsey, the dog made a bow,
The dame said, Your servant, the dog said Bow wow.

There can be little doubt that the great publisher of the
Seven Dials, next to children's books, had his mind mostly
centered upon the chronicling of doubtful scandals, fabulous
duels between ladies of fashion, "cooked" assassinations,
and sudden deaths of eminent individuals, apochryphal
elopements, real or catch-penny account of murders, impossible robberies, delusive suicides, dark deeds and public
executions, to which was usually attached the all-important
and necessary "Sorrowful Lamentations," or ".Copy of
Affectionate Verses," which, according to the established
custom, the criminal composed in the condemned cell
the night before his execution, after this manner :—

" A LL you that have got feeling hearts, I pray you now
attend
To these few lines so sad and true, a solemn silence lend ;
It is of a cruel murder, to you I will unfold ——
The bare recital of the tale must make your blood run cold."

Or take another and stereotyped example, which from
time to time has served equally well for the verses *written
by* the culprit—Brown, Jones, Robinson, or Smith :

"THOSE deeds I mournfully repent,
But now it is too late,
The day is past, the die is cast,
And fixed is my fate.
Young men be taught by my dreadful fate,
Avoid the paths I have trod,
And teach yourselves in early years
To love and fear your God."

Occasionally the Last Sorrowful Lamentations contained
a "Love Letter"—the criminal being unable, in some
instances, to read or write, being no obstacle to the com-

position. Written according to the street patterer's statement: "from the depths of the condemned cell, with the condemned pen, ink, and paper." This mode of procedure in "gallows" literature, and this style of composition, have prevailed for from fifty to sixty years.

Then they would say: "Here you have also an exact likeness of the murderer taken at the bar of the Old Bailey!" when all the time it was an old woodcut that had been used for every criminal for the last forty years.

"There's nothing beats a stunning good murder after all," said a " running patterer " to Mr. Henry Mayhew, the ingenious author of " London Labour and London Poor." It is only fair to assume that Mr. James Catnach shared in the sentiment.

The Battle of Waterloo—this last, or fifteenth of the decisive battles at which Napoleon I. was finally overthrown, took place 18th of June, 1815. There can be no doubt that there were many street-ballads written to commemorate this great historical event, but we have only succeeded in obtaining two examples. From the first, which is in eighteen stanzas, we make a selection as follows :

The Battle of Waterloo.

A T ten o'clock on Sunday the bloody fray begun,
It raged hot from that moment till the setting of the
sun,
My pen, I'm sure, can't half relate the glory of that day,
We fought the French at Waterloo & made them run away.

On the 18th day of June, eighteen hundred and fifteen,
Both horse and foot they did advance, most glorious to be
seen,   [did blow,
Both horse and foot they did advance, and the bugle horn
The sons of France were made to dance on the plains of
Waterloo.

Our Cavalry advanced with true and valiant hearts,
Our Infantry and Artillery did nobly play their parts,
While the small arms did rattle, and great guns did roar,
And many a valiant soldier bold lay bleeding in his gore.

Napoleon like a fighting cock, was mounted on a car,
He much did wish to represent great Mars the god of war,
On a high platform he did stand, and loudly he did crow,
He dropp'd his wings and turned his tail to us at Waterloo.

The valiant Duke of Brunswick fell in the field that day,
And many a valiant officer dropp'd in the awful fray,
And many British soldiers lay wounded in their gore,
Upon the plains of Waterloo,—where thundering cannons
    roar.

Lord Wellington commanded us, all on that glorious day,
When many poor brave soldiers in death's cold arms did
    lay ;—
Where small arms they did rattle, and cannons loudly roar,
At Waterloo, where Frenchmen their fate did much deplore.

Now tender husbands here have left their wives to mourn,
And children weeping, cry—when will our dads return ?
Our country will dry up their tears, we feel rejoiced to know
They will reward each soldier bold, who fought at Waterloo.

When Bonaparte he did perceive the victory we had won,
He did lament in bitter tears, saying, O my darling son !
I will set off for Paris straight, and have him crown'd also,
Before they hear of my defeat on the plains of Waterloo.

So unto George our gracious king my voice I mean to raise
And to all gallant commanders I wish to sing their praise,
The Duke of York and family and Wellington also,
And the soldiers brave they fought that day on the plains of
Waterloo.

J. Catnach, Printer, 2, Monmouth Court, 7 Dials.
CARDS, BILLS, &C., *Printed on very Reasonable Terms.*

From the other example we select the first and two concluding stanzas as a fair specimen of the whole :

'TWAS on the 18th day of June Napoleon did advance,
The choicest troops that he could raise within the
bounds of France ;
Their glittering eagles shone around and proudly looked the
foe,
But Briton's lion tore their wings on the plains of Waterloo.

We followed up the rear till the middle of the night,
We gave them three cheers as they were on their flight ;
Says Bony, d——n those Englishmen, they do bear such a
name,
They beat me here at Waterloo, at Portugal, and Spain.

Now peace be to their honoured souls who fell that glorious
day,
May the plough ne'er raise their bones nor cut the sacred
clay ;
But let the place remain a waste, a terror to the foe,
And when trembling Frenchmen pass that way they'll think
of Waterloo.

J. Pitts, Printer, 6, Great St. Andrew Street.

'Few cases ever excited greater interest in the public mind or caused more street-papers to be sold than that of Eliza Fenning, a domestic servant, aged twenty-one, who was indicted at the Old Bailey, April the 11th, 1815, for administering arsenic into some yeast dumplings, with intent to kill and murder Mr. and Mrs. Turner, her master and mistress, and the rest of the family. The public took a great interest in her case, and universally she was believed to be innocent, but the jury in a few minutes brought in a verdict of *Guilty*. Thousands of persons, after examining the evidence adduced at the trial, did not hesitate to express their opinions very strongly upon the subject of the case ; and many of the lower orders assembled in the front of Mr. Turner's house, in Chancery Lane, where he carried on the business of a law stationer, hooting and hissing, and otherwise expressing their indignation at what they conceived to be an unjust prosecution of their servant. The mob continued to assemble for many weeks, and it was not until the police had taken very vigorous measures against them, that they were finally dispersed.

Mr. Hone published a narrative of the case, with a portrait of the poor girl; this was replied to, and there continued much contention upon the matter. The medical man who had given evidence on the trial, suffered considerably in his practice.

Four months elapsed between her conviction and execution. So many circumstances, which had developed themselves subsequently to the trial, had been communicated to the Secretary of State by highly respectable persons who interested themselves in her favour, that a reprieve was confidently expected. At length the order for her execution was received.

From the moment the poor girl was first charged with the poisoning, she never faltered in her denial of the crime, and rather courted than shunned an investigation of her case, and on the fatal morning, the 26th of July, 1815, when at the foot of the gallows, a 'gentleman who had greatly interested himself in her behalf, abjured her, in the name of that God in whose presence she was about to appear, if she knew anything of the crime for which she was about to suffer to make it known, when she replied distinctly and clearly, " Before God, then, I die innocent !"   The question was again put to her by the Reverend Mr. Vazie, as well as by the ordinary, and finally by Oldfield, a prisoner who suffered with her, and to each she repeated, " I am innocent." These were her last words.*

Thousands accompanied her funeral ; and the public still sympathizing with the unhappy parents, a subscription was entered into for their benefit.

On the cessation of the protracted war which consigned Napoleon to St. Helena, Great Britain found herself subject to those temporary domestic difficulties which always succeed a sudden return from hostilities to peace.   The revulsion was felt by nearly every individual in the kingdom ; agriculture, trade, and commerce became, for the instant, almost torpid, and thousands of the labouring classes were thrown out of employment.

On the 15th of November, 1816, a meeting of about 30,000 persons, including Mr. Henry Hunt, the Radical leader, took place in Spa Fields—then a large uninclosed space—to vote an address from the distressed manufacturers to the Prince Regent ; a second meeting, on the 2nd of December, following, terminated in an alarming riot, the shops of several gunsmiths were attacked for arms by the rioters, and in the shop of Mr. Beckwith, on Snowhill, Mr. Platt was wounded, and much injury was done before the

---

* In the "Annual Register," for 1857, p. 143, it is stated, on the authority of Mr. Gurney, that she confessed the crime to Mr. James Upton, a Baptist minister, shortly before her execution.

tumult was suppressed. For this riot, John Cashman, the seaman, was hanged, March 12th, 1817, and, to make the dreadful ceremony as awfully impressive as possible, it was ordered that he should suffer in front of Mr. Beckwith's shop, where the crime for which his life was forfeited, had been committed. This circumstance materially benefitted the producers and workers of street-literature.

The sensation excited throughout the country by the melancholy death of the Princess Charlotte, on the sixth day of November, 1817, was an event of no ordinary description, and even at the present day is still vividly remembered. It was, indeed, a most unexpected blow, the shining virtues, as well as the youth and beauty of the deceased, excited an amount of affectionate commiseration, such as probably had never before attended the death of any royal personage in England.

In the Princess Charlotte the whole hopes of the nation were centered. As the only child of the Prince Regent and Caroline of Brunswick, she was regarded as the sole security for the lineal transmission to posterity of the British sceptre, her uncles, the Dukes of Clarence, Kent, Cumberland, and Cambridge being then all unmarried. Well-grounded fears were entertained that through her death the inheritance of the Crown might pass from the reigning family, and devolve on a foreign and despotic dynasty. These apprehensions were dispelled by the subsequent marriage of the Duke of Kent and the birth of the Princess Victoria, who, in her actual occupancy of the throne, has realised all the expectations which the nation had been led to entertain from the anticipated accession of her cousin.

In May, 1816, the Princess Charlotte was married to Prince Leopold of Saxe-Coburg. Their union had been the result of mutual attachment, not of political expediency, and in the calm tranquillity of domestic life, they enjoyed a degree of happiness such as has not often been the lot of royal personages. The Princess's approaching confinement was looked forward to by the nation with affectionate interest, but without the least apprehension as to the result. Early in the morning of Tuesday, the 4th of November, she was taken ill; the expresses were sent off to the great officers of State, including the Archbishop of Canterbury and the Lord Chancellor, who immediately attended. Everything seemed to go on favourably till the evening of the following day, when, at nine o'clock, the Princess was delivered of a still-born child. This melancholy circumstance, however, did not appear to affect the Princess so seriously as to give any cause for alarm, and about midnight it was deemed expedient to leave her to repose and the attentions of the nurse, Mrs. Griffiths. Ere half-an-hour elapsed, the latter observed such an alarming change in her patient that she at once summoned Prince Leopold and the medical attendants, Sir Richard Crofts and Drs. Baillie and Sims, who hurried to the chamber. The Princess became rapidly worse.

*   *   *   *   *   *   *

In her last agonies—in that awful moment when the scenes of this earth and all their grandeur were to close upon her for ever—scenes in which she had experienced the height of terrestrial bliss—the Princess grasped the hand of him who had ever been the object of that bliss. It was not the warm grasp of life: it was the convulsive one of death. Her head fell on her bosom, and breathing a gentle sigh she expired.

After the grief of the nation had somewhat subsided, the feeling of sorrow was succeeded by one of anger. It was said that the medical attendants of the Princess had mismanaged the case, and a carelessness and neglect, it was affirmed, had been shown which would have been scandalous had the fate of the humblest peasant woman been concerned. Extreme caution must be observed in dealing with these popular reports, considering the general propensity in human nature to slander, and the tendency to find in the deaths of eminent personages food for excitement and marvel. There really appears to have been some blundering in the case, but that this was the occasion of the Princess's death, we have no warrant for believing. It is a curious circumstance that Sir Richard Croft, the physician against whom the public odium was chiefly directed, committed suicide ere many months had elapsed.

We have given the above outline of the life and circumstances of the death of Princess Charlotte, to show how likely such an event, and at such a time, would affect the interests of producers of broadsides of news for the streets. The Seven Dials Press was busily engaged in working off "papers" descriptive of every fact that could be gleaned from the newspapers, and that was suitable for street sale. Catnach was not behind his compeers, as he published several statements in respect to the Princess's death, and *made* the following lines *out of his own head!* And had, continued our informant—a professional street-ballad writer—" wood enough left for as many more."

> "She is gone! sweet Charlotte's gone!
> Gone to the silent bourne;
> She is gone, she's gone, for evermore,—
> She never can return.
>
> She is gone with her joy—her darling Boy,
> The son of Leopold blythe and keen;
> She Died the sixth of November,
> Eighteen hundred and seventeen."

A parallel to the feeling of the public mind at the early and unexpected death of the Princess Charlotte has only appeared in recent years on the occasion of the demise of the consort of our beloved sovereign—the good Prince Albert.

G 2

The year 1818, proved a disastrous one to Catnach, as in addition to the extra burden entailed on him in family matters, he had, in the ordinary way of his trade, printed a street-paper reflecting on the private character and on the materials used in the manufacturing of the sausages as sold by the pork butchers of the Drury Lane quarter in general, and particularly by Mr. Pizzey, a tradesman carrying on business in Blackmore Street, Clare Market, who caused him to be summoned to the Bow Street Police Court to answer the charge of malicious libel, when he was committed to take his trial at the next Clerkenwell Sessions, by Sir Richard Burnie, where he was sentenced to six months' imprisonment. An official copy—*verbatim, et literatim, et punctuatim*—of the Indictment is now subjoined :—

Middlesex. The Jurors, For our Lord the King upon their Oath present that before and at the time of the committing of the offence hereinafter next mentioned and from thence hitherto Divers Liege Subjects of our said Lord the King to wit Thomas Pursell and John Gray resided and dwelt and still do reside and dwell in divers to wit two dwelling-houses situate and being in a certain public Street and Highway called Drury Lane in the County of Middlesex and divers other Liege Subjects of our said Lord the King to wit Thomas Pizzey Richard Hollings John Caspar Shum and John Shum during that time resided and dwelt and still reside and dwell in divers to wit four other dwelling houses situate and being in the neighborhood of Drury Lane aforesaid to wit in the Parish of St. Clement Danes in the said County of Middlesex and the said persons respectively during the time aforesaid exercised and carried on and still do exercise and carry on in the said dwelling-houses respectively the Trade and Business of a Pork Butcher and Seller of Pork to wit in the Parish of St. Clement Danes aforesaid in the County of Middlesex aforesaid nevertheless one James Catnach late of the Parish of St. Giles in the Fields in the County of Middlesex aforesaid Printer being a person of an evil wicked and malicious mind and disposition and unlawfully wickedly and maliciously devising contriving and intending as much as in him lay to cause it to be suspected and believed that one of the Pork Butchers and Sellers of Pork in the Neighborhood of Drury Lane aforesaid had been and was guilty of the misconduct hereinafter next mentioned and to stir up and irrate the minds of the Liege Subjects of our Lord the now King against the Porkbutchers in Drury Lane aforesaid and the neighborhood thereof and further contriving to scandalize vilify and defame vex barrass oppress and wholly ruin the said Thomas Pursell and John Gray and Thomas Pizzey Richard Hollings John Caspar Shum and John Shum respectively and to hinder and prevent the Leige Subjects of our said Lord the King from dealing or having any transactions with the said Thomas Pursell John Gray Thomas Pizzey Richard Hollings John Caspar Shum and John Shum in the way of their said respective trades and business on the first day of June in the Fifty eighth year of the reign of our Sovereign Lord George the Third by the Grace of God of the United Kingdom of Great Britain and Ireland King Defender of the Faith with force and arms at the Parish of Saint Giles in the Fields in the County of Middlesex aforesaid unlawfully and maliciously did print compose and publish and cause to be published a second false scandalous malicious and defamatory libel of and concerning such Pork Butchers containing therein the false scandalous malicious defamatory and libellous matter and words following that is to say—"*Another dreadful discovery ! Being an account of a number of Human Bodies found in the Shop of a Pork Butcher. We have just been informed of a most dreadful and horrible discovery revolting to every feeling of humanity and calculated to inspire sentiments of horror and disgust in the minds of every Individual. On Saturday night last the Wife of a Journeyman Taylor went into the Shop of a Butcher* (meaning the Shop of the said Thomas Pizzey) *in the Neighborhood of D——L——*(thereby then and there meaning Drury Lane and the said shop of the said Thomas Pizzey aforesaid) *to buy a piece of Pork. At the time the Master* (meaning the said Thomas Pizzey) *was serving a man came into the Shop* (meaning the said last mentioned Shop) *carrying a Sack. The woman thought by the appearance of the man that he was a Body Snatcher and when she left the Shop* (meaning the said Shop) *she* (meaning the said woman) *communicated her suspicions to an acquaintance she met with : the news of this soon spread abroad and two Officers went and searched the house* (meaning the house of which the said Shop was part and parcel) *and to their inexpressible horror found two dead bodies* (meaning human Bodies) *wrapped up in a sack great flocks of people were assembled from all parts of the Town at Marlborough Street in expectation of the offender having a hearing. Catnach* (meaning the said James Catnach) *Printer 2 Monmouth Court* (thereby then and there meaning that the person carrying on business in the said Shop as such Porkbutcher as aforesaid had caused and procured two dead human bodies to be brought into his said shop with intent to endeavour to sell the same as and for Pork) and the Jurors aforesaid on their oath aforesaid further say that by means and on account of the said false scandalous malicious and defamatory libel having been so published as aforesaid afterwards to wit on the first day of June in the fifty eighth year aforesaid and on divers days and times afterwards at the Parish of St. Clement Danes aforesaid in the County of Middlesex aforesaid divers to wit Two hundred Subjects of our said Lord the King whose names are to the Jurors aforesaid as yet unknown did riotously and tumultuously meet together to disturb the peace of our said Lord the King near to the said Dwelling house of the said Thomas Pizzey in the neighborhood of Drury Lane aforesaid to wit in the Parish of St. Clement Danes aforesaid to wit in Blackmore Street there and being so assembled and met together did then and there break and enter the said Shop of the said Thomss Pizzey and did break divers to wit ten windows of and belonging to the said shop and Dwelling house of the said Thomas Pizzey and did then in the said Shop unlawfully and against the will of the said Thomas Pizzey stay and continue for a long space of time to wit for the space of twelve hours on each of the said days assaulting and insulting the said Thomas Pizzey and Elizabeth his Wife and others of his family and his servants there and making a great noise and disturbance therein and hindered and prevented the said Thomas Pizzey from exercising and carrying on his said trade and business of a Pork Butcher therein and by means and on account of the publishing of the said libel as aforesaid. To the great damage scandal infamy and disgrace of the said Thomas Pursell John Gray and the said Thomas Pizzey Richard Hollings John Caspar Shum and John Shum respectively In contempt of our said Lord the King and his Laws. To the evil and pernicious example of all others and against the peace of our said Lord the King his Crown and Dignity. And the Jurors aforesaid on their Oath aforesaid do further present that before and at the time of the committing of the offence by the said James Catnach as hereinafter mentioned and from thence hitherto there have and still are divers to wit ten persons residing and carrying on respectively the trade and business of Pork Butchers and Sellers of Pork in Drury Lane aforesaid and in the neighborhood thereof to wit in the Parish of St. Clement Danes aforesaid in the County aforesaid.

SECOND COUNT.—**And the Jurors** aforesaid on their oath aforesaid do further present that the said James Catnach unlawfully wickedly and maliciously devising contriving and intending as much as in him lay to stir up and irritate the minds of the liege Subjects of our said Lord the King against the said last mentioned persons so carrying on their said Trade and Business of Pork Butchers and Dealers in Pork as aforesaid and to scandalize vilify defame oppress and wholly ruin the same persons and to hinder and prevent the liege Subjects of our said Lord the King from dealing and having any transactions with the same persons in the way of their said trades and business on the day and year first aforesaid at the Parish of St. Giles in the Fields aforesaid in the County of Middlesex aforesaid unlawfully and maliciously did print compose and publish and cause to be printed and published a certain other false scandalous malicious and defamatory libel containing therein the false scandalous malicious defamatory and libellous matter and words following of and concerning one of the said Pork Butchers to the great damage scandal infamy and disgrace of the said Thomas Pizzey in the way of his said trade and business in contempt of Our said Lord the King and his laws to the evil example of all others and against the Peace of Our said Lord the King his Crown and Dignity.

True Bill.

20th June : The Defendant remanded to new Prison at Clerkenwell at his own request.

8th September retracts plea and Confesses.

To be imprisoned in the House of Correction at Clerkenwell in this County for six months and committed accordingly.

During Catnach's incarceration his mother and sisters, aided by one of the Seven Dials bards, carried on the business, writing and printing off all the squibs and street ballads that were required. In the meanwhile the Johnny Pitts' crew printed several lampoons on " Jemmy Catnach." Subjoined is a portion of one of them that has reached us, *vivâ voce*, of the aforesaid professional street-ballad writer :—

Jemmy Catnach printed a quarter sheet—
  It was called in lanes and passages,
That Pizzey the butcher, had dead bodies chopped,
  And made them into sausages.

Poor Pizzey was in an awful mess,
  And looked the colour of cinders—
A crowd assembled from far and near,
  And they smashed in all his windows.

"Now Jemmy Catnach's gone to prison;
    And what's he gone to prison for?
For printing a libel against Mr. Pizzey,
    Which was sung from door to door.

"Six months in quod old Jemmy's got,
    Because he a shocking tale had started,
About Mr. Pizzey who dealt in sausages
    In Blackmore Street, Clare Market."

Misfortunes are said never to come singly, and so it proved to the Catnach family, for while Jemmy was *doing* his six months in the House of Correction at Clerkenwell, we find in the pages of the *Weekly Dispatch* for January 3, 1819, and under POLICE INTELLIGENCE, as follows :—

CIRCULATING FALSE NEWS.—At Bow Street, on Wednesday, Thomas Love and Thomas Howlett were brought to the office by one of the patrole, charged with making a disturbance in Chelsea; in the morning, by blowing of horns, with a most tremendous noise, and each of them after blowing his horn, was heard to announce with all the vociferation the strength of his lungs would admit of:—" The full, true, and particular account of the most cruel and barbarous murder of Mr. Ellis, of Sloane Street, which took place, last night, in the Five Fields, Chelsea." The patrole, knowing that no such horrid event had taken place, had them taken up. The papers in their possession, which they had been selling at a halfpenny each, were seized and brought to the office with the prisoners. But what is most extraordinary, the contents of the papers had no reference whatever to Mr. Ellis ! They were headed in large letters, " A HORRID MURDER," and the murder was stated to have been committed at South Green, near Dartford, on the bodies of Thomas Lane, his wife, three children, and his mother. The murderer's conduct was stated very particularly, although, in fact, no such event occurred. The magistrate severely censured the conduct of the whole parties. He ordered the prisoners to be detained, and considered them to be very proper subjects to be made an example of. On Thursday these parties were again brought before the Magistrate, together with Mrs. Catnach [the mother] the printer of the bills, which gave a fictitious statement of the horrid murder said to be committed at Dartford. She was severely reprimanded. The two hornblowers were also reprimanded and then discharged.

At a Manchester Reform Meeting—since known as the "Peterloo Massacre"—held on the 16th of August, 1819, the assembly consisted of from 60,000 to 100,000 persons — men, women, and children. Mr. Henry Hunt, an extreme politician—Radical Hunt*—took the chair ; he had spoken but a few words, when the meeting was suddenly assailed by a charge of the Manchester cavalry, assisted by a Cheshire regiment of yeomanry, and a regiment of hussars. The unarmed multitude were in consequence driven one upon another, by which eleven were killed, and about 600 ridden over by the horses, or cut down by their riders. Hunt, for his share in this affair, was indicted as the ringleader, and sentenced to three years' imprisonment in Ilchester gaol. Following is the first stanza of one of the many street ballads published on the subject :—

PETERLOO.

"See ! see ! where freedom's noblest champion stands,
Shout ! shout ! illustrious patriot band,
Here grateful millions their generous tribute bring,
And shouts for freedom make the welkin ring,
While fell corruption, and her hellish crew
The blood-stained trophies gained Peterloo."

---

* In the Commons he first took his station, and there
Some weighty discussion he quickly did hear.
On radical Hunt cast his eye quite elate,
" *The friend of the people*,"—their great advocate,
But, alas ! Satan found to his utter dismay,
That he, like a weathercock, turn'd any way ;
That his honour was formed of the most brittle stuff,
And his arguments only were cloaks to a puff
For his "REAL MATCHLESS BLACKING," and "FINE ROASTED
    CORN."
So Satan turned from him, enraged and in scorn.
    "Satan in Parliament ; or, a Fruitless Search after Honesty."

The busy year of 1820 was a very important one to
Catnach, in fact the turning-point in his life. The Duke
of Kent, fourth son of George III. and father to Queen
Victoria, died on the 23rd of January—the event was of
sufficient consequence to produce an elegy for street. sale.
The Duke of Kent was not a politician, he seldom appeared
beyond the shade of private life, or presiding at the
anniversaries of some of the great charitable institutions,
in many of which he took a particular interest. His social
virtues were many, and he was very charitable ; but in his
military capacity, the rigour of his discipline often reached
the verge of cruelty. In no command with which he was
ever trusted could he scarcely be tolerated ; and although
he might be amiable in the eyes of his intimate friends, and
died regretted by his dependants, yet the army had imbibed
a hatred of his name, and he was not considered as the
soldier's friend. Six days after the death of the Duke of
Kent—viz., on the 29th of January, 1820, George III. died,
and that event set the " Catnach Press " going night and day
to supply the street papers, containing "Full particulars," &c.

> " Mourn, Britons mourn! Your sons deplore,
>   Our Royal Sovereign is now no more,"

was the commencement of a ballad written, printed, and
published by J. Catnach, 2 Monmouth Court, 7 Dials.
Battledores, Lotteries, and Primers sold cheap. Sold by
Marshall, Bristol, and Hook, Brighton.

The strong constitution of his Majesty had supported him
to within a few weeks of his decease, in spite of the
dreadful malady under which he laboured. Early in the
month of January, symptoms of decay began to manifest
themselves. His sufferings were not protracted, and the
approach of death was not embittered by pain. No lucid
interval had cheered or distracted the last moments of his
life ; his long reign on earth was ended.

The royal body was committed to the family vault in St. George's Chapel, at Windsor, on the 16th of February, amidst a concourse of the great and the noble of the' land. The usual ceremony of proclamation and salutation announced the accession of George IV., and another important era commenced.

Immediately following these events came the Cato Street conspiracy. On the 24th of February the newspapers contained the startling intelligence that, on the previous evening, a party of eleven men, headed by Arthur Thistlewood, who was already known as a political agitator, had been apprehended at a stable in Cato Street, an obscure place in the locality of Grosvenor Square, on a charge of being concerned in a conspiracy to assassinate the greater part of the King's Ministers while at a cabinet dinner at Lord Harrowby's, and to excite an insurrection in the metropolis, and that, in the conflict that took place on their apprehension, one of the police officers, named Smithers, had been shot to the heart by one of the conspirators. The truth of the intelligence was soon confirmed by the proceedings which took place before the magisterial authorities ; and in due course all the parties were put on their trial at the Old Bailey, on a charge of high treason, Arthur Thistlewood, the leader, being the first tried on the 17th of April; the Lord Chief Justice Abbott presiding. The names of the other prisoners were—William Davidson, a man of colour ; James Ings, John Thomas Brunt, Richard Tidd, James William Wilson, John Harrison, Richard Bradburn, James Shaw Strange, and Charles Cooper, of whom the first four, together with Thistlewood, were executed as traitors on May 1st.

Exactly half-an-hour after they had been turned off, the executioner appeared on the scaffold, accompanied by a man whose lineaments were concealed by a crape mask, and the ceremony of decapitation was proceeded with, amidst expressions of horror and disgust from the assembled multitude. One by one the corpses were detached from the beam, and being laid on a bench prepared for the purpose, the operator, with the most perfect skill, detached the head almost in a single cut, and holding it up to public gaze, the executioner pronounced these words—" Behold the head of a traitor !" The head and body were then deposited in a coffin and removed ; but the rush of blood at each decapitation was so great that the end of the scaffold had the aspect of a slaughter house. The other portion of the sentence—as to the drawing on hurdles and quartering of the bodies—had been dispensed with. It is the last occasion on which such a spectacle—harrowing as it was without these additional horrors—has been witnessed in this country.* The six remaining prisoners were respited during his Majesty's pleasure.

The Cato Street conspiracy proved a rich harvest to all concerned in the production of street literature, in the midst of which there was a very sharply contested election for the City of Westminster, which was determined on Saturday, 24th March, at three o'clock. The numbers stood as under :—

Sir Francis Burdett...............	5,327
J. Cam Hobhouse, Esq.	4,884
Hon. G. Lamb	4,436

There was no lack of street-papers, squibs, and ballads thrown off by the " Seven Dials Press."

---

* The person who decapitated Thistlewood and the other traitors, it appears from Sheriff Parkins, was a resurrection man who obtained bodies for the hospitals. When asked if he could perform the task of cutting off the heads, he replied, "Oh, yes ; that he could do it very well, as he was in the habit of cutting off heads for the purpose of obtaining teeth."—*The News*, October 1, 1820.

"Oh, Cammy Hobby is the man,
And so is daddy Sir Franky, O ;
The Hon. G. Lamb is going mad
And kicking like a donkey, O."
"Oh, the naughty Lamb—
The miserable sinner, O ;
We 'll have him roast and boil'd,
And cut him up for dinner, O."

During the whole time of the election party spirit ran very high. A real lamb's head with a real rat in its mouth, was stuck upon the top of a pole. From the rat's tail hung a cock's comb. On the lamb's head was placed a lawyer's wig, surmounted with a fool's cap. On a board immediately below the head, was inscribed in front—" Behold the ratting Lamb, with a cock's comb at his tail." On the other side, the inscription was—

" If silly Lambs will go ratting,
'Tis fit they get this sort of batting."

Catnach came in for a fair share of the work, and he found himself with plenty of cash in hand, and in good time to increase his trade-plant to meet the great demand for the street-papers that were in a few months to be published daily, and in reference to the ever-memorable trial of Queen Caroline ; then it was that his business so enormously increased as at times to require three or four presses going night and day to keep pace with the great demand for street papers, which contained a very much abridged account of the previous day's evidence, and taken without the least acknowledgement from an early procured copy of one of the daily newspapers.

Caroline Amelia Elizabeth, Queen Consort of England, was born 17th May, 1768. She was the daughter of

Charles William Ferdinand, hereditary Prince of Brunswick-Wolfenbüttle, and the Princess Augusta, eldest sister of King George III. Soon after the French Revolution, the marriage of the heir-apparent to the Crown of England began to be regarded as a subject of great national import-ance, and negotiations for an alliance with the Princess Caroline of Brunswick, were entered into. On the 20th of December, 1794, Caroline became, by contact, Princess of Wales, and in the month of April following, accompanied by her mother and a numerous retinue, she departed from Brunswick, and was received with great magnificence at the English Court. On the 8th of April, 1795, the marriage was celebrated between George, Prince of Wales, and Caroline, of Brunswick. The royal pair, however, were not well assorted, and they lived only a short time together. On the 7th of January, 1796, a daughter was born—the Princess Charlotte—and a few months after a formal sepa-ration took place between the Prince and Princess of Wales, and she lived by herself in a country residence at Black-heath, the object of much sympathy, the people regarding her as the victim of her husband's love of vice. Reports to her discredit, led the King, in 1808, to cause investigation to be made into her conduct, which was found to be impru-dent but not criminal. In 1814 she obtained leave to visit Brunswick and the coasts of the Mediterranean, and lived for some time on the Lake of Como, an Italian, by name Bergami, being all the while in her company. On the death of George III., January, 1820, her Highness, as Consort of George IV., became Queen of England, but she was offered an annuity of £50,000 sterling to renounce the title and live abroad.

From a *brochure* entitled the " GREEN BAG ; or, a Dainty Dish to set before a King," illustrated by G. Cruikshank, we take the opposite page and woodcut.

"My lord, I dare not make myself so guilty,
To give up willingly that noble title
Your master wed me to : nothing but death
Shall e'er divorce my dignities."—*King Henry VIII.*

And so they sent a MESSENGER,
    To meet the Queen halfway ;
And give her FIFTY THOUSAND POUNDS
    If she abroad would stay ;
And never more be call'd a Queen,
    Or any such a thing,
But leave them with their dainty dish
    To set before the King.

The offer of compromise was indignantly refused by the Queen, and she made a triumphal entry into London, on the 6th of June. Whereupon the Government instituted proceedings against her for adultery, which commenced on the 17th of August, 1820, and continued until Friday, 10th of November, when Lord Liverpool, the Prime Minister, withdrew the Bill of Divorce, on the double ground of the majority (nine) and the unconstitutionality and inexpediency of the Bill. Still she was virtually found guilty, inasmuch as she was not allowed to share in the coronation of his Majesty, George IV., being turned away from the door of Westminster Abbey. This was a grievous disappointment to her, and a great blow to her pride, the Whig portion of the community having pretended to regard her as an ill-used innocent woman more for the purpose of enlisting the sympathy of the commonality, to be twisted into indignation against the King and Tory government of the day.

There emanated from the press, chiefly during the progress of the trial, numerous caricatures and political squibs, songs, &c., illustrated by Cruikshank and others, most of which have now become very rare. Although these were mostly on the part of the Queen, others on the King's side were in every respect superior in point of merit. It is a remarkable fact that one man in his way, by his infinite wit, did more on behalf of the Crown, than the combined efforts of the democratic party against it. We allude to Theodore Hook, who opened his campaign against the Queen by a thin octavo, which at the time made considerable noise. It was entitled, "Tentamen; or, an Essay towards the History of Whittington and his Cat," by Dr. Vicesimus Blinkinsop, I.L.D., F.R.S., A.S.S., &c. The Whittington, of course, was no other than Alderman Wood, and Caroline was the Cat. "Throughout the whole *libellus*," says Lockhart, "there was a prodigious rattle of puns and conundrums, but the strong points of the case against

Whittington and Co., were skilfully brought out nevertheless.
Hook being as yet quite *in obscuro*, nobody suspected him.
It was pretty generally ascribed to the manufacturers of the
'New Whig Guide.'"

"Tentamen" was followed by several similar pamphlets,
chiefly in verse, all directed against Alderman Wood and
other supporters of the Queen, and all published in the
year 1820, by Wright, of Fleet Street. They are also to
be distinguished by a caricature likeness of the celebrated
Alderman, which appears on the whole of them.

This was the prelude to "John Bull." The most important event with which the name of Theodore Hook stands
connected is unquestionably the establishment of the "John
Bull" newspaper, at the close of 1820. The universal,
instantaneous, and appreciable effect produced on the

H

great political movements of the day by its appearance, is perhaps unparalleled in the history of periodical literature.*

Many of the "John Bull" songs, in construction and even in execution, were very little different from those which Hook used to improvise in the course of a festive evening. It has been said, by one who knew him, that a person who never witnessed that marvellous performance could not take a better notion of what it was than from such a piece as "Mrs. Muggins' Visit to the Queen," in thirty-one stanzas, commencing :—

" Have you been to Brandenburgh,—Heigh, Ma'am, ho, Ma'am?
> You 've been to Brandenburgh, ho?
> — Oh, yes, I have been, Ma'am,
> To visit the Queen, Ma'am,
> With the rest of the gallanty show——show;
> With the rest of the gallanty show.

> *   *   *   *   *   *

And who were attending her—Heigh, Ma'am, ho, Ma'am ?
> Who were attending her, ho?
> Lord Hood, for a man,
> For a Maid, Lady Anne,
> And Alderman Wood for a beau——beau,
> And Alderman Wood for a beau.

There were several other clever attacks by Theodore Hook, in the pages of " John Bull," upon the Queen and her friends, which covered them with ridicule. One of them in particular, entitled "Hunting the Hare," was very severe :—

> "Would you hear of the triumph of purity?
> Would you share in the joy of the Queen?
> List to my song ; and, in perfect security,
> Witness a row where you durst not have been.

---

* Works of Theodore Hook. Chatto and Windus : Piccadilly.

All kinds of Addresses,
From collars of S.S.'s
To vendors of cresses,
    Came up like a fair;
And all thro' September,
October, November,
And down to December,
    They hunted this Hare.

*   ..   *   *   *   ..

Verdant green-grocers, all mounted on Jack-asses
  (Lately called Guildfords, in honour of Fred),
Sweet nymphs of Billingsgate, and tipsy as Bacchuses,
  Roll'd in like porpoises, heels over head !

And better to charm her,
Three tinkers in armour,
All hired by Harmer,
    Brave Thistlewood's friend ;
Those stout men of metal,
Who think they can settle
The State, if a kettle
    They're able to mend."

This political squib, which is in fourteen stanzas, had
such an effect on the female portion of the Queen's friends
as actually, in a great measure, to cause to be put down those
absurd exhibitions, which under the name of levées and
under the auspices of "Absolute Wisdom"—*i.e.* Sir Matthew
Wood—her Majesty was so injudicious as to countenance.*
    While Theodore Hook was writing on the side of the
" King and Constitution" in the columns of the "John Bull"

---

* The Queen has given notice that addresses will still be received at
Brandenburgh-house ; but, on account of the lateness of the season, she
requests they may be accompanied by small deputations only.—*The
News*, Nov. 5, 1820.

newspaper, Mr. William Hone, a political pamphleteer and
compiler of popular antiquities, and who defended himself
successfully in three trials for profane libel in publishing
parodies on the Church Liturgy, &c., published a series of
bold political pamphlets and satires, among which there is
one on the side of the Queen that soon became very popular
and ran through many editions. It bears the title of "NON
MI RECORDO!" and has three illustrations by George
Cruikshank, one being a burlesque portrait of the valet
Bergami, who, when any pertinent question was put to him
by Mr. Henry Brougham, as counsel for the defence,
invariably gave the very convenient reply "*Non mi
recordo*"—*i.e.*, " I do not remember."

Who are you ?   "*Non mi recordo.*"
What countryman are you—a foreigner or an Englishman?
"*Non mi recordo.*"

This trial was the means of bringing forward, as Attorney-General for the Queen, Mr. Henry Brougham, who was afterwards raised to the Woolsack and the Peerage, and so long and well-known as Lord Brougham. Mr. Thomas, afterwards Lord Denman, acted as Solicitor-General. His conduct, in behalf of the Queen, was so highly approved of by the London citizens, that they presented him with the freedom of their city.

Mr. Brougham occupied two days in the delivery of his address. "Those only who listened to his oration," says a contemporary writer, "can form an adequate idea of its splendour and dignity." So just and appropriate is the following summary of the trials to which her Majesty had been successively exposed, that it is copied into these pages for the purpose of presenting a condensed view of her sufferings.

"It was always," said Mr. Brougham, "the Queen's sad fate to lose her best stay, her strongest and surest protector, when danger threatened her; and, by a coincidence most miraculous in her eventful history, not one of her intrepid defenders was ever withdrawn from her without that loss being the immediate signal for the renewal of momentous attacks upon her honour and her life. Mr. Pitt, who had been her constant friend and protector, died in 1806. A few weeks after that event took place, the first attack was levelled at her. Mr. Pitt left her as a legacy to Mr. Perceval, who became her best, her most undaunted, her firmest protector. But no sooner had the hand of an assassin laid prostrate that minister than her Royal Highness felt the force of the blow, by the commencement of a renewed attack, though she had but just been borne through the last by Mr. Perceval's skilful and powerful defence of her character. Mr. Whitbread then undertook her protection, but soon that melancholy catastrophe happened which all good men of every political party in the State, he believed, sincerely and universally lamented. Then came, with Mr. Whitbread's dreadful loss, the murmuring of that storm which was so soon to burst, with all its tempestuous fury, upon her hapless and devoted head. Her child still lived, and was her friend ; her enemies were afraid to strike, for they, in the wisdom of the world, worshipped the rising sun. But when she lost that amiable and beloved daughter, she had no protector ; her enemies had nothing to dread. Innocent or guilty, there was no hope ; and she yielded to the entreaty of those who advised her residence out of this country. Who, indeed, could love persecution so steadfastly as to stay and brave its renewal and continuance, and harass the feelings of the only one she loved so dearly, by combating such repeated attacks, which were still reiterated after the record of the fullest acquittal ? It was, however, reserved for the Milan Commission to concentrate and condense all the threatening clouds which were prepared to burst upon her ill-fated head ; and, as if it were utterly impossible that the Queen could lose a single protector without the loss being instantaneously followed by the commencement of some important step against her, the same day which saw the remains of her venerable sovereign entombed—of that beloved sovereign who was from the outset her constant father and friend—that same sun which shone upon the monarch's tomb ushered into the palace of his illustrious son and successor one of the perjured witnesses who were brought over to depose against her Majesty's life."

Nor should the following bold, yet correct, and indeed inimitable peroration to this incomparable speech be omitted :—

" Such, my lords," said Mr. Brougham, " is the cause now before you, and such is the evidence by which it is attempted to be upheld. It is evidence inadequate to prove any proposition ; impotent, to deprive the subject of any civil right ; ridiculous, to establish the least offence ; scandalous, to support charges of the highest nature; monstrous, to ruin the honour of the Queen of England. What shall I say of it, then, as evidence to support a judicial act of legislature—an *ex post facto* law? My lords, I call upon you to pause. You stand on the brink of a precipice. If your judgment shall go out against the Queen, it will be the only act that ever went out without effecting its purpose; it will return to you upon your own heads. Save the country—save yourselves. Rescue the country—save the people of whom you are the ornaments, but, severed from whom, you can no more live than the blossom that is severed from the root and tree of which it grows. Save the country, therefore, that you may continue to adorn it; save the crown, which is threatened with irreparable injury; save the aristocracy, which is surrounded with danger; save the altar, which is no longer safe when its kindred throne is shaken. You see that, when the Church and the Throne would allow of no Church solemnity in behalf of the Queen, the heart-felt prayers of the people rose to Heaven for her protection. I pray Heaven for her, and here I pour forth my fervent supplications at the Throne of Mercy, that mercies may descend on the people of this country richer than their rulers have deserved, and that your hearts may be turned to justice."

While Hone, Hodgson, Fairburn, Dolby, and others, were publishing on the Queen's side, the printers of street literature—"Went in a rum'un, sir, for the Queen, Alderman Wood, and the People, sir. Yes, sir; and many's the good belly-full of food, nailed and pelted boots, hats, coats, trousers, and waistcoats, as was got out of Queen Caroline's *crim. con.* case, sir; and that 'ere Bergami chap, sir, the foreign cove, as was her *waley,* and did all her writing for her, and yet couldn't remember nothing after all. So Muster Harry Brougham called him *Non mi recordo,* because he wouldn't, or couldn't, remember nothing at all.

It always struck me, sir, that there was a great deal more *on*
his head than bear's grease ; and he wasn't a bad-looking
chap, sir, if the pictures of him didn't tell lies.   Ah ! those
was *the* days, and nights, too, for the flying stationers and
standing patterers, sir.   Those were the times when Old
Jemmy Catnach, as you're a-talking of, made his money, sir."

Great as was the demand, the printers of street literature
were equal to the occasion, and all were actively engaged in
getting out "papers," squibs, lists of various trade deputations
to the Queen's levées, lampoons and songs, that were almost
hourly published, on the subject of the Queen's trial.   The
following is a selection from one which emanated from the
" Catnach Press," and was supplied to us by John Morgan,
a Seven Dials bard, and who added that he had the good
luck—the times being prosperous—to screw out half-a-crown
from Old Jémmy for the writing of it.   " Ah ! sir," he continued, " it was always a hard matter to get much out of
Jemmy Catnach, I can tell you, sir.   He was, at most times,
a hard-fisted one, and no mistake about it.   Yet, sir, some-
how or another, he warn't such a bad sort, just where he
took.   A little bit rough and ready, like, you know, sir.   But
yet still a ' nipper.'   That's just about the size of Jemmy
Catnach, sir.   I wish I could recollect a little more of the
song, but you 've got the marrow of it, sir :—

> 'And when the Queen arrived in town,
>   The people called her good, sirs ;
> She had a Brougham by her side,
>   A Denman, and a Wood, sirs.

> ' The people all protected her,
>   They ran from far and near, sirs,
> Till they reached the house of Squire Byng,
>   Which was in St. James's Square, sirs.

' And there my blooming Caroline,
　　About her made a fuss, man,
　And told her how she had been deceived
　　By a cruel, barbarous husband.'"

Street papers continued to be printed and sold in connection with Queen Caroline's trial up to the date of her
death, in the month of August, 1821.

A COPY OF VERSES IN PRAISE OF QUEEN CAROLINE.

" YE Britons all, both great and small,
　　Come listen to my ditty,
　Your noble Queen, fair Caroline,
　　Does well deserve your pity:

Like harmless lamb that sucks its dam,
  Amongst the flowery thyme,
Or turtle dove that's given to love:
  And that's her only crime.
Wedlock, I ween, to her has been
  A life of grief and woe;
Thirteen years past she's had no rest,
  As Britons surely know.
To blast her fame, men without shame,
  Have done all they could do;
'Gainst her to swear they did prepare
  A motley, perjured crew.
Europe they seek for Turk or Greek,
  To swear her life away,
But she will triumph yet o'er all,
  And innocence display.
Ye powers above, who virtue love,
  Protect her from dispair,
And soon her free from calumny,
  Is every true man's prayer."

J. Catnach, Printer, 2, Monmouth Court, 7 Dials.

Immediately following the Queen's death, there were published a whole host of monodies, elegies, and ballads in her praise. Catnach made a great hit with one entitled "Oh! Britons Remember your Queen's Happy Days," together with a large broadside, entitled "An Attempt to Exhibit the Leading Events in the Queen's Life, in Cuts and Verse. Adorned with Twelve splendid Illustrations. Interspersed with Verses of Descriptive Poetry. Entered at Stationers' Hall. By Jas. Catnach, Printer, 7 Dials. Price 2d." A copy is preserved in the British Museum. Press Mark. *Tab.* 597, *a,* 1—67, and arranged under CATNACH,

from which we select two pieces as a fair sample of Jemmy's
" poetry-making ! "—Which please to read carefully, and
" Mind Your Stops!" quoth John Berkshire.

An Elegy on the Death of the Queen.

CURS'D be the hour when on the British shore,
 She set her foot—whose loss we now deplore ;
For, from that hour she pass'd a life of woe,
And underwent what few could undergo :
And lest she should a tranquil hour know,
Against her peace was struck a deadly blow ;
A separation hardly to be borne,
Her only daughter from her arms was torn !
And next discarded—driven from her home,
An unprotected Wanderer to roam !
Oh, how each heart with indignation fills,
When memory glances o'er the train of ills,
Which through her travels followed every where
In quick succession till this fatal year !
Here let us stop—for mem'ry serves too well,
To bear the woes which Caroline befel,
Each art was tried—at last to crush her down,
The Queen of England was refus'd a crown !
Too much to bear—thus robb'd of all her state
She fell a victim to their hate !
" They have destroy'd me,"—with her parting breath,
She died—and calmly yielded unto death.
Forgiving all, she parted with this life,
A Queen, and no Queen—wife, and not a wife !
To Heaven her soul is borne on Seraph's wings,
To wait the Judgment of the KING of Kings ;
Trusting to find a better world than this,
And meet her Daughter in the realms of bliss.

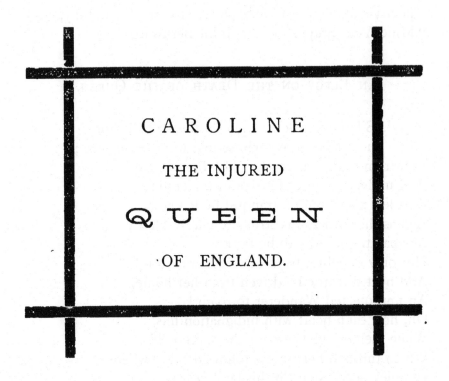

CAROLINE

THE INJURED

QUEEN

·OF ENGLAND.

Beneath this cold marble the "Wanderer" lies,
   Here shall she rest 'till "the Heavens be no more,"
'Till the trumpet shall sound, and the Dead shall arise
   Then the perjurer unmask'd will his sentence deplore.
Ah! what will avail then, Pomp, Titles, and Birth,
   Those empty distinctions all levell'd will be,
For the King shall be judg'd with the poor of the earth,
   And, perhaps, the poor man will be greater than he.
Until that day we leave Caroline's wrongs,
   Meantime, may "Repentance" her foes overtake;
O grant it, kind POWER, to whom alone it belongs.
   AMEN.   Here an end of this Hist'ry we make.

Quod.   JAS. C–T–N–H, Dec. 10th, 1821.

DEATH OF HER MAJESTY

THE

QUEEN OF ENGLAND.

Wednesday, August 7, 1821.

The tragedy of the persecutions and death of a Queen is at length brought to an awful close; and thousands—we may say millions—of eyes will be suffused in tears, when they shall read that CAROLINE OF BRUNSWICK is no more. The greatest, perhaps the best woman of her day, sunk by what may be called a premature death, on Tuesday Evening.

At half-past eleven o'clock the following bulletin was issued :—

" Her Majesty departed this life at twenty-five minutes past ten o'clock this night.

" M. BAILLIE.   PELHAM WARREN.
" H. AINSLIE.   HENRY HOLLAND.
" W. G. MATON.

" *Brandenburgh House, August 7.*"

J. Pitts, Printer, 6, Great St. Andrew Street.

· In the early part of the year 1821, the British public were informed through the then existing usual advertising mediums that there was about to be published, in monthly parts, " Pierce Egan's Life in London; or, The Day and Night Scenes of Jerry Hawthorn, Esq., and his elegant friend Corinthian Tom, accompanied by Bob Logic, the Oxonian, in their Rambles and Sprees through the Metropolis. Embellished with Scenes from Real Life, designed and etched by I. R. and G. Cruikshank, and enriched with numerous original designs on wood by the same Artists."

Some time previous to its appearance a great taste had exhibited itself amongst fashionable bloods for sporting works—books upon the chase, upon racing, upon boxing, and " sport" generally.   The demand soon brought an excellent supply, and " Boxiana," in its own peculiar department, at once became a great favourite.   Artists, too, arose, who devoted all their powers to hunting subjects, to racing favourites, and to pugilistic encounters.   Amongst these the names of Alkén, Dighton, Heath, Brooke, Rowlandson, &c., became very popular.   One day it occurred to the editor of " Boxiana" that if Londoners were so anxious for books about country and out-of-door sports, why should not Provincials and even Cockneys themselves be equally anxious to know something of " Life in London?" The editor of " Boxiana" was Mr. Pierce Egan, who, as the literary representative of sport and high life, had already been introduced to George IV. ; the character of the proposed work was mentioned to the King, and his Gracious Majesty seems to have heartily approved of it, for he at once gave permission for it to be dedicated to himself.   The services of Messrs. Robert and George Cruikshank were secured as illustrators, and on the 15th of July, 1821, the first number, price one shilling, was published by Messrs. Sherwood, Neely, and Jones, of Paternoster Row.   This sample, or first instalment, of the entire work was quite enough for society to judge by. It took both town and country by storm. It was found to be the exact thing in literature that the readers of those days wanted. Edition after edition was called for—and supplied, as fast as the illustrations could be got away from the small army of women and children who were colouring them. With the appearance of numbers two and three, the demand increased, and a revolution in our literature, in our drama, and even in our nomenclature began to develope itself. All the announcements from Paternoster Row were of books, great and small, depicting life in London; dramatists at once turned their attention to the same subject, and tailors, bootmakers, and hatters, recommended nothing but Corinthian shapes, and Tom and Jerry patterns.*

Immediately Messrs. Sherwood and Co. issued the first shilling number of Mr. Egan's work, out came Jones and Co., of Finsbury Square—the successors of the famous Lackington, who would have been shocked at the very idea of such a work—with the following, published in sixpenny numbers :—

---

* The late John Camden Hotten's Introduction to the new edition of "Life in London." Chatto & Windus : Piccadilly.

"REAL LIFE IN LONDON;

Or, The Rambles and Adventures of BOB TALLYHO, Esq., and his cousin, the Hon. TOM DASHALL, through the Metropolis, exhibiting a Living Picture of Fashionable Characters, Manners, and Amusements in High and Low Life, by an Amateur. Embellished and illustrated with a series of Coloured Prints, designed and engraved by Messrs. Heath, Alkén, Dighton, Brooke, Rowlandson, &c."

As may be readily conceived, the stage soon claimed "Tom and Jerry." The first drama founded upon the work was from the pen of Mr. Barrymore, and thus announced in the bill :—"Royal Amphitheatre. Extraordinary Novelty and Eccentric Production. Monday, Sept. 17, 1821, at half-past six o'clock precisely, will be presented, never acted, an entirely New, Whimsical, Local, Melo-Dramatic, Pantomimical Drama, with new scenery, dresses, and mechanical changes, founded on Pierce Egan's popular work, which has lately engrossed the attention of all London, called 'LIFE IN LONDON; or, Day and Night Scenes of TOM and JERRY, in their Rambles and Sprees through the Metropolis.'" The piece prepared for stage representation by Mr. W. Barrymore.

"Corinthian Tom, Mr. Gomersal; Jerry Hawthorn, Mr. Jones; and Bob Logic, Mr. Herring."

The second dramatic version was written for the Olympic Theatre, by Charles Dibden, and thus set forth in the bill :— "Olympic Theatre. On Monday, Nov. 12, 1821, and following evenings, will be presented a new Extravaganza of Fun, founded on Pierce Egan's highly popular work, and interspersed with a variety of Airs and Graces, called 'LIFE IN LONDON.'

"Tom (a Capital of the Corinthian Order) Mr. Baker.

"Jerry Hawthorn (out of Order, and more of the Composite than the Corinthian, never intended for the Church, though fond of a Steeple chase), Mr. Oxberry, and Logic (a Chopping Boy, full of wise saws and modern-instances), by Mr. Vale."

Mr. Moncrieff appeared as the third on the list of dramatists, and it was announced at the Adelphi Theatre in the following style :—" On Monday, Nov. 26th, 1821, will be presented for the first time, on a scale of unprecedented extent (having been many weeks in preparation under the superintendence of several of the most celebrated Artists, both in the *Ups and Downs* of Life, who have all kindly come forward to assist the Proprietors in their endeavours to render the Piece a complete out-and-outer), an entirely new Classic, Comic, Operatic, Didactic, Aristophanic, Localic, Analytic, Panoramic, Camera-Obscura-ic Extravaganza Burletta of Fun, Frolic, Fashion, and Flash, in three acts, called 'TOM and JERRY; or, LIFE IN LONDON.' Replete with Prime Chaunts, Rum Glees, and Kiddy Catches, founded on Pierce Egan's well-known and highly popular work of the same name, by a celebrated extravagant erratic Author. The music selected and modified by him from the most eminent composers, ancient and modern, and every Air furnished with an attendant train of Graces. The costume and scenery superintended by Mr. I. R. Cruikshank, from the Drawings by himself and his brother, Mr. George Cruikshank, the celebrated Artists of the original Work.

"Corinthian Tom, Mr. Wrench ; Jerry Hawthorn, Mr. W. Burroughs ; Logic, Mr. Wilkinson ; Jemmy Green, Mr. Keeley ; Dusty Bob, Mr. Walbourn ;* African Sal, Mr.

---

* Pierce Egan wrote—"The personification of 'Dusty Bob,' by the above actor, has been unanimously decided by the public, to be one of the greatest triumphs of the histrionic art ever exhibited upon the stage. The first tragedian of the day, with the utmost liberality, gave it as his opinion, that, during the whole course of his theatrical life, he had never seen any performance equal to it. Also, a comic actor of the greatest celebrity, exclaimed! 'Good heaven ! is it possible ? Do my eyes deceive me ? Most certainly it is a real *dustman* they have got upon

Sanders; Billy Waters, Mr. Paulo; Kate, Mrs. Baker; Sue,.
Mrs. Waylett, &c., &c."

---

the stage.   I am very sorry the profession has descended so low as to be
compelled to resort to the streets to procure a person of that description
to sustain the character.' "

Walbourn as "Dusty Bob," was drawn and engraved by George
Cruikshank, and sold at the Adelphi Theatre ; and he kept, during and
after the run of the piece, the "Maidenhead" public house, in Maiden
Lane, Battle Bridge.   The house, previous to his taking it, was doing a
small trade ; but when he became the landlord, he put out a sign with
a portrait of himself in the above character, painted in oil, by George
Cruikshank ; after that "Dusty Bob," together with "Black Sal,"
became to be by-words, and drew together many of the "Dusty"
fraternity; for near to the house was Smith's dust yard, at which hundreds
were employed, male and female.

THE LITERARY DUSTMAN.

My dawning genus fust did peep,
  Near Battle Bridge 'tis plain, sirs—
You recollect the cinder heap,
  Vot stood in Gray's Inn Lane, sirs?
'Twas there I studied picturesque,
  Vhile I my bread vos yarning,
And there inhalin' the fresh *breeze*,
  I sifted out my larnin' !
    They calls me Adam Bell, 'tis clear,
      (As Adam vos the fust man),
    And by a co—in—side—ance queer,
      Vy, I 'm the fust of dustmen !—
        A Literary Dustman !

The "Old Pub" of fifty years ago is now the *Victoria* tavern,
Great Northern Railway; Maiden Lane, is York Road, and Battle
Bridge is known as King's Cross, from a statue of George IV.—a most
unartistic piece of work—taken down in 1842.

Great sculptors all conwarse wi' me,
  And call my taste diwine, sirs—
King George's statty at King's Cross
  Vas built from my design, sirs.
    The Literary Dustman !

" This piece," says Mr. Moncrieff, " obtained a popularity,
, and excited a sensation, totally unprecedented in theatrical
history : from the highest to the lowest, all classes were
alike anxious to witness its representation. Dukes and
dustmen were equally interested in its performance ; and
Peers might be seen mobbing it with apprentices to obtain
admission. Seats were sold for weeks before they could be
occupied ; every theatre in the United Kingdom, and even
in the United States, enriched its coffers by performing it,
and the tithe portion of its profits would for ever have
rendered it unnecessary for its author to have troubled the
public with any further productions of his Muse. It
established the fortunes of most of the actors engaged in its
representation and gave birth to several newspapers. The
success of ' The Beggar's Opera,' ' The Castle Spectre,'
and ' Pizarro,' sunk into the shade before it. In the *furore*
of its popularity, persons have been known to travel post
from the farthest part of the kingdom to see it ; and five
guineas have been offered in an evening for a single seat."

Besides the authors already mentioned, Tom Dibden,
Farrell, and Douglas Jerrold, each produced dramas upon
the popular theme, and during the seasons of 1821-2,
" Life in London " was performed with great *éclat*, at ten
theatres in and around the metropolis, to overflowing houses.
But Pierce Egan at length became tired of the successes of
the playwrights in using his book, and resolved to try his own
hand at a dramatic version—or as he termed it, " to take a
leaf out of his own book "—and the AUTHOR's PIECE was
" got up " and performed for the first time at Sadler's Wells,
under the respectable management of Mr. Egerton, on
Monday, April 8, 1822 with most decided success.

It was thus announced by Mrs. Egerton in the address
written for the occasion by T. Greenwood, Esq. :—

> " To-night, my friends, this modern taste to meet,
> We show you JERRY at his country seat ;
> Then up to town transport the rustic beau,
> And show him ' Life in London,' HIGH and LOW."

Corinthian Tom, Mr. Elliott; Jerry Hawthorn, Mr. Keeley ; and Bob Logic by Mr. Vale.

The Burletta of TOM and JERRY had been repeated so often all over the kingdom, and particularly in the Metropolis, that the performers, notwithstanding the great applause they nightly received in the above piece, absolutely became tired and worn-out with the repetition of their characters, when the following piece of satire, written by T. Greenwood, Esq., was published, entitled " The Tears of Pierce Egan, Esq., for the Death of 'Life in London ;' or, the Funeral of Tom and Jerry, dedicated to Robert and George Cruikshank, Esqs. Price Two Shillings, with an engraving by George Cruikshank."

> " Beat out of the Pit and thrown over the Ropes,
> TOM and JERRY resign'd their last breath,
> With them, too, expired the Managers' hopes,
> Who are left to deplore their sad death !

> " Odd and various reports of the cause are about,
> But the real one was *this*, I opine : ·
> They were run to a *standstill*, and, therefore, no doubt,
> That the cause was a rapid *decline*.

> " When Death showed his *Nob*, out of *Time* they were beat,
> And neither would come to the *scratch ;*
> They hung down their heads and gave up the last heat,
> Not prepared with the Spectre to *match*.

> " All wept at the FUNERAL ! the FANCY and all—
> Some new, but a great many mended :
> And EGAN, while CRUIKSHANK and *Bob* held the pall,
> As *Chief-Mourner* in person attended ! ! !"

"Their *Sprees* and their *Rambles* no more shall amuse,
 Farewell to all nocturnal parleys:
The Town felt regret as the bell tolled the news, ·
 And no one rejoiced—but the *Charleys !*

"A monument, too, their kind Patrons will raise,
 Inscribed on—' Here lies TOM and JERRY,
Who, departing the *stage* to their immortal praise,
 ONE THOUSAND NIGHTS made the *Town merry* !!!'

"May their souls rest in peace, since they've chosen to flit, ⸍
 Like other great heroes departed ;
May no mischief arise from the *sudden* exit,
 Nor PIERCE EGAN die—*broken-hearted !* "

In reference to the above, Pierce Egan states in "The Finish to the Adventures of Tom, Jerry, and Logic," that Catnach, in less than twelve hours after the publication, produced a pirated edition for street sale, for twopence.

BLACK SAL AND DUSTY BOB.

The original work, "Life in London," went through several editions in a very short time, and the plates, by the Brothers Cruikshank, were considered so full of amusement that they were transferred to a variety of articles without any loss of time. The lady taking her *gunpowder* was enabled to amuse her visitors with the adventures of *Tom* and *Jerry* on her highly-finished tea-tray. The lovers of Irish *Blackguard* experienced à double zest in taking a pinch from a box, the lid of which exhibited the laughable phiz of the eccentric BOB LOGIC. The country folks were delighted with the handkerchief which displayed TOM getting the best of a Charley, and DUSTY BOB and BLACK SAL "all happi-ness!" The *Female of Quality* felt interested with the lively scene of the light fantastic toe at Almack's, when playing with her fan; and the *Connoisseur*, with a smile of satisfaction on his countenance, contemplated his screen, on which were displayed the motley groups of high and low characters continually on the move in the metropolis.

·Mr. Pierce Egan, in his *"Finish,"* states that he reckoned no less than sixty-five separate publications, which he enumerates *in extenso*, all derived from his own work, and adds, with his usual amount of large and small CAPITALS and *italics*—"We have been *pirated*, COPIED, *traduced;* but unfortunately, not ENRICHED by our indefatigable exertions; therefore NOTORIETY must satisfy us, instead of the smiles of FORTUNE. Our efforts have given rise to numerous productions in the market of literature, yet we can assert, with a degree of confidence hitherto unshaken, that none of our *imitators* have dared to think for themselves during the long period of seven years, neither have they shown any originality upon the subject of 'LIFE IN LONDON ;' but who have left it—*disinterested* souls!—to the Author and Artist to put a CLIMAX to the adventures of ·TOM, JERRY, and LOGIC." The last remark is in reference to the publication of "The Finish" to the Adventures of Tom, Jerry, and Logic, seven years after the date of "The Life in London."

Brighton, of course, had its version of "Life in London."

The theatre was then under the management of Mr. Samuel —or as he was commonly known, Jerry Sneak Russell, from the inimitable manner in which he personated that character in Foote's farce of "The Mayor of Garrat." We have a copy of the play-bill of the period before us, and as we think the manager's remarks and the selection of criticisms are in their way curious, we here append them, including the cast of characters.

THEATRE ROYAL, BRIGHTON.

LAST NIGHT BUT ONE.

TOM AND JERRY.

In announcing the successful piece of "Tom and Jerry" for this evening, the manager feels great satisfaction in being able to quote in its favour the following observations from the critiques in the London and other newspapers. "The scenery, dresses, &c., are good throughout, and much credit is due to the manager for the style in which it is got up. It is with pleasure we remark that this piece has been most judiciously and with a very proper feeling freed from the impurities of dialogue, which rendered it improper to meet the delicate ear of the gentler sex. We therefore venture, without subjecting ourselves to reproach, to recommend our readers to see 'Life in London,' to witness an exposure of many impositions practised in real life, and be made 'Fly' (the plain English of *au fait)* to the *multum in parvo* phrases which are now introduced into passing conversations."

"BRIGHTON.—The theatre at this place has just produced its 'Tom and Jerry' with great success, and we may say, deservedly, every objectionable point that might be thought to infringe on decorum having been most ingeniously suppressed without any diminution of the whim and fire of its varied and entertaining scenes. This regard to propriety argues much discretion, and seems to meet the approbation of the *beau monde* resorting hither, for the theatre is, graced with abundance of fashion and beauty."

" The ' Tom and Jerry' of the Brighton Theatre has good scenery, good acting, and what in such a piece is perhaps still better, good and chaste dialogue to recommend it ; it has been cleansed of its impurities without injuring its life and spirit. As thus represented, it cannot raise a blush on the cheek of the most fastidious female."

On Wednesday evening, September 12, 1822, will be reproduced the highly popular and amusing Burletta of

TOM AND JERRY.

Corinthian Tom	Mr. Power.
Bob Logic	...Mr. Chapman.
Jerry Hawthorn	... Mr. Russell.
Squire Hawthorn	...Mr. Chambers.
Tattersal	Mr. Mortimer.
Yorkshire Cove	... Mr. Hatton.
Primefit	... Mr. Julian.
Bill Chaunt	...Mr. Whatford.
Dusty Bob	... Mr. Starmer
Mr. Mace ... (Landlord of all Max in the East)	... Mr. Jenkins.
Billy Waters	Mr. Sheen.

Mr. Muff ... Mr. Collier.   Gammoning Jack ... Mr. Mills.
Snoozy ... Mr. Cole.   Trifle ... Mr. Dale.
Little Jemmy ... Master Williams.   Chaffing Sam ... Mr. Wiber.

Tom Belcher	... Mr. Jones.
President of the Daffy Club	Mr. Campbell.
Huntsmen, Watchmen, Villagers, Cadgers, &c., &c.	
Corinthian Kate	Miss M. Cooke.
Hon. Mrs. Gadabout	Mrs. Clarke.
Patty Primrose	...Miss Carr.
Mary	Miss Cramer.
Hon. Mrs. Trifle ... ... , ...	Miss Grosette.
Fortune Teller	Mrs. Grosette.
Mrs. Allright	Miss H. Grosette.
African Sal ... ... , ...	...Miss Black.

Country Lasses, Ladies at Almack's in the West, &c., &c.
Prospectus of Scenery, &c., &c., as before.

To conclude with the Romantic Melo-Drama of
VALENTINE and ORSON.

Valentine ... ... Mr. Power.
Orson ... ... Mr. S. Chapman.

[Creasy, Printer, *Gazette* Office, Brighton.

Jemmy Catnach, true to his line of life, soon joined what
Pierce Egan designates as the "Mob of Literary Pirates,"
who irritate the poor author almost to madness, blast his
prospects, impose on the unwary by their imitations, and
render his cash account all but nugatory, and just as he may
be congratulating himself on the success of his genius,
receiving the smiles of Fame, and a *trifling sweetener* from
Threadneedle Street, as a reward for his exertions, he may
be attacked by *Sappers* and *Miners*—those pickers and
stealers who do not absolutely come under the denomination
of *pickpockets*, yet *thieves* to all intents and purposes, and,
certainly *robbers* of the most unprincipled description—a
set of Vampires *living* upon 'the brains' of other persons,
and dare not to think for themselves."

Catnach brought out a "whole sheet" of letter-press for street-sale, entitled "Life in London," with twelve woodcuts, which are reduced and very roughly executed copies of the centre figures of the original plates by the Brothers Cruikshank—but all in reverse. The letter-press matter consists of flash songs, and a poetical epitome of the plot and design of the original work of "Life in London." And taking it as it stands, and from where it emanated, rather a creditable performance, particularly when we take into consideration—as duly announced by the street-patterer, that it was "Just printed and pub—lish—ed, all for the low charge of twopence."

On the rarity of this Catnachian and pirated edition of "Life in London" it is superfluous to enlarge, and it is easy to account for this circumstance, if we reflect that the broadside form of publication is by no means calculated for preservation; hundreds of similar pieces printed for street-sale must have perished. The more generally acceptable a broadside or street ballad became, and was handed about for perusal, the more it was exposed to the danger of destruction. No copy of Catnach's version is preserved in the British Museum, therefore, and for the reason above stated, it must be considered as a great "Literary Rarity."*

---

* Our thanks are due, and are hereby given to Mr. Crawford John Pocock, of Cannon Place, Brighton, for the loan and use of his—what we feel almost inclined to consider—unique copy of Catnach's broadside of "Life in London," and who, on our incidentally mentioning to him that we had failed to discover a copy in the British Museum, or in the stock of several well-known booksellers, at once, and in the most unreserved manner, informed us that not only did he possess a copy of the broadside we were in search of, but that it was very much at our service to aid us in perfecting our work. This was so much like the true and genuine Book Collector, and apart from that of the order "Curmudgeon," that we take this opportunity of publicly thanking him on behalf of ourselves and readers, who are thus enabled to peruse a faithful reprint of this rarity in street-literature.

THE SPREES OF

TOM, JERRY, AND LOGICK;

A New Song, of Flash, Fashion, Frolic, and Fun.

COME all ye swells and sporting blades who love to see good fun,
    Who in the dark, to have a lark, a mile or two would run;
Here's a dish of entertainment which cannot fail to please,
The rigs of Tom and Jerry, and all their jolly sprees.
    With their dash along, flash along, to Life and London haste away,
    Where sprees and rambles, larks and gambols, is the time of day.

    From Hawthorn-Hall young Jerry came to see his cousin Tom,
And with his friend Bob Logick acquainted soon became,
Then to cut a dash, he learns the flash, to act high life and low,
And up and down through all the town at night they rambling go.

    In a morning at Tattersall's you may them often see,
'Mong jockies, grooms, and chaunters, a knowing company;
In the afternoon they're lounging in Burlington Arcade,
And at night they're at the Opera, a Ball, or Masquerade.

Among the milling kiddy coves young Jerry took delight,
And was always first to raise a purse to have a glorious fight,
A Fancy blade he then became, and his courage ran so high,
That in his room, he floor'd his groom, and black'd his valet's eye.

Then off to Leicester-fields they'd march, the Strand, or Drury-lane,
Among the sporting ladies to carry on the game,
They'd take them to a gin-shop and treat them round so civil,
Then spur them on to fight and scratch each other like the devil.

While rambling up and down one night they came to Temple-Bar,
And to have a spree, they did agree, 'gainst the Charlies to make war,
Then in the twinkling of an eye a watch-box was upset,
The Watchy roar'd till all was blue, but out he could not get.

They smash'd their lanterns, kick'd their shins, and did their
　　pipkins crack,
And laid them down so neatly one by one upon their backs,
The prigs and sporting ladies all joined in the row,
But Jerry, Tom, and Logick by the pigs [watchmen] were ta'en in tow.

Then to the Holy Land they went disguis'd from top to toe,
To see the Beggar's Opera where all the Cadgers go,
With Mahogany Bet they had a lark, Black Moll, and Dumpling Kate,
And treated all the apple-women with a yard of tape [gin].

Now, with your leave good folks I will conclude my flashy song,
I hope you 're entertained, and I 've not detain'd you long,
And Logick, Tom, and Jerry, do cordially unite,
To thank you for your patronage, and wish you all Good Night,
　　　　　　　　With their dash along, &c.

LIFE IN LONDON.

FROM over the hills and far away,
　　Where rustic sports employ each day,
Young Jerry came, with cousin Tom,
. To see the rigs of London Town. .
　　Of all that e'er he did or saw, .
　　A faithful picture here we draw.

CUT I.—JERRY IN TRAINING FOR A SWELL.

NOW Jerry must needs be a swell,
His coat must have a swallow-tail,
And Mr. Snip, so handy, O,
Soon rigg'd him out a Dandy, O.
Then hey for Life and London Town,
To swagger Bond Street up and down,
And wink at every pretty maid
They meet in Burlington Arcade.

CUT II.—TOM AND JERRY AMONG THE LADIES.

L ADIES, your most humble servants,
     Tom and Jerry stand before you.
Our blood is thrilling, you 're so killing ;
     At once we love you and adore you.
Let us softly sit beside you ;
     Trust us, you will quickly own,
That love's alarms hath sweeter charms
     Than joys e'er yet to mortal known.

CUT III.—Jerry Loses at Play.

A T St. James's they dine, when, flush'd with new wine
     To the Gaming Tables they reel,
Where blacklegs and sharps, often gammon the flats,
     As their pockets do presently feel.
Success at first Jerry delighted,
     But ere the next morning he found
That his purse was most cleverly lighted
     Of nearly Five Thousand Pounds.

CUT IV.—JERRY LEARNING TO SPAR.

NOW Jerry 's become a Fancy blade,
　　To Jackson's he often goes,
And to shew his skill in the milling trade,
　　He crack'd poor Logick's nose.
He gloried in having a turn-up,
　　And was always the first in a lark,
To bang and wallop the Charlies,
　　And pommil them in the dark.

CUT V.—TOM AND JERRY AT A FORTUNE-TELLERS.

HERE lives a Fortune-Telling Gipsy,
    Wrinkled, crabbed, grim and old;
And Tom and Jerry's fancy ladies
    Are gone to get their Fortunes told.
They slily view'd them, and pursued them,
    For to have some glorious fun.
Behind the curtain, see them sporting,
    This is Life in London Town.

CUT VI.—BEGGAR'S OPERA. TOM, JERRY, AND LOGICK AMONG
       THE CADGERS IN THE HOLY LAND.

NOW to keep up the spree, Tom, Jerry, and Logick,
    Went disguis'd to the Slums in the Holy Land;
Through each crib and each court, they hunted for sport,
    Till they came to the BEGGAR'S OPERA so nam'd;
But sure such a sight they had never set sight on,
    The quintessence of Tag, Rag, and Bob-Tail was there:
Outside of the door Black Molly was fighting,
    And pulling Mahogany Bet by the hair.
There was cobblers and tailors, sweeps, cadgers, and sailors,
    Enough to confound Old Nick with their din;
There was bunters, and ranters, and radical chaunters,
    Clubbing their half-pence for quarterns of gin.

Some were descrying the traps [officers] of Red Lion,*
    Some were preparing their matches for sale;
And a surly old duchess, with one of her crutches,
    Had floor'd a blindman for capsizing her ale.
A tinker was bawling, a dustman was hauling
    His drunk wife to bed, whom he 'd given a black eye,
For the which Mother Drake, shook her fist in his face,
    And pray'd that his Last Dying Speech she might cry.
Our blades stood delighted, and view'd all around them,
    When in popp'd Black Billy [Waters] as brisk as a bee,
He struck up his fiddle, they all gather'd round him,
    And chaunted this CLASSICAL stave in high glee.

SONG OF THE CADGERS IN THE HOLY LAND.

COME, let us dance and sing,
    While fam'd St. Giles' bells shall ring,
Black Billy scrapes the fiddle string,
    Little Jemmy fills the Chair.
Frisk away, let 's be gay,
This is Cadger's holiday;
While knaves are thinking, we are drinking,
    Bring in more gin and beer.
        Come, let us dance and sing, &c.

    Here 's Dough-boy Bet, and Silver Sall,
      Dusty Bob, and Yankee Moll,

---

* In Red Lion Square is the office of the Mendicity Society—the terror of beggars and impostors.—"I say, my lads, what do you think happened to me the other day? I vas carried up afore the—the—vot d 'ye call it—Mantikity Society, and vot do you think they did? Vy, they slapped a pick-axe into vone of my mauleys, and a shovel into the other, and told me to vork. I said, gemmon, says I, I can't vork, 'cause vy, I vas too veak; so I bolted off, and in sich a 'urry that I left both my crutches behind, so now I ain't got no tools to vork with."

K

And Suke, as black as any pall,
　　The pinks of the Holy Land.
Now, merry, merry, let us be,
There's none more happier sure than we,
For what we get we spend it free,
　　As all must understand!
　　　　Come, let us dance, &c.

Now he that would merry be,
　　Let him drink and sing as we,
In palaces you shall not see,
　　Such happiness as here.
Then booze about, our cash an't out,
Here's sixpence in a dirty clout;
Come, landlord, bring us in more stout,
　　Our pension-time draws near.
　　　　Come, let us dance, &c.

CUT VII.—Night Scene. Tom and Jerry upsetting the
Charlies.

HARK ! the watchman springs his rattle,
　　Now the midnight lark 's begun ;
Boxes crashing, lanthorns smashing,
　　Mill the Charlies—oh ! what fun.

Pigs are hauling, girls are bawling,
　　Wretch, how durst you bang me so,
My sconce you 've broken—for your joking
　　You shall to the watch-house go.

CUT VIII.—Brought before the Magistrate.

AN' please your Worship here 's three fellows
　　Been hammering of us all about ;
Broke our boxes, lanterns, smellers,
　　And almost clos'd our peepers up.
Our pipkins broke, Sir,—'tis no joke, Sir,
　　Faith, we 're crush'd from head to toe ;
We 're not the men, Sir !—Hold your tongue, Sir,
　　You must find bail before you go !

CUT IX.—Tom, Jerry, and Logick in a Row.

ERCY! what a din and clatter
    Breaks the stillness of the night,
Lamps do rattle—'tis a battle,
    Quick; and let us see the sight,
Old and young at blows like fury,
    Tom and Jerry leads the row,
Milling, flooring all before them,
    This is Life in London, boys.

CUT X.—Scene in a Gin-Shop.

HERE some is tumbling and jumping in,
　　And some are staggering out;
One's pawn'd her smock for a quartern of gin,
　　Another, her husband's coat.
Behold, Mr. Tom and Jerry,
　　Have got an old bawd in tow,
They sluic'd her with gin, 'till she reel'd on her pins,
　　And was haul'd off to quod for a row.

CUT XI.—POOR LOGICK IN THE FLEET.

ALL in the Fleet poor Logick's moor'd,
　　His swaggering's now at an end,
And Tom and Jerry are gone on board,
　　Their friendly assistance to lend.
Now, their sprees and gambols are closed,
　　For, Logick has vow'd and swore,
When he's from Limbo safe loosed,
　　He'll marry—and rake no more.

CUT XII.—Jerry Going Back to the Country.

T HREE merry boys were Logick, Tom, and Jerry,
 And many funny larks they have seen ;
Now Logick's got a wife, so has Tom, and Mr. Jerry
 Is going back to Devonshire again.
Farewell, gay London, the country calls me home again,.
 Where my pretty Susan at my absence does complain ;
Yet, Jerry kindly wishes to all his friends health, peace, and
 joy,
 The coach moves on—the play is done—Good-bye, Good-
 bye.
 Quod. JAS. C–N–H, March 23, 1822.

With the "Life in London," its language became the
language of the day ; drawing-rooms were turned into
chaffing cribs, and rank and beauty learned to *patter slang.*

As we have before observed, "Life in London" was
dedicated by permission to George IV., and it is a circumstance in itself which looks singular enough in this Victorian
age, that royalty should have condescended to have had
such a work dedicated to it ; one paragraph, which we are

about to quote, strikes us as being a very peculiar and free-and-easy style for an author to address himself to a King of England.   It is as follows :—

"Indeed, the whole chapter of 'Life in London' has been so repeatedly perused by your Majesty in such a variety of shapes, from the elegant A, the refined B, the polite C, the lively D, the eloquent E, the honest F, the stately G, the peep-o'-day H, the tasteful I, the manly J, the good K, the noble L, the stylish M, the brave N, the liberal O, the proud P, the long-headed Q, the animated R, the witty S, the flash T, the knowing U, the honourable V, the consummated W, the funny X, the musical Y, and the poetical Z,—that it would only be a waste of your Majesty's valuable time to expatiate further upon this subject."

One notable effect of " Life· in London," particularly in its dramatised form, must be recorded.   It broke the heart of poor Billy Waters, the one-legged musical negro, who died in St. Giles's workhouse, on Friday, March 21, 1823, whispering with his ebbing breath, a mild anathema, which sounded very much like : " Cuss him, dam Tommy Jerry." Poor Billy, who was born in America, and lost his leg by falling from the top-sail yard to the quarter deck, in the Ganymede sloop of war, under the command of Sir John Purvis, endeavoured up to the period of his last illness, to obtain for a wife and two children what he termed " An honest living by scraping de cat-gut !" by which he originally collected considerable sums of money at the West-end of the town, where his ribbon-decked cocked hat and feathers, with the grin on his countenance, and sudden turn and kick out of his wooden limb, and other antics and efforts to please, excited much mirth and attention, and were well rewarded from the pockets of John Bull.   The burden of Billy's ditty " From noon to dewy eve," and from January to December was :—

> Kitty will you marry me,
> Kitty will you cry—
> Kitty will you marry me,
> Kitty will you cry ! cry—cry !

Billy became unfortunate—his occupation gone. The fickle British public refused to be as liberal as they had been, which he attributed to the production of "Tom and Jerry," with whom he was made to take his Madeira and Champagne, also to complain when he had "No capers cut for de leg ob mutton, *Bah!*" "No real turtle, but de mock turtle ! No lem'un to him weal, no hoysters to him rum'-steak. Vat !" he was made to exclaim, "Vat's dat I hears ! No sassingers to de turkey ?— de Alderman vidout him chain. Damme, Landlord, me change my hotel to-morrow."

However, by a combination of events, Billy became very poor, and was obliged, prior to his going into the workhouse, to part with his old friend, the fiddle, for a trifling sum at the pawnbroker's ; and the wooden *pin* (leg) which had so often supported Billy, would have shared the same fate, but its extensive service had rendered it worthless though it had twice saved poor Billy from the penalties of the *Treadmill.* He received a trifling pension after he left the naval service.

A short time prior to his death, Billy Waters was elected King of a party of Beggars in St. Giles's, in consequence of his notoriety.

> Of all the occupations,
> A beggar's life's the best ;
> For whene'er he's weary,
> He 'll lay him down and rest.
> And a begging we will go, we'll go, we'll go;
> And a begging we will go '

There was a jovial beggar,
He had a wooden leg.
And a begging we will go ! &c.

Billy was considered of sufficient public importance, when in the *flesh*, to be moulded and well *baked* by a Potter, who, taking up and moistening a lump of clay, said, " *Be ware !*" and then turned Billy out in one of his happiest moods and positions, with a broad grin on his black *mug*—a perfect image, suitable for a chimney or sideboard ornament ; which found a ready sale at the time of its manufacture, but has now become very rare in perfect condition, and, much coveted by collectors to add to their Class, or Section of " ENGLISH CHARACTERS." Specimens of this style of ware are exhibited at the Brighton Free Public Library, by Henry Willett, Esq.

How delightful Pierce Egan's book was to the youths of England, and how eagerly all its promised feasts of pleasure were devoured by them, Thackeray has told us in his " Roundabout Papers—DE JUVENTUTE"—in the " Cornhill Magazine" for October, 1860.

Mr., afterwards Sir William Cubitt, of Ipswich, erected a treadmill at Brixton Gaol, and soon afterwards in other large prisons. A street ballad on the subject was issued from the " Catnach Press" and had a most unprecedented sale, keeping the pressmen and boys working for weeks—

"And we're all treading, tread, tread, treading,
And we're all treading at fam'd Brixton Mill."

The treadmill—that " terror to evil doers"—excited much attention, and the inventor's name gave rise to many jokes on the subject among such of the prisoners who could laugh at their own crimes, who said that they were punished by the *cubit !* The following punning ditty was very popular at the period :—

The Treadmill.

This Brixton Mill 's a fearful ill,
    And he who brought the Bill in,
Is threatn'd by the *cribbing* coves,
    That he shall have a *milling*.
They say he shew'd a simple pate,
    To think of felons mending :
As every *step* which here they take,
    They 're still in crime *ascending*.

And when releas'd, and in the streets
    Their former snares they 're spreading,
They swear 'tis Parliament, which wills
    They must their old ways *tread in*.
The Radicals begin to think
    ·'Twill touch the Constitution,
For as the *wheel* moves round and round,
    It brings a *Revolution*.

But though these snarlers show their teeth,
    And try to vex the nation,
Their actions soon are *tried* and *judg'd*,
    ·And *grinding* is their station.
The *Gambling swells*, who near St. James'
    Have *play'd* their double dealings,
Say 'tis not fair that Bow-street should
    Thus *work* upon their feelings.

Tom, Jerry, Logic, three prime sprigs,
    Find here they cannot *come* it,
For though their *fancy* soars aloft,
    They ne'er will reach the *summit*.
Corinthian Kate and buxom Sue
    Must change their *warm* direction,
For if they make one *false step* more
    They 'll have *Cold Bath Correction*.

The moon-struck youths who haunt the stage,
  And spend their master's siller,
Must here play to another tune,
  'Tis called the *Dusty Miller.*
Ye bits of blood (the watchman's dread)
  Who love to floor a *Charley,*
As you delight to strip and fight,
  Come forth and *mill* the *barley.*

John Barleycorn's a stout old blade,
  As every man puts trust in,
And you will make no *meal* of him,
  But he'll give you a *dusting.*
But here we'll stay, for *puns* they say,
  Are bad as stealing purses
And I to *Brixton* may be sent,
  To *grind* some *floury verses.*

A STEP IN THE WRONG DIRECTION.

A mournful and affecting
COPY OF VERSES
on the death of
ANN WILLIAMS,
Who was barbarously and cruelly murdered by her sweetheart,
W. JONES, near Wirksworth, in Derbyshire, July, 1823.

William Jones, a young man aged 20, has been fully committed to Derby gaol for the murder of his sweetheart, under circumstances of unheard of barbarity. The poor victim was a servant girl, whom under pretence of marriage he seduced. On her proving with child the villain formed the horrid design of murdering her, and carried his diabolical plan into execution on Monday evening last. The following verses are written upon the occasion, giving a complete detail of this shocking affair :—

Come all false hearted young men
  A~d listen to my song,
'Tis of, a cruel murder,
  That lately has been done
On the body of a maiden fair
  The truth I will unfold,
The bare relation of this deed
  Will make your blood run cold.
Near Wirksworth town in Derbyshire,
  Ann Williams she did dwell,
In service she long time had lived,
  Till this to her befel.
Her cheeks were like the blushing rose
  All in the month of May,
Which made this wicked young man
  Thus unto her did say:
Nancy, my charming creature,
  You have my heart ensnared,
My love is such I am resolved
  To wed you I declare.
Thus by his false deluding tongue
  Poor Nancy was beguil'd,
And soon to her misfortune,
  By him she proved with child
Some days ago this damsel fair
  Did write to him with speed,
Such tenderness she did express
  Would make a heart to bleed.
She said, my dearest William,
  I am with child by thee,
Therefore, my dear, pray let me know
  When you will marry me.
The following day at evening,
  This young man did repair,
Unto the town of Wirksworth,
  To meet his Nancy there.
Saying, Nancy dear, come let us walk,
  Among the flowery fields,
And then the secrets of my heart
  To you I will reveal.
O then this wicked young man
  A knife he did provide,
And all unknown to his true love
  Concealed it by his side.
When to the fatal spot they came,

These words to her did say:
  All on this very night I will
Your precious life betray.
On bended knees she then did fall,
  In sorrow and despair,
Aloud for mercy she did call;
  Her cries did rend the air;
With clasped hands and uplift eyes
  She cried, Oh spare my life,
I never more will ask you
  To make me your wedded wife.
O then this wicked young man said,
  No mercy will I show;
He took the knife all from his side,
  And pierced her body through.
But still she smiling said to him.
  While trembling with fear,
Ah! William, William, spare my life;
  Think on your baby dear.
Twice more then with the bloody knife
  He ran her body through,
Her throat was cut from ear to ear,
  Most dreadful for to view;
Her hands and arms and beauteous face
  He cut and mangled sore,
While down upon her milk white breast
  The crimson blood did pour.
He took the shawl from off her neck,
  And round her body tied,
With pebble stones he did it fill,
  Thinking the crime to hide.
O then into the silver stream
  He plunged her straightway,
But with her precious blood was stained,
  Which soon did him betray.
O then this young man taken was,
  And into prison sent,
In ratling chains he is confin'd,
  His crime for to lament,
Until the Assizes do come on
  When trembling he must stand,
Reflecting on the deed he's done;
  Waiting the dread command.
Now all you thoughtless young men
  A timely warning take;
Likewise ye fair young maidens,
  For this poor damsel's sake.
And Oh beware of flattering tongues,
  For they'll your ruin prove;
So may you crown your future day,
  In comfort, joy, and love

Printed at J Pitts, Wholesale Toy and Marble Warehouse, 6. Great St. Andrew Street, Seven Dials.

THURTELL MURDERING MR. WEARE.

Catnach's next "great go" was the "Full, True, and
Particular Account of the Murder of Weare by Thurtell
and his Companions, which took place on the 24th of
October, 1823, in Gill's Hill Lane, near Elstree, in Hertfordshire.—Only One Penny." There were eight formes set
up, for Old Jemmy had no notion of stereotyping in those
days, and pressmen had to recover their own sheep-skins,
and struggled away at the two-pull squeezer at the rate of
200 or 300 copies an hour, and considered that wonderful!
But by working night and day for a week they managed to
get off about 250,000 copies with the four presses, each
working two formes at a time. The horrible details of the
murder, together with the daring character of the perpetrator,

was sufficient to rouse a feeling of indignation in the breast of every well-thinking individual in the kingdom. The number of copies which Catnach printed on this occasion was enormous.

Catnach made over £500 by Weare's murder and Thurtell's trial and execution. There were no newspapers in those days to give working people particulars of what was going on, except a few at 7d. and 8½d. a copy, and these only circulated amongst the rich and merchants. And after the thing had well got wind, "the trade," if such a ragged, dirty crew of newsmen as those who assembled by hundreds could be called by so respectable a name, completely filled up Little Earl Street, and there was great difficulty in passing in or out of the shop, so Old Jemmy had to resort to the plan of taking the money in his shop and then giving the hawkers a ticket to go round to Monmouth Street, where he had another shop, which was used as a warehouse, and this helped to divide the crowd, who cursed and swore, and created such a terrible riot because they could not get served directly, that the whole neighbourhood was quite alarmed.

If the sale of the first account of the murder of Weare surprised "the establishment," and put their rapid printing process to the proof, the trial out-did it tenfold, for when the affair had got thoroughly known, and was looked for on a certain day, the demand was tremendous! Besides his own four presses, Catnach set two other printers to work, each of whom set two presses going on it, and so managed to turn out nearly 500,000 copies of the trial in about eight days. But Catnach deeply regretted this step, for he lost more than he gained by the attempt to meet the demand; for, besides giving his competing friends an idea of the good thing that was to be made by these penny sheets, it set them to cheat him; for they opened a mart themselves with his sheets, and sold away as fast as they could, and kept the money afterwards, never giving Catnach a penny after using his paper as well; for in the confusion there was no check kept upon the deliveries, there being no time to count, the white paper went in by ream and the printed sheets came out by the heap, till they were all gone.

At this particular time he got quite enamoured with the idea of illustrating. So great was the demand for the latest news connected with the murder, that the publisher siezed the opportunity of raising the price of some of the special sheets from a penny to twopence. This, according to Jemmy's idea, was only just, seeing the great amount of extra expense he was incurring by illustrating; but of all the specimens of art, those which the great publisher of Monmouth Court used on this occasion, have a right to be ranked amongst the most hideous which this or any other country has produced. They were entirely destitute of taste or genius. As the trial progressed, and the case became more fully developed, the public mind became almost insatiable. Every night and morning large bundles were despatched to the principal towns in the three kingdoms.

An old "paper worker" repeated to Mr. Henry Mayhew, from memory, the first and second "Death Verses" on the "broad-sheet," of the "Life, Trial, Confession and Execution" of John Thurtell, for the murder of Weare :—

"Come, all good Christians, praise the Lord,
    And trust to Him in hope.
God, in his mercy, John Thurtell sent
    To hang from Hertford gallows rope.

Poor Weare's murder the Lord disclosed—
    Be glory to his name :
And Thurtell, Hunt, and Probert, too,
    Were brought to grief and shame."

Then added, "That's just the old thing, sir; and its quite

in Old Jemmy Catnach's style, for he used to write werses—anyhow, he said he did, for I've heard him say so, and I've no doubt he did in reality—it was just his favourite style, I know, but the march of intellect put it out of doors."

Another street ballad informed the British public that:—

> "Thurtell, Hunt, and Probert, too, for trial must now prepare,
> For that horrid murder of Mr. William Weare."

Mr. Weare lived at No. 2, in Lyon's Inn, Strand, London. The following, taken from a contemporary ballad, was attributed to Theodore Hook:—

> "They cut his throat from ear to ear,
>   His brains they battered in ;
> His name was Mr. William Weare,
>   He dwelt in Lyon's Inn."

Lyon's Inn, lately demolished, was an old Inn of Chancery, belonging in former days to the Inner Temple. It faced Newcastle Street on its eastern side, between Wych Street and Holywell Street ; a "short cut" led to it from the Strand to the latter street, the site of which is well defined to this day by a carved lion's head, always painted red, attached to the premises, No. 37. This side entrance was through Horne Court, on the opposite side of Holywell Street and next to an inn known as the "Dog Tavern"—a house where Samuel Pepys frequently had "a liquor up," and "to comfort myself did drink half-a-pint of mulled sack"—and which had been an hostelry for some 250 years at least before its demolition in 1864, for the purpose of carrying out a building speculation of the Strand Hotel Company (Limited)—a scheme which ended in a failure, except to the few. The Globe Theatre and Opera Comique now occupy a portion of the site of the former Lyon's Inn.

So popular—or as we should say, "sensational "—was the
murder of Weare by Thurtell, that little Williams (or Boiled
Beef Williams, as ·he was called, by reason of being associated with the once famous Boiled Beef House in the Old·
Bailey, and who, although living at the time within the ·
rules of the King's Bench, became the lessee of the Surrey
Theatre) just after the murder gave a representation of the

"Gaming is robbery in masquerade."

tragic scene in a piece called "The Gamblers," produced
on Monday, the 17th of November, 1823, and absolutely,
to give greater *éclat* to the performance, purchased the horse
and the "identical chaise" in which the murder was first
attempted to be committed, and in which Thurtell drove
Weare down to the lonely cottage in Gill's Hill Lane ; also
"the identical sofa" on which Thurtell slept the night of
the murder, and "the identical table" round which the
party supped, appeared on the stage.   The allusions in
this drama to the dreadful event, were too palpable to be

overlooked by the professional gentlemen retained by the family of Thurtell, for his defence, at the approaching trial, and in reference to this fact we find in, "The News" of November 22nd, 1823, the following :—

COURT OF KING'S BENCH, WEDNESDAY, NOV. 19, JOHN THURTELL'S DEFENCE.

IN THE MATTER OF JOHN THURTELL.

Mr. CHITTY, being called on, rose and said, "I am instructed to move your Lordships on behalf of John Thurtell, a prisoner in jail on a charge of murder, for a rule calling on Llewellyn Williams, the proprietor of the Surrey Theatre to show cause why a criminal information should not be exhibited against him, for a high misdemeanour, tending to pervert the course of justice, and prevent the prisoners accused of murder from having an impartial trial. My Lords, he has advertised all over London, and represented in his theatre, the alleged circumstances of this very crime. There is an actor who personates Thurtell; he is shown in company with the deceased, and he is represented in the act of committing murder. There was last night a large audience to witness this scandalous performance, and the excitement of feeling, when the actor who performs the murderer is secured, was quite unexampled, and could scarcely be believed as occurring in this country. The hand-bill announced the performance for the whole week.

THE LORD CHIEF JUSTICE.—How do you prove Mr. Williams to be the proprietor.

Mr. CHITTY.—My Lord, he has admitted himself to be so ; and I move also against the printer, whose name is affixed to the play-bill.

THE LORD CHIEF JUSTICE.—Take a rule to show cause.

L 2

On the 24th of November, Mr. Denman and Mr. Barne-well, on behalf of the proprietor, and Mr. Marryatt, on behalf of the printer, appeared to show cause against the rule. The matter underwent a long discussion, and ultimately the rule was discharged as far as related to the printer, and made absolute with regard to the proprietor and manager of the theatre.

The following is George Ruthven's account of the apprehension of Thurtell and the others in the horrible murder.

"After it had been ascertained that it was human blood and human hair on the pistol, and Hunt and Probert were in custody, I left in order to secure John Thurtell. I found him at Mr. Tetsall's, at the sign of the Coach and Horses, Conduit Street, Hanover Square. I said—

"'John, my boy, I want you.'

"'What for, George?' said he.

"I replied, 'Never mind; I'll tell you presently.'

"Thurtell had been anticipating various proceedings against him for setting his house on fire in the City, by Mr. Barber Beaumont, on behalf of the County Fire Office. It was highly probable that he suspected I wanted him on that charge. He, however, prepared to accompany me. My horse and chaise were at the door. He got in, and I handcuffed him to one side of the rail of my trap. I drove on towards Hertford. On the road, nothing could be more chatty and free than the conversation on the part of Thurtell. If he did suspect where I was going to take him, he played an innocent part very well, and artfully pretended total ignorance. We had several glasses of grog on the road. When we arrived, I drove up to the inn where Probert and Hunt were in charge of the local constables.

"'Let us have some brandy and water, George,' said Thurtell, after we had shaken hands with his associates. I went out of the room to order it.

"'Give us a song,' said Thurtell; and Hunt, who was a beautiful singer, struck up,

" ' Mary, list, awake ! '

" I paused, with the door in my hand, and said to myself, ' Is it possible that these men are murderers.' "

The circumstances immediately attending the murder are so fully and so well detailed in the proper channels that we need not here say more than that the trial took place at Hertford on the 5th January, 1824.

The prisoners who stood indicted were John Thurtell and Joseph Hunt. The latter was at the time well known as a public singer and was somewhat celebrated for the talent which he possessed. Both prisoners were found guilty, but Hunt was reprieved and subsequently ordered to be transported for life. Thurtell, who fully confessed to the crime, was executed in front of Hertford gaol on Friday, the 9th of January, 1824.

As before observed, Catnach cleared over £500 by this event, and was so loth to leave it, that when a wag put him up to a joke, and showed him how he might set the thing a-going again, he could not withstand it, and so about a fortnight after Thurtell had been hanged, Jemmy brought out a startling broad-sheet, headed, "WE ARE ALIVE AGAIN !" He put so little space between the words "WE" and " ARE," that it looked at first sight like " WEARE." Many thousands were bought by the ignorant and gullible public, but those who did not like the trick called it a " catch penny," and this gave rise to this peculiar term, which ever afterwards stuck to the issues of the " Seven Dials' Press," though they sold as well as ever.

Probert, who had been mixed up in the affair, was admitted as King's evidence and discharged at the rising of the Court. He subsequently met the fate he so richly deserved, for, having been found guilty at the Old Bailey of horse stealing, he was executed there on the 20th of June, 1825.

THE CONFESSION AND EXECUTION OF

JOHN THURTELL

AT HERTFORD GAOL,

On Friday, the 9th of January, 1824.

THE EXECUTION.

Hertford, half-past twelve o'clock.

This morning, at ten minutes before twelve, a bustle among the javelin-men stationed within the boarded enclosure on which the drop was erected, announced to the multitude without that the preparations for the execution were nearly concluded The javelin-men proceeded to arrange themselves in the order usually observed upon these melancholy but necessary occurrences. They had scarcely finished their arrangements, when the opening of the gate of the prison gave an additional impulse to public anxiety

When the clock was on the stroke of twelve, Mr Nicholson, the Under-Sheriff, and the executioner ascended the platform, followed on to it by Thurtell, who mounted the stairs with a slow but steady step. The principal turnkey of the gaol came next, and was followed by Mr Wilson and two officers. On the approach of the prisoner being intimated by those persons who, being in an elevated situation, obtained the first view of him, all the immense multitude present took off their hats.

Thurtell immediately placed himself under the fatal beam, and at that moment the chimes of a neighbouring clock began to strike twelve. The executioner then came forward with the rope, which he threw across it. Thurtell first lifted his eyes up to the drop, gazed at it for a few moments, and then took a calm but burned survey of the multitude around him He next fixed his eyes on a young gentleman in the crowd, whom he had frequently seen as a spectator at the commencement of the proceedings against him. Seeing that the individual was affected by the circumstance, he removed them to another quarter, and in so doing recognised an individual well known in the sporting circles, to whom he made a slight bow

The prisoner was attired in a dark brown great coat, with a black velvet collar, white corduroy breeches, drab gaiters and shoes. His hands were confined with handcuffs, instead of being tied with cord, as is usually the case on such occasions, and, at his own request, his arms were not pinioned. He wore a pair of black kid gloves, and the wrists of his shirt were visible below the cuffs of his coat. As on the last day of his trial, he wore a white cravat. The irons, which were very heavy, and consisted of a succession of chain links, were still on his legs, and were held up in the middle by a Belcher handkerchief tied round his waist.

The executioner commenced his mournful duties by taking from the unhappy prisoner his cravat and collar. To obviate all difficulty in this stage of the proceedings, Thurtell flung back his head and neck, and so gave the executioner an opportunity of immediately divesting him of that part of his dress. After tying the rope round Thurtell's neck, the executioner drew a white cotton cap over his countenance, which did not, however, conceal the contour of his face, or deprive him entirely of the view of surrounding objects.

At that moment the clock sounded the last stroke of twelve. During the whole of this appalling ceremony, there was not the slightest symptom of emotion discernible in his features; his demeanour was perfectly calm and tranquil, and he behaved like a man acquainted with the dreadful ordeal he was about to pass, but not unprepared to meet it. Though his fortitude was thus conspicuous, it was evident from his appearance that in the interval between his conviction and his execution he must have suffered much. He looked careworn; his countenance had assumed a cadaverous hue, and there was a haggardness and lankness about his cheeks and mouth, which could not fail to attract the notice of every spectator.

The executioner next proceeded to adjust the noose by which Thurtell was to be attached to the scaffold. After he had fastened it in such a manner as to satisfy his own mind, Thurtell looked up at it, and examined it with great attention. He then desired the executioner to let him have fall enough The rope at this moment seemed as if it would only give a fall of two or three feet. The executioner assured him that the fall was quite sufficient. The principal turnkey then went up to Thurtell, shook hands with him, and turned away in tears. Mr Wilson, the governor of the gaol, next approached him. Thurtell said to him, " Do you think, Mr Wilson, I have got enough fall ?" Mr Wilson replied, " I think you have, Sir. Yes, quite enough." Mr Wilson then took hold of his hand, shook it, and said, " Good bye, Mr Thurtell, may God Almighty bless you." Thurtell instantly replied, " God bless you, Mr Wilson, God bless you." Mr Wilson next asked him whether he considered that the laws of his country had been dealt to him justly and fairly, upon which he said, " I admit that justice has been done me—I am perfectly satisfied."

A few seconds then elapsed, during which every person seemed to be engaged in examining narrowly Thurtell's deportment. His features, as well as they could be discerned, appeared to remain unmoved, and his hands, which were extremely prominent, continued perfectly steady, and were not affected by the slightest tremulous motion.

Exactly at two minutes past twelve the Under-Sheriff, with his wand, gave the dreadful signal—the drop suddenly and silently fell—and

JOHN THURTELL WAS LAUNCHED

INTO ETERNITY.

Printed at J. Pitts, Wholesale Toy and Marble Warehouse, 6, Great St. Andrew Street, Seven Dials.

On the 10th of September, 1824, Henry Fauntleroy, of the firm of Marsh, Stracey, Fauntleroy, and Graham, bankers, in Berners Street, was apprehended in consequence of its being discovered that in September, 1820, £10,000 3 per cent. stock, standing in the names of himself, J. D. Hume, and John Goodchild, as trustees of Francis William Bellis, had been sold out under a power of attorney, to which the names of his co-trustees and some of the subscribing witnesses were forged. It was soon ascertained that the extent to which this practice had been carried was enormous, no less than £170,000 stock having been sold out in 1814 and 1815 by the same fraudulent means.

The payments of the banking house were immediately suspended, and a commission of bankruptcy was the result.

Mr. Fauntleroy's private conduct became now the subject of general conversation, and the street papers were daily filled with most exaggerated statements of the depravity of his habits. He was said to be a libertine, a deep gamester, and most profusely extravagant, but much of what was thus stated was afterwards refuted. He married a young lady of a respectable but not opulent family, named Young, who had previously borne him a child; but though he was persuaded thus far to redeem her character, he did not live with her after the day of their union, and to this unhappy circumstance is probably to be attributed much of that occasional excess which was magnified into the grossest libertinism.

It was for defrauding his wife's family that he was executed, the case selected by the Bank for prosecution being that of having forged the name of Frances Young, spinster, to a power of attorney, under which was sold the sum of £5,000 3 per cent. consols.

There were certain transactions which Fauntleroy did, which only came to light after he was apprehended, and

which tended to show the extent of his designs, and the
unscrupulous manner in which he was determined to perpe-
trate his frauds.

The trial took place on the 30th of October. At seven
o'clock the doors leading to the court-house of the Old
Bailey were besieged. The jury being sworn, the clerk
read the first indictment, which charged Henry Fauntleroy,
with forging a deed with intent to defraud Frances Young
of £5,000 stock. The Attorney-General told the jury that
although the Bank of England only intended to prosecute
in this case, the most extraordinary circumstance was that
amongst the prisoner's private papers contained in a tin box
there had been found one in which he acknowledged to
having forged different sums which, added together, amounted
to £120,000, and adduced a reason for his conduct, which
was also in the prisoner's handwriting. The statement was
followed by this declaration :—" In order to keep up the
credit of our house, I have forged powers of attorney for
the above sums and parties, and sold out to the amount
here stated, and without the knowledge of my partners. I
kept up the payments of the dividends, but made no entries
of such payments in our books. The Bank began first to
refuse to discount our acceptances, and to destroy the credit
of our house ; the Bank shall smart for it."

The Attorney-General then called his witnesses, who
confirmed in every point his statement of the case, after
which the prisoner read his defence, giving a lengthened
statement of the disasters and vicissitudes of the Bank with
which he had, and his father before him, been connected.
He was found Guilty of uttering, and sentenced to Death.

During the whole of the stages of the examination of the
prisoner before the magistrates, and also before the judges
who tried him, every advantage, in the shape of getting news,
was resorted to. There were several circumstances connected
with the case before the apprehension of Fauntleroy which,

by some means, got to the ear of Catnach, who made the
most of his knowledge by publishing many "papers" in
connection therewith. The principal portion of the metropolitan press were at this time above giving ear to mere idle
gossip, and there was a delicacy about the matter which
required every caution and consideration, as the criminal
was a man who had maintained a good standing in the
world; he resided in one of the most fashionable streets in
the metropolis, and had an establishment in the Western
Road, Brighton, where his mother and sister resided during
the fashionable season; and he moved in the gay and select
circles of London life. When these things are considered,
it is not surprising that so much interest should have been
taken in the career of one who had been regarded and
respected by the citizens of the greatest city in the world.

Every exertion was used by Mr. Fauntleroy's counsel, his
case being twice argued before the Judges, but both
decisions were against him; and on the 30th November,
1824, his execution took place. The number of persons
assembled was estimated at nearly 100,000. Every window
and roof which could command a view of the dreadful
ceremony was occupied, and places from which it was impossible to catch a glimpse of the scaffold were blocked up
by those who were prevented, by the dense crowd before
them, from advancing further.

The station in society of this unfortunate man, and the
long-established respectability of the banking-house, in which
he was the most active partner, with the vast extent of
the forgeries committed, gave to his case an intensity of
interest which has scarcely ever been equalled, and during
the whole time it was pending afforded plenty of work for
the printers and vendors of street literature, and Catnach's
advanced position, which was now far beyond all his compeers, caused him to get the lion's share. Every incident in
the man's character, history, and actions was taken advan-

tage of. The sheets, almost wet from the press, were read by high and low ; by those who lived and revelled in marble halls and gilded saloons, as well as by those who throng our large towns and centres of industry.

The *faux pas* of Edmund Kean, the eminent actor, with the wife of Alderman Cox, a proprietor and member of the Committee of Management of Drury Lane Theatre, in 1825, led to a lawsuit, on the termination of which Kean was compelled to pay £800 damages, proved a rich harvest for the street ballad singers. Catnach printed one that became for the time very popular and commanded for some months a large sale. It was entitled :—

COX *versus* K EAN ;

OR

LITTLE BREECHES.

——o——

" With his ginger tail he did assail, and did the prize obtain,
This Merry Little Wanton Bantam Cock of Drury Lane—
.LITTLE BREECHES."

Our tragedian being completely overwhelmed by an aldermanic Coxonian tornado, and hissed from the stages of Drury Lane and Edinburgh, was ordered by his forensic doctors to breathe the air of the broad Atlantic and visit the United States for the second time. After two seasons he returned ; but though favourably received once more, his career was near its end. In 1833 he was announced to play the part of Othello, his son Charles being cast for Iago. Kean struggled through the opening scenes of the play, but when he came to the speech, " Villain, be sure you prove my love,"—Act iii., sc. 3.—he sank exhausted upon his son's shoulder, and was led off the stage. This was his last appearance. He died at Richmond, May 15, 1833.

The parliamentary election of 1826 for the county of Northumberland, the principal seat of which was at Alnwick, gave early promise of being severely contested. There were four candidates in the field, namely, Henry Thomas Liddell, now first Earl of Ravensworth, of Ravensworth Castle, county Durham ; Mr. Matthew Bell, of Woolsingham, Northumberland ; Mr. Thomas Wentworth Beaumont, and Lord Howick, now Henry the third Earl Grey, K.G. The nomination of the candidates took place on Tuesday, June 20th, 1826, and the polling continued till July 6th, when the result was as follows :—

Liddell...	...	...	...	...	1562
Bell ...	...	...	...	...	1380
Beaumont	...	...	...	...	1335
Howick	...	...	...	...	977

Lord Howick retired some time before the close of the poll, and was returned to the same Parliament for Winchelsea, and sat 1826—30.

This contest was the greatest political event in the history of the county. It is estimated that it cost the candidates little short of £250,000, and presented the peculiar feature of a Whig and a Tory coalescing together. Liddell and Bell were both Tories, yet each of them coalesced with one of the other party.

Now, as we have before observed, Mr. Mark Smith, who at the present time of writing, carries on the business of printer and bookseller of Alnwick,* and James Catnach were fellow apprentices, both being bound to learn the art of printing to the elder Catnach on the same day, and afterwards worked together for a short time with Mr.

---

* Wanted, an Apprentice to the Printing Business, who may be made a Freeman of Alnwick.—Apply to Mr. M. Smith.—*The Alnwick Journal*, May, 1877.

Joseph Graham, the printer at Alnwick. This early-formed acquaintanceship continued throughout the remaining portion. of Catnach's life, and whenever Mr. Mark Smith went to London in after years he always visited Jemmy's house.

During the time Catnach was in business, several Alnwick young men who had made their way to the metropolis, which was then considered to be almost a necessary step in order to get more insight and experience in their respective trades, called upon him at Monmouth Court, when he always gave them a hearty welcome and a "cup o' kindness." Many of these young Northumbrians and their newly-formed London friends, when the labours of the day were over, made it their business to meet at the house of the printer and afterwards adjourn to a neighbouring tavern, and there they used to sing or hear sung ballads that had been composed and printed during the day, and at parting would have their pockets filled with the latest productions from his press. At these meetings several very amusing scenes often occurred. Jemmy was a bit of a poet; he had courted the Muses; although, if we are to take some of the pieces which appeared in the "awfuls" as specimens of poetic genius, we are afraid they will not reach the standard of the present day. When seated beside his friends he was particularly fond of reading aloud to them his latest productions; and it was amusing to see the flush of pride pass over his face when any of the company were so musically endowed as to be able to sing the verses to a tune of any kind.

Mr. James Horsley, Mr. Mark Smith, and Mr. Thomas Robertson are now nearly all that remain of Jemmy Catnach's old Alnwick friends. Mr. John Robertson, who was so fond of fun, and who could relate so many amusing stories of Catnach and his eccentricities, has long been dead. He was in London when Jemmy was imprisoned for libelling Pizzey, the sausage maker of Blackmore Street, Drury Lane. Mr. Thomas Robertson, who for upwards of fifty years has carried on an extensive business in Alnwick as cabinet maker, was, when in London, a constant visitor at the house of Catnach, and with whom he spent many evenings. Mr. Thomas Robertson, who had a fine voice, used to sing the tune over while Jemmy composed. Many a ballad was thus produced : the elaboration of the ideas, the length of lines, and the setting of the type all going on simultaneously, " Sing that over again, Tom," was a frequent request, when the verse and music did not satisfy Jemmy's ear, and after repeated efforts, it was pronounced fit for the national taste, and then printed off for immediate sale.

Mr. Robertson is still a hearty old man, and fond of relating stories of his younger days.

It was in consequence of the continued friendship existing between Mr. Mark Smith and Jemmy Catnach that the latter had often expressed a desire to serve his fellow-apprentice, should circumstances occur to render it necessary. The Alnwick election of 1826 promised to be a good one as regarded printing, and Mr. Smith anticipating a difficulty in getting through his work, applied to Catnach to know if he could render him any assistance. The result was that Jemmy at once proffered to go to Alnwick and take with him a small hand-press. After his arrival he seldom went out of the house. He kept remarkably close to his work, so much so that Mr. Smith was greatly surprised at the change which had come over his friend. He had his meals with Mr. Smith and his family, but he rigidly adhered to the custom which had governed his actions when in London, by always sitting down without a coat on, or, in what people term, "shirt sleeves." He worked early and late, as besides addresses, squibs, &c., they had to get out the state of the poll every afternoon shortly after four o'clock. The number of addresses and squibs, in prose and verse, during this memorable election was enormous. The whole, when collected together, forms four good-size volumes. The principal printers in Alnwick at this time, and who were engaged by the candidates, were Smith, Davison, and Graham. But there was a great deal of printing done at Newcastle, Gateshead, North Shields, Morpeth, and other towns.

A recent writer in a serial article in "The Alnwick Journal," which he entitles "Reminiscences of Alnwick, by a Native," writes as follows on this memorable election and other local matters of the same period :—

"During the contested election of 1826, on a Saturday afternoon, there came on a thunderstorm, accompanied by a tremendous fall of rain, which swept down Clayport Bank, choked the grates a little below the Union Court, then continuing onward carrying all before it; when it came to the foot of the street, part of the flood broke into the Market Place, to the amazement of the clerks in the polling booths, who were up to their knees in an instant, while the other portion overwhelmed the wares of the muggers, which were spread on the ground for sale; and a crate containing a child was carried down to the low end of the shambles before it could be rescued, which was done at last at great risk. The frantic behaviour of the poor mother, the pots, dishes, straw, cart covers, horse trappings, and the necessaries belonging to camp life, all driven higglede-pigglede along, made this an exciting scene, not to be forgotten by those who witnessed it. The spoils of the flood landed in the slack opposite the residence of Messrs. Moffat the hatters, which was a low old-fashioned place. The brothers, together with a traveller, were sitting in a room adjoining their shop when in rushed the water, upsetting the table at which they were sitting, and carrying away all that would swim, amongst which were two £5 notes. Subsequently one of them was found sticking to a grate in the wall at the foot of the yard. Contrast this and the ricketty place adjoining, once occupied by Thomas Finlay with his hack horses and gigs to let, with the present beautiful range of shops where energy and business habits seem to prevail."

There can be but little doubt but that all who were professionally engaged at this election made a good thing out of it. The money spent upon printing alone must have been very great. And nearly all the public-houses in Alnwick were made "open houses," as well as most of those in the principal towns throughout the county. And old

people talk to this day with a degree of pride of "those ·
good old times" that existed at the Parliamentary elections
previous to the passing of the Reform Bill of 1832. As
far as Catnach was concerned, he merely went to help to pay
off a deep debt of gratitude owing by him to the Smith
family for many past favours to his own family when they
were in dire distress in *auld lang syne.* Besides, Jemmy
was now getting towards that state known as being "comfortably well-to-do," and the trip was a change of air—a bit
of a holiday and a visit to the town of his birth. And as
he had buried his mother in London during the early part
of the year, he took the opportunity to erect in the parish
churchyard, that which at once stands as a cenotaph and a
tombstone, bearing the following inscription :—

> JOHN, Son of JOHN CATNACH,
> Printer, died August 27th,
> 1794, Aged 5 years and 7 months.
> JOHN CATNACH died in
> LONDON, 1813, Aged 44.
> MARY, his wife died Jany.
> 24th, 1826, Aged 60 years,
> Also John, Margaret, and
> Jane Catnach, lie here.*

Catnach's mother, we are upon good authority informed,
laboured under melancholia, a disease which is characterised
by dejection of spirits, fondness for solitude, timidity, fickle-
ness of temper, and great watchfulness. The mind pursues
one object or train of thought which in general bears a near
relation to the patient, or to his or her affairs, which are
viewed with great and unfounded apprehension. This
painful state of mind is often attended by a strong propensity to suicide. Mrs. Catnach became all but an imbecile,

---

* The above copied *verbatim* by Mr. George Skelly, of Alnwick,
November 14th, 1876.

and one night she fell in the fire and was so burnt that she
died from the effects a few weeks afterwards.   She was
buried in the churchyard of St. Giles in the Fields.

During Catnach's absence from London on the Alnwick
election, his old rivals—the Pitts family—were, as usual,
concocting false reports, and exhibiting lampoons, after the
following manner :—

> Poor Jemmy with the son of Old Nick,
>   Down to Northumberland he's gone ;
> To take up his freedom at Alnwick,
>   The why or the wherefore's known to none.

> Before he went, he washed in soap and sud.
>   The Alnwick folks they found the fiddle ;
> Then they dragged poor Jemmy through the mud,
>   Two foot above his middle.

The above was in allusion to the old ceremony of being
dragged through the dirty pool to be made a Freeman of
the town of Alnwick.   But, as far as Catnach was concerned,
there is no truth whatever in the matter, but was simply "a
weak invention of the enemy."   In the first place, owing to
some doubt we entertained on the subject, through the
somewhat contradictory statements given us, we made it our
business to communicate with Mr. George Skelly, of Alnwick,
to whom we must tender our grateful thanks for the kindness
and promptness which have characterised his actions during
the time we have been engaged on this work.   He then, at
our solicitation, searched the town records of the list of
Freemen, and reported that the name of James Catnach
does not occur.   Then, again, it was in the latter part of
June and the beginning of July in the same year that
Catnach was at Alnwick, and the ceremony of making
freemen always took place on St. Mark's Day, April 25th,

or at least two months earlier. Thus the statement of the
Pitts party was—

> " As false
> As air, as water, as wind, as sandy earth,
> As fox to lamb, as wolf to heifer's calf,
> Pard to the hind, or step-dame to her son."

Catnach, as the high priest of the literature of the
streets, surrounded by trade rivals, " stood like a man at
a mark with a whole army shooting at him," but he was
as firm as a rock and with the strength of a giant, and as
Hyperion to a Satyr defied them all.

"Admission to the freelege," writes Mr. Tate, in his
" History of Alnwick," " was obtained by birthright or by
apprenticeship to a freeman, or by election by the Four-
and-Twenty (*i.e.*, Town Councillors). All the legitimate
sons of freemen are now entitled to be made free, wheresoever born or whether before or after their fathers'
admission to the freelege; and this has been the usage
during the last two centuries. Every freeman can take
apprentices to his own trade, who at the expiration of
seven years' servitude, are entitled to become free.

The form of the freeman's oath has varied; in the
earlier part of the seventeenth century, when the admissions
were made at the Courts Leet, it appears to have included
fealty to the lord of the manor; but subsequently it was as
follows :—

You shall faith and true allegiance bear to our sovereign lord,
the King, shall sweare that you shall maintaine from time to time, and
att all times hereafter as needs shall require all the immunities,
freedoms, rights, and privileges of this towne and burrough, and in all
things shall behave yourself as a good and faithful freeman of this towne.

But when articles were proposed to bring to an end the
great lawsuit between the Earl of Northumberland and the
Corporation, the Four-and-Twenty agreed, in 1759, " that

for the future, fealty shall be added to and continued in the
oath, if his lordship insists thereon," his lordship did insist,
and this absurd and useless clause was added to the oath.

The fees of admission were, from 1611 to 1677, 4d. and
a pottle of burnt wine from the eldest son of a freeman,
5s. and a pottle of burnt wine from younger sons and
apprentices, in addition to the court fees; in 1677 the fee
for the second son of a freeman was reduced to 2s. 6d., and
in 1687 the pottle of wine was converted into a money payment of 2s. 6d. In 1697 the fees were for the eldest son
5s. to the town, and for the younger sons and apprentices
7s. 6d. ; but in 1700, 9s. were added to all these fees, on
account of the expense incurred by the Corporation in
making and upholding some great dykes or fences across
the moor ; and these amounts continue to be paid at the
present time, out of which, however, 1s. is returned to each
young freeman to drink the health of the Chamberlain.
Notwithstanding the entire disconnection of the freelege
from the effete court leet, an official from the Castle makes
application for 8d. to the bailiff and 8d. to the sergeants for
every admission.

The ceremony of making freemen is described as follows,
in Hone's "Every Day Book;" but we refer those of our
readers who desire a more elaborate and exhaustive
description, to Tate's "History of Alnwick," vol. ii.,
page 241 :—

" When a person takes up his freedom he is led to a pond known by
the name of the *Freeman's Well*, through which it has been customary
for the freemen to pass from time immemorial before they can obtain
their freedom. This is considered so indispensable, that no exception
is permitted, and without passing this ordeal the freedom would not be
conferred. The pond is prepared by proper officers in such a manner
as to give the greatest possible annoyance to the persons who are to pass
through it. Great dykes, or mounds, are erected in different parts, so
that the candidate for his freedom is at one moment seen at the top of
one of them only up to his knees, and the next instant is precipitated

into a gulf below, in which he frequently plunges completely over head. The water is purposely rendered so muddy that it is impossible to see where these dykes are situated, or by any precaution to avoid them. Those aspiring to the honour of the freedom of Alnwick are dressed in white stockings, white pantaloons, and white caps. After they have reached the point proposed, they are suffered to put on their usual clothes, and then obliged to join in a procession, and ride round the boundaries of the freeman's property—a measure which is not a mere formality for parade, but absolutely indispensable, since, if they omit visiting any part of their property it is claimed by his grace the Duke of Northumberland, whose stewards follow the procession to note if any such omission occurs. The origin of the practice of travelling through the pond is not known. A tradition is current that King John was once nearly drowned upon the spot where this pond is situated, and saved his life by clinging to a holly tree ; and that he determined, in consequence, thenceforth, that before any candidate could obtain the freedom of Alnwick, he should not only wade through this pond, but plant a holly tree at the door of his house on the same day ; and this custom is still scrupulously observed."

Although Alnwick has undergone important changes since the close of the last century, yet they are trifling in comparison with what the freemen have effected within a very short period, by converting into a productive tract of land, that which, but a few years ago, was a marshy barren waste, where, although furze flourished in the greatest luxuriance, the grass, even in the most favoured seasons, resembled in colour what is commonly called invisible green. Here some ragged looking quadrupeds, which the freemen dignified with the name of sheep, were left to eke out a miserable existence. These ravenous animals were widely known beyond their own territory; the highest fences being insufficient to restrain their predatory habits ; and therefore the cultivation of the moor has perhaps been a greater boon to the neighbouring proprietors than it may ultimately prove to the freemen themselves.

From time immemorial the freemen of Alnwick appear to have regarded themselves as an oppressed and injured body. At one time we find them complaining of being

M 2

plundered by the lord of the manor, and at another of being grossly deceived by the Four-and-Twenty; and, if we may trust to rumour, we learn that even amongst themselves the greatest harmony does not always prevail; for we are told that at their meetings or guilds physical as well as moral force is not unfrequently resorted to in support of their arguments.

.The following document will furnish some idea of the state of feeling which at that period prevailed between themselves, the Four-and-Twenty, and the Lord of the Manor :—

"Hexham, December 11, 1781.

"*To the Petitioning Freemen of the Borough of Alnwick.*

"And it came to pass as I journeyed northwards, that behold I met with sages arrayed some in leather, some in woollen aprons, and some almost Adamites.

"And I said unto them, Whither go ye?

"And they answered and said, We be select men of a confused number, immersed in our Pool of Bethesda, 'and we go to seek our patrimony, a large tract of country, of which we have been bereaved by unrighteous men, who have usurped an authority unknown to our forefathers, and we go in search of means to redeem our birthright.

"And, lo! to that end we have heretofore laid our grievances before the beautiful young man, the Chief of the Stewards of our Prince, at the Castle, who hath promised to do whatever seemeth meet unto us, and behold, we sojourn thither.

"Then said I, Beware whom ye trust, and confide not in the promises of designing Princes, nor their fair promising agents.

"Your inheritance is the gift of the good old King John, who, to preserve peace and to prevent the unruly rage of the multitude, hath wisely appointed perpetual Stewards to rule over you, which Stewards have been found faithful.

"Attempt not therefore to alienate your property, but with all sobriety conform to the mode prescribed by your bountiful donor, which hath preserved it inviolate to your ancestors and their posterity for so many generations; cease, therefore, your lawless altercations.

"At this, my friendly admonition, some cursed the day they listened to the advice of evil counsellors, and returned to their homes; but others, having no reason of their own and being unable to withstand mine, murmured thereat, and went their ways, the Lord knows whither.

"Howbeit, after some days, behold I met these pretended sages near the great man's gates, having their faces covered with shame and confusion.

"And I said unto them, Oh ! ye wicked and perverse individuals, how long will ye continue to distress your own families and disturb the peace of your benefactors ! Wot ye not that ye are all in the wrong !

"And they answered and said, We have laid our grievances before the great man, who hath spurned at our application and accosted us thus :—

"Oh ! ye drunkenest of all drunken freemen, so audaciously to enter these gates with such wicked proposals ! Conscious I am that all my civilities have been treated with unparalleled ingratitude ; and, to ruin my reputation with my respectable neighbours, you now impudently solicit me to be a principal in an unlawful act against them, in direct violation of the terms prescribed by our royal donor.

"Wot ye not that it is my duty to study the interests of my family, and to conciliate the friendship of my neighbours; but not such vagabonds as you are.

"Go your ways, then, and with dutiful submission implore the forgiveness of your lawful superiors, the Four-and-Twenty, whom ye have so wickedly bely'd.

"And, till this my mandate you have obeyed, never shall your ungodly lust be gratified with a single horn of ale from my cellar. And go directly, lest a worse course should fall upon ye.

"And they submissively answered and said, Lo ! we go and do as thou hast commanded."

Alnwick does not appear to have ever achieved the distinction of being a Parliamentary borough. It, however, claims the dignity, without sharing the advantages, of being the county town of Northumberland. It also boasts of having a Corporate existence, but is bereft of the chief functionary which confers dignity on a Corporation. That body, on all public questions, seems to exercise a sort of divided authority with the Board of Health, except with regard to railway communication, over which the latter appears to claim exclusive jurisdiction.*

---

* "ALNWICK, and the Changes it has undergone during the last 50 years." A Lecture by J. A. Wilson, Esq.

The destruction of the Royal Brunswick Theatre, Well Street, Wellclose Square, East London, on the 29th of February, 1828, by the falling in of the walls, in consequence of too much weight being attached to the heavy cast-iron roof, made a rare nine days' wonder for the workers of street-papers. Fortunately the catastrophe happened in the day-time, during the rehearsal of "Guy Mannering," and only fifteen persons perished, viz :—

Mr. D. S. Maurice, one of the Proprietors,

Mr. J. Evans ... *Bristol Observer*,	Mr. J. Purdy ... *Blacksmith*,
Miss Mary A. Feron ... *Actress*,	Messrs. J. Miles, W. Leader,
Miss Freeman ... *Corps de ballet*,	A. W. Davidson, M. Miles,
Mr. E. Gilbert ... *Comedian*,	and J. Abbott, ..., *Carpenters*,
Mr. J. Blamire ... *Property Man*,	J. Levy, *A Clothesman* (accident-
Mr. G. Penfold ... *Doorkeeper*,	ally passing).
Miss Jane Wall ... *A Visitor*,	

"Oh yes, sir! I remember well the falling of the Brunswick Theatre, out Whitechapel way. It was a rare good thing for all the running and standing patterers in and about ten miles of London. Every day we all killed more and more people—in our "Latest Particulars." One day there was twenty persons killed, the next day thirty or forty, until it got at last to be worked up to about a hundred, and all killed. Then we killed all sorts of people, Duke of Wellington, and all the Dukes and Duchesses, Bishops, swell nobs and snobs we could think of at the moment."

During the season 1828, Mr. Fawcett, stage manager of Covent Garden Theatre, imposed upon himself the Herculean task of checking the immorality of the age, the first notice of which appeared in the "Globe" newspaper, and was to this effect :—

"We are glad to learn that Mr. Fawcett, the manager of Covent Garden Theatre, has appointed Mr. Thomas, the active constable, serving in his own right, to superintend some new arrangements which have been made to exclude from the theatre the profligate females of a certain class, whose conduct has frequently been such as to create disgust among the respectable part of the audience. Mr. Thomas is also authorised to remove from the house any female, however superior in her grade to those against whom the new regulation is intended principaly to apply, if she is found offending by language, or gesture against the rules or Propriety."

The natural consequence of such an injunction against the vested rights of those connected with the *demi-monde* was a torrent of squibs, lampoons, and street ballads, and to use the words of our informant, the Seven Dials' Press was "All alive oh!" and every "flying stationer," of London, jubilant.

THE GRAND BLOW UP !!!

OR,

THE

BATTLE OF COMMON GARDEN.

A New Farce,

BY STAGE-MANAGER FAWCETT.

" MR. F. is it true,
We 're indebted to you
For new rules for preserving decorum ?
One would think, to be sure,
Since you 're grown so demure,
That you should be one of the *Quorum*.

" Can't you manage the Stage
Without letting your rage
Extend to Saloons and the Lobbies ? .
You 've enough if you stop
But behind your " new drop ".
To do—and that 's one of your hobbies.

" Behind curtain and scene,
And in the Room Green,
'Tis your place to keep actresses decnt,
They are surely worse there,
When breeches they wear,
And of late there 's a monstrous incease in 't

" In this novel *fantique*,
Are you with them in leagu ?
If you are, it is not acting properl ;
For what right have they,
First their legs to display,
And then to enjoy a monopoly ?

*   *   *   *   *   *

" Say, who could advise
Such a project so wise,
Of morals he 'd surely a high   se !

Was it ' C—lm—n the Younger,'
Who younger no longer,
Now checks by his license all license ? "

To be followed every evening by

THE HYPOCRITE.

Doctor Cantwell and Mawworm   Mr. Morality Fawcett ! !
Old Lady Lambert...   ...   ...   Mr. C–lm–n the Younger !
☞ No money returned after the rising of the curtain.

Printed by J. Catnach, 2 and 3, Monmouth Court, 7 Dials, where may
be obtained all the old and new Songs of the day, Children's Books, &c.

In Dyot Street, St. Giles's—now George Street, after
George Prince of Wales—but called Dyot Street after
Richard Dyot, Esq., a parishioner of St. Giles's in the
Fields—lived that most notorious and world-renowned
lodging-house keeper "Mother Cummins," so well known to
all the Bucks about town, in their hot youth, when George
the Third was King.

Oh, she lives snug in the Holy Land,
Right, tight, and merry in the Holy Land,
   Search the globe round, none can be found
So *accommodating!* as Old Mother Cummins
                           Of the Holy Land.

'It is related that Major Hanger accompanied George IV.
to a beggar's carnival in St. Giles's. He had not been there
long when the Chairman, Sir Jeffery Dunston, addressing
the company, and pointing to the then Prince of Wales,
said " I call upon that 'ere gemman with a shirt for a song."
The Prince, as well as he could, got excused upon his friend
promising to' sing for him, and he chanted in prime style
a flash ballad full of "St. Giles's Greek," for which he received
great applause.' The Major's health having been drank with
nine times nine, and responded to by him, wishing them" good
luck till they were tired of it," he departed with the Prince
to afford the company time to fix their different routes for
the ensuing day's business.

The Song of The Young Prig.

MY mother she dwelt in Dyot's Isle, (*a*)
   One of the canting crew, (*b*) sirs ;
And if you 'd know my father's style,
   He was the Lord *Knows-who*, sirs !
I first held horses in the street, .
   But being found defaulter,
Turned rumbler's flunky (*c*) for my meat,
   So was brought up to the halter.
Frisk the cly, (*d*) and fork the rag, (*e*)
   Draw the fogles plummy, (*f*)
Speak to the tattler, (*g*) bag the swag, (*h*)
   And finely hunt the dummy. (*i*)

2

My name they say is Young Birdlime,
   My fingers are fish-hooks, sirs ;
And I my reading learnt betime,
   From studying pocket-books, (*k*) sirs.
I have a sweet eye for a plant, (*l*)
   And graceful as I amble,
Fine draw a coat-tail sure I can't,
   So kiddy is my famble. (*m*)
     Frisk the cly, &c.

(*a*) Dyot's Isle, *i.e.*, Dyot Street, which with the surrounding neighbourhood was afterwards desecrated to the purposes of twopenny to sixpenny lodging houses, and so well known collectively as St. Giles's Holy Land, or Rookery, but a very great portion of the district has lately been pulled down to make way for street and sanitary improvements in that quarter. (*b*) Beggars. (*c*) A cad, or *footman*, to hackney coaches, to water the horses, &c. (*d*) To pick a pocket. (*e*) Lay hold of the notes or money. (*f*) Draw out the handkerchiefs dexterously. (*g*) Steal a watch. (*h*) Pocket the chain and seals. (*i*) Adroitly search for a pocket-book. (*k*) Pocket-books are called "readers." (*l*) An intended robbery. (*m*) Having a practical and skilful hand.

3

A night-bird, (*a*) oft I'm in the cage, (*b*)
  But my rum chants ne'er fail, sirs,
The dubsman's (*c*) senses to engage,
  While I tip him leg-bail, (*d*) sirs.
There's not, for picking, to be had,
  A lad so light and larky, (*e*)
The cleanest angler on the pad, (*f*)
  In daylight or the darkey. (*g*)
    Frisk the cly, &c.

4

And though I don't work capital, (*h*)
  And do not weigh my weight, (*i*) sirs,
Who knows but that in time I shall,
  For there's no queering fate, sirs.
If I'm not lagged to Virgin-nee, (*k*)
  I may a Tyburn show be, (*l*)
Perhaps a tip-top cracksman be, (*m*)
  Or go on the high toby. (*n*)
    Frisk the cly, &c.

Catnach, like many others connected with the getting up
of news broadsides and fly-sheets, did not always keep
clear of the law. The golden rule is a very fine one, but,
unfortunately, it is not always read aright; in some cases
injured innocence flies at extremes. For years the press
of this country has been a powerful agency, making its

(*a*) A disorderly vagabond. (*b*) The round-house. (*c*) Gaoler.
(*d*) Running away. (*e*) Frolicsome. (*f*) Expert street robber.
(*g*) The night. (*h*) Commit any offence punishable with death.
(*i*) The £40 payable on capital conviction. (*k*) Transported.
(*l*) Hanged. (*m*) House-breaker. (*n*) Turn highwayman.

influence felt in every nook and corner in the land. As a counteract to this, the character of the subject is rigidly protected by statute laws. The nice points that are constantly arising in our law courts in regard to defamation of character, are numerous, and in many cases novel and entertaining. Catnach for a long time had been living upon unfriendly terms with a party connected with the management of one of Mother Cummins' lodging-house establishments in the immediate neighbourhood, so out of spite printed a pamphlet, purporting to be the "Life and Adventures of Old Mother Cummins." Here Catnach had reckoned without his host, by reason of his not taking into consideration the extensive aristocratic and legal connection Mother Cummins had for her friends and patrons. The moment she was made acquainted with the "dirty parjury" that Jemmy Catnach had printed and caused to be publicly circulated, she immediately gave instructions to *her* Attorney-General to prosecute the *varmint*, when a warrant was applied for and obtained to search the premises of the Seven Dials printer. But Catnach got the news of the intended visit of the Bow Street Runners, and naturally became alarmed from having a vivid recollection of the punishment and costs in the case of the Drury Lane sausage makers, so the forme containing the libellous matter was at once broken up—"pied," that is, the type was jumbled together and left to be properly distributed on a future occasion. What stock of the pamphlets remained were hastily packed up and carried off to the "other side of the water" by John Morgan, one of Catnach's poets! while another forme, consisting of a Christmas-sheet, entitled "The Sun of Righteousness," was hurriedly got to press, and all hands were working away full of assumed innocence when the officers from Bow Street arrived at Monmouth Court, when, after a diligent search, they had very reluctantly to come to the conclusion that they were "a day behind the fair," and that the printer had been a little too sharp for them this time.

From " Bell's Life in London," for March 23, 1828, we take the following article, headed in large italic capitals :—

DEATH AND FUNERAL OF MOTHER CUMMINS.

"The venerable landlady of the notorious lodging house in George Street, St. Giles's, Old Mother Cummins, departed this life in the beginning of last week, and was carried to the grave on Saturday, followed by an immense number of the inhabitants of the Holy Land. She had come over from Ireland, about fifty years ago, in the twenty-ninth year of her age, and having entered into matrimonial bonds with the *gintleman* who now survives her, she took a 'bit of a shed,' in the most obscure part of the Irish regions, and by letting a few beds in shares, without any scrupulousness as to the difference of sex between those who occupied them, contrived to put together as much money as enabled her to speculate more extensively in the accommodation line. She, at last, was able to make up forty beds, and the moderate terms on which she allowed her customers to repose recommended half-pay officers and others of the needy class to her sheets very frequently. She always boasted of the security of property in her mansion, and she took the most effectual means of maintaining that character, by clapping a padlock upon the door of each room, as soon as she received her demand. Her rooms were let furnished at an expense of from sixpence to two shillings per night, so that a bricklayer's labourer and an Oxford student sometimes heard each other snore. Mr. Cummins used to assist in the management of the concern. He was a check upon her liberality, which was really great, to the poor half-starved wretches in the neighbourhood, but he never dared to interfere, in any serious degree, with her arrangements. Thirty years ago, Mother Cummins took a house in Pratt's Place, Camden Town, in which she resided, for the purpose of superintending the extensive washing of her establishment, and she regularly, every week, drove to town for the linen and woollen in which her customers were wont to repose. Her washerwomen were all decent Irishwomen, and upon the wash-days, she was the best customer of the Southampton Arms ; but she has gone for ever ! . She died a most excellent Catholic, never having, as she declared on her death bed, eaten a bit of meat on a Friday, since she was born. After having been 'waked' in the usual way, her remains were allowed the benefit of the air of Heaven, all the windows in the house having been thrown up, and open they remained until the body

was half way to its everlasting home.   On the Saturday morning, the
neighbourhood of Pratt's Place was in the greatest bustle.   The
solemnity which would have been observed in the case of another
individual, was thrown aside for bustle and merriment, as if to hail the
departure of a gentle spirit for more pure and delightful regions.   Even
her widower, whose health seemed to flag a good deal, and who was
carried to his carriage in his night-cap, as if he was on his journey to
eternity through the hands of a certain important functionary of the
law, appeared to partake of the general happiness.   The procession
moved along until it reached St. Giles's Church, where all the rookeries
behind Meux's brewhouse, seemed to have disgorged their contents.
After the last duties were performed, several glasses of gin were handed
into the mourning coaches, and towards the conclusion of the day, a
general row took place, and many an eye was closed up, and nose
distorted, before the police could interfere with effect."

Immediately after Mother Cummins's death and funeral,
the following announcement appeared :—

Published this Day, Price Sixpence, embellished with a
humorous Coloured Plate,

THE LIFE AND CAREER OF

MOTHER CUMMINS,

The celebrated Lady Abbess of St. Giles's ; with a curious
Description, Regulations, &c., of her singular Establishment.
An account of her Funeral, &c.   Interspersed with nume-
rous Anecdotes of Living Characters, Visitors of Mother
Cummins's Nunnery,—Capt. Shiels and the Forty-four Nuns
—Poll Hankey and Sir Charles Stanton,—Jane Sealey and
an Illustrious Person, &c.—With an Account of some of
the principal Nuns of the Establishment ; particularly
Mrs. Throgmorton and Lord Al...n..y—Bell Chambers
and the D... of Y...,—Miss Wilkinson and Captain
Featherstone—Marianne Hempstead, the Scotch Beauty—
Miss Weltern Davis and the Rev. Mr. H...l..y Be..rs..d
—Mary Thomas, the Female Chimney-Sweep, and Captain
T...t...s, &c.

POET'S CORNER.

"There is a pleasure in poetic pains,
Which only Poets know."

"Yonder, sir, is Mr. Gooséquill, a 'Seven Dials Bard,' who came to town with half-a-crown in his pocket, and his tragedy, called the 'Mines of Peru,' by which he of course expected to make his fortune. For five years he danced attendance on the manager, in order to hear tidings of its being 'cast,' and four more in trying to get it back again. During the process he was groaned, laughed, whistled, and nearly kicked out of the secretary's room, who swore (which he well might do, considering the exhausted treasury of the concern) that he knew nothing about, nor ever heard of, the 'Mines of Peru.' At last Mr. Goosequill, being shown into the manager's kitchen, to wait till he was at leisure, had the singular pleasure of seeing two acts of the 'Mines of Peru' daintily fastened round a savoury capon on the spit, to preserve it from the scorching influence of the fire.

"'This was *foul* treatment,' I observed, and I ventured to ask how he had subsisted in the meanwhile? 'Why, he first made an agreement with a printer of ballads in Seven Dials,' who, finding his inclinations led to poetry, expressed his satisfaction, telling him that one of his poets had lost his senses, and was confined in Bedlam, and another was dazed with drinking drams. An agreement was made, and he earned five-pence-three-farthings per week as his share of this speculation with the muses. But his profits were not always certain. He had often the pleasure of supping with Duke Humphrey, and for this reason he turned his thoughts to prose; and in this walk he was eminently successful, for during a week of gloomy weather he published an *apparition*, on the *substance* of which he subsisted very comfortably for a month. He often makes a good meal upon a monster. A *rape* has frequently afforded him great satisfaction, but a *murder*—an out-and-out *murder* —if well timed, is board, lodging, and washing, with a feast of nectared sweets for many a day.'"*

Jack Randall, the *Nonpareil* of the ring, died at his house, the Hole-in-the-Wall, Chancery Lane, on Wednesday, March 12th, 1828, aged 34. Jack was an *Anglo-Irishman*, and first drew his breath in the Hibernian colony of St. Giles. He was the hero of sixteen prize battles, and left the ring undefeated. At this period it was considered he had received not less than £1,200 by his good fortune, but "easy got, easy gone"—as fast as it was received it was spent, until prudence suggested the expediency of laying the foundation of something substantial for his family, and he accordingly closed his bargain for the Hole-in-the-Wall, under the patronage of General Barton, his friends giving him a pipe of wine, instead of a piece of plate, to commence operations. From henceforth he pursued the business of a publican, and was highly respected by all ranks of the *Fancy*. Tom Moore, the Irish poet, was a frequenter

---

* "Real Life in London; or, The Rambles and Adventures of Bob Tallyo, Esq., and his Cousin, the Hon. Tom Dashall." *See* page 112.

N

of his house, and it was there that he picked up most of his material for his " Tom Cribb's Memorial to Congress," &c. The liberality of his friends, however, added to his own predilection for *daffey*, gradually paved the way to the " break up " of his constitution, and for the last few months of his life he was but the shadow of his former self.

From a ballad of the period entitled, " *A Fancy Elegy on the death of Jack Randall,*" we selected as follows :—

" ALAS ! poor Jack lies on his back,
    As flat as any flounder :
Although he died of a *bad inside*,
    No *heart* was ever *sounder.*

" The *Hole-in-the-Wall* was once his *stall*,
    His *crib* the *Fancy* name it :
A *hole in the ground* he now has found,
    And no one else will claim it.

" But too much *lush* man's strength will crush,
    And so found poor Jack Randall :
His fame once bright as morning light,
    Now 's out, like *farthing candle.*

"Good bye, brave Jack !—if each thy track
  Would follow—barring drinking—
What a *noble race* would our country grace,
  Firm, loyal, and *unshrinking.*"

Four years after the Thurtell and Weare affair, namely,
in the month of April, 1828, another "sensational" murder
was discovered—that of Maria Marten, by William Corder,
in the Red Barn, at Polstead, in the county of Suffolk.
The circumstances that led to the discovery of this most
atrocious murder were of an extraordinary and romantic
nature, and manifest an almost special interposition of
Providence in marking out the offender. As the mother of
the girl had on three several nights dreamt that her daughter
was murdered and buried in Corder's Red Barn, and as this
proved to be the case, an additional "charm" was given to
the circumstance. And the "Catnach Press" was again
set working both day and night to meet the great demand
for the "Full Particulars." The first broad-sheet worked
off on the subject was as follows :—.

ATROCIOUS MURDER OF A YOUNG WOMAN IN SUFFOLK.
SINGULAR DISCOVERY OF THE BODY FROM A DREAM.

THE RED BARN.

THE SCENE OF THE MURDER, AND WHERE THE BODY OF MARIA MARTEN WAS FOUND CONCEALED.

A murder, rivalling in cold-blooded atrocity that of Weare, has been brought to light within a few days, at Polstead, in the county of Suffolk. The circumstances which have reached us are as follows:—

Maria Marten, a fine young woman, aged twenty-five, the daughter of a mole catcher in the above village, formed an imprudent connexion, two or three years ago, with a young man, named William Corder, the son of an opulent farmer in the neighbourhood, by whom she had a child. He appeared much attached to her, and was a frequent visitor at her father's. On the 19th of May last she left her father's house, stating, in answer to some queries, that she was going to the Red Barn to meet William Corder, who was to be waiting there with a chaise to convey her to Ipswich, where they were to be married. In order to deceive observers—Corder's relations being hostile to the connection—she was to dress in man's attire, which she was to exchange in the barn for her bridal garments. She did not return at the time expected, but being in the habit of leaving home for many days together, no great alarm was expressed by her parents. When, however, several weeks had elapsed, and no intelligence was received of their daughter, although William Corder was still at home, the parents became anxious in their inquiries. Corder named a place at a distance where he said she was, but that he could not bring her home for fear of displeasing his friends. Her sister, he said, might wear her clothes, as she would not want them. Soon after this, Corder's health being impaired, he, in real or pretended accordance with some advice he had received, resolved on going abroad. Accordingly, he left home in September last, expressing a great anxiety before he left to have the barn well filled. He took with him about £400. Several letters have been received by his mother (a widow) and sister, as well as by the Martens, in which he stated that he was living with Maria in the Isle of Wight. These, however, bear the London post-mark. He regularly desired that all his letters should be burnt, which request was not complied with. Strange surmises lately gained circulation throughout the neighbourhood, and one person stated, as a singular circumstance, that on the evening when Maria Marten disappeared, he had seen Corder enter the Red Barn with a pick-axe. The parents became more and more disturbed and dissatisfied, and these fears were still more strongly agitated by the mother dreaming, on three successive nights last week, that her daughter had been murdered, and buried in the Red Barn. She insisted that the floor of the barn should be upturned. On Saturday, Marten, the father, with his mole-spade and a neighbour with a rake, went to examine the barn, and soon, near the spot where the woman dreamt her daughter lay buried, and only about a foot and a half under ground, the father turned up a piece of a shawl which he knew to have belonged to his daughter, and his assistant with his rake pulled out part of a human body. Horror struck, the unhappy father and his neighbour staggered from the spot. The remains were afterwards disinterred, the body being in a state of decomposition. The pelisse, shawl, Leghorn bonnet, and shoes, were, however, distinctly identified as those once belonging to Maria Marten. The body has been closely inspected, but owing to its decayed state, no marks of violence have, we understand, been discovered, except some perforations in the bones of the face, which appear as if made by small shot. There can be but little doubt left but that this unfortunate young woman fell a victim to her unhallowed passion, and was inhumanly butchered by the monster upon whom she relied for future protection as a husband. The barn is well situated for such a deed of horror, being a full quarter of a mile from any human habitation. An inquest was held before W. Weyman, Esq., Coroner for the Liberty, on Sunday last, and adjourned till Friday, in the hope that some intelligence may be gained of Corder to lead to his apprehension. The murdered remains were buried on Sunday night, at Polstead, in the presence of an immense concourse of spectators.

Printed by j. Catnach, 2, Monmouth Court, 7 Dials.

———

Immediately following the above, another broad-sheet was printed and published with the gratifying announcement of the apprehension of the murderer! And the sale continued unabatingly for both town and country, every paper-worker making great profits by the sale ; and "The Catnach Press" still working with all their strength. Subjoined we give a *verbatim* copy of the second broad-sheet that was issued :—

ATROCIOUS MURDER OF A YOUNG WOMAN
IN SUFFOLK.
SINGULAR DISCOVERY OF THE BODY
FROM A DREAM.
APPREHENSION OF THE MURDERER AT EALING, MIDDLESEX.

LIKENESS OF WILLIAM CORDER.

On Tuesday William Corder was brought before Matthew
Wyatt, Esq., at Lambeth Street Police Office, in custody of
Lea, the officer, charged with the perpetration of as dark
and foul a murder as perhaps ever stained the annals of

crime.   Its accomplishment took place nearly a twelvemonth since ; and on the morning of yesterday, far from the scene of his diabolical offence, while sitting in imaginary security, the culprit was taken into custody.

His unfortunate victim was an inhabitant of Polstead, in Suffolk,—her name was Maria Marten ; and the prisoner appears to have been impelled to the frightful act by fear of the discovery of some former offence.   He was brought up for a short examination prior to his transmission to Suffolk. His age he stated to be twenty-four.   His dress was fashionable, and when taken into custody he, in conjunction with his wife, kept a boarding school for ladies at the Grove House, Ealing Lane, Middlesex.   Many rumours are afloat relative to his crime, but the real particulars, as far as they have as yet transpired, are as follows :—

For some years past the prisoner, who is a person of some property, and at the time of the committal of the offence with which he is charged was resident at Polstead, kept company with the unfortunate deceased, the daughter of a small farmer living in the vicinity of that village.   An illicit intercourse was the consequence of their acquaintance, and a child the fruit of their connexion.   This, it is rumoured, was murdered by the prisoner, and the mother. being aware of the revolting event, made use of it by a threat of discovery to extort from her paramour a promise of marriage.   On the 19th of May last, he called at her father's house and then expressed his willingness to have the ceremony performed, but in order that it might be private, and as much concealed as possible, he said his wish was to have it celebrated by license, and not by banns.

From that period up to Saturday week the parents heard no more of their daughter.   Some weeks since the mother had several dreams, which very much agitated her mind. On three several nights she dreamt that her daughter was murdered and buried on the right hand bay, as she calls it, of the further side of Corder's Red Barn. This was found to be the case.

On the discovery of the body, which has thrown the village of Polstead into the greatest excitement, W. Weyman, Esq., the coroner at Bury St. Edmunds, at once instituted an inquiry, and from the circumstances that came out of it, he was induced to despatch Ayres, a constable, in pursuit of the prisoner. He arrived in town on Monday, and having applied at Lambeth Street Office for assistance, the business was placed in the hands of Lea, who certainly has discharged his office with intelligence, activity, and industry. With a loose clue afforded him by the county constable, he traced the prisoner first to Gray's Inn Terrace, and from there through a number of intermediate places to his residence in Ealing Lane, near Brentford, where he apprehended him. A degree of stratagem was necessary to obtain an entrance, and he procured it by representing that he had a daughter whom he was anxious to place under .the care of his .wife. On going in, he found him in the parlour with four ladies, at breakfast. He was in his dressing gown, and had a watch before him, by which he was minuting the boiling of some .eggs. . Lea called him on one side, and told him that he was a London police officer, and come to apprehend him upon a most serious charge.

Printed by J. Catnach, 2, Monmouth Court, 7 Dials.

The trial of Corder took place at the Shire Hall, Bury St. Edmunds, on the 7th of August, before the Lord Chief Baron (Alexander). The prisoner pleaded *"Not Guilty,"* and the trial proceeded. On being called on for his defence, Corder read a manuscript paper. He declared that he deeply deplored the death of the unfortunate deceased, and he urged the jury to dismiss from their minds all that prejudice which must necessarily have been excited against him by the foul imputations which had been cast upon him by the public press, &c. Having concluded his address, the Lord Chief Baron summed up, and a verdict of *"Guilty"* was returned, and he was executed outside Bury gaol on Monday, August 10th, 1828. The Last Dying Speech and Confession had an enormous sale—estimated at 1,166,000 —a *fac simile* copy of which, with the " Lamentable Verses," said to have been written by Old Jemmy Catnach, will be found on the opposite page, reproduced on a smaller scale from the original, by the Litho-Zincographic Process, of which we have given examples. Others will follow.

CONFESSION AND EXECUTION OF

WILLIAM CORDER,

THE MURDERER OF MARIA MARTEN.

Since the tragical affair between Thurtell and Weare, no event has occurred connected with the criminal annals of our country which has excited so much interest as the trial of Corder, who was justly convicted of the murder of Maria Marten on Friday last.

THE CONFESSION.

"Bury Gaol, August 10th, 1828 —Condemned cell.
"Sunday evening, half-past Eleven.

"I acknowledge being guilty of the death of poor Maria Marten, by shooting her with a pistol. The particulars are as follows:—When we left her father's house, we began quarrelling about the burial of the child: she apprehended the place wherein it was deposited would be found out. The quarrel continued about three quarters of an hour upon this sad and about other subjects. A scuffle ensued, and during the scuffle, and at the time I think that she had hold of me, I took the pistol from the side pocket of my velveteen jacket and fired. She fell, and died in an instant. I never saw her even struggle. I was overwhelmed with agitation and dismay:—the body fell near the front doors on the floor of the barn. A vast quantity of blood issued from the wound, and ran on to the floor and through the crevices. Having determined to bury the body in the barn (about two hours after she was dead. I went and borrowed a spade of Mrs Stow, but before I went there I dragged the body from the barn into the chaff-house, and looked the barn. I returned again to the barn, and began to dig a hole, but the spade being a bad one, and the earth firm and hard, I was obliged to go home for a pickaxe and a better spade, with which I dug the hole, and then buried the body I think I dragged the body by the handkerchief that was tied round her neck. It was dark when I finished covering up the body. I went the next day, and washed the blood from off the barn-floor. I declare to Almighty God I had no sharp instrument about me, and no other wound but the one made by the pistol was inflicted by me. I have been guilty of great idleness, and at times led a dissolute life, but I hope through the mercy of God to be forgiven. WILLIAM CORDER."

Witness to the signing by the said William Corder,
JOHN ORRIDGE.

Condemned cell, Eleven o'clock, Monday morning,
August 11th, 1828.

The above confession was read over carefully to the prisoner in our presence, who stated most solemnly it was true, and that he had nothing to add to or retract from it.—W. STOCKING, chaplain; TIMOTHY R. HOLMES, Under-Sheriff.

THE EXECUTION.

At ten minutes before twelve o'clock the prisoner was brought from his cell and pinioned by the hangman, who was brought from London for the purpose He appeared resigned, but was so weak as to be unable to stand without support, when his cravat was removed he groaned heavily, and appeared to be labouring under great mental agony. 'When his wrists and arms were made fast, he was led round towards the scaffold, and as he passed the different yards in which the prisoners were confined, he shook hands with them, and speaking to two of them by name, he said, "Good bye, God bless you." They appeared considerably affected by the wretched appearance which he made, and "God bless you !" "May God receive your soul !" were frequently uttered as he passed along. The chaplain walked before the prisoner, reading the usual Burial Service, and the Governor and Officers walking immediately after him The prisoner was supported to the steps which led to the scaffold; he looked somewhat wildly around, and a constable was obliged to support him while the hangman was adjusting the fatal cord. There was a barrier to keep off the crowd, amounting to upwards of 7,000 persons, who at this time had stationed themselves in the adjoining fields, on the hedges, the tops of houses, and at every point from which a view of the execution could be best obtained. The prisoner, a few moments before the drop fell, groaned heavily, and would have fallen, had not a second constable caught hold of him. Everything having been made ready, the signal was given, the fatal drop fell, and the unfortunate man was launched into eternity. Just before he was turned off, he said in a feeble tone, "I am justly sentenced, and may God forgive me"

The Murder of Maria Marten.
BY W CORDER.

COME all you thoughtless young men, a warning take by me,
And think upon my unhappy fate to be hanged upon a tree;
My name is William Corder, to you I do declare,
I courted Maria Marten, most beautiful and fair.

I promised I would marry her upon a certain day,
Instead of that, I was resolved to take her life away.
I went into her father's house the 18th day of May,
Saying, my dear Maria, we will fix the wedding day.

If you will meet me at the Red-barn, as sure as I have life,
I will take you to Ipswich town, and there make you my wife;
I then went home and fetched my gun, my pickaxe and my spade,
I went into the Red-barn, and there I dug her grave.

With heart so light, she thought no harm, to meet him she did go
He murdered her all in the barn, and laid her body low;
After the horrible deed was done, she lay weltering in her gore,
Her bleeding mangled body was buried beneath the Red-barn floor.

Now all things being silent, her spirit could not rest,
She appeared unto her mother, who suckled her at her breast,
For many a long month or more, her mind being sore oppress'd,
Neither night or day she could not take any rest.

Her mother's mind being so disturbed, she dreamt three nights o'er,
Her daughter she lay murdered beneath the Red-barn floor;
She sent the father to the barn, when he the ground did thrust,
And there he found his daughter mingling with the dust.

My trial is hard, I could not stand, most woeful was the sight,
When her jaw-bone was brought to prove, which pierced my heart quite;
Her aged father standing by, likewise his loving wife,
And in her grief her hair she tore, she scarcely could keep life.

Adieu, adieu, my loving friends, my glass is almost run,
On Monday next will be my last, when I am to be hang'd,
So you, young men, who do pass by, with pity look on me,
For murdering Maria Marten, I was hang'd upon the tree.

Printed by J. Catnach, 2 and 3, Monmouth Court.—Cards, &c , Printed Cheap.

Mr. James Grant, in the second series of his popular work, the "Great Metropolis," has a sketch of one Mr. Curtis, an eccentric person, whose taste for witnessing executions, and for the society of persons sentenced to death, was remarkable. He had been present at every execution in the metropolis and its neighbourhood for the last quarter of a century. He actually walked before breakfast to Chelmsford, which is twenty-nine miles from London, to be present at the execution of Captain Moir. For many years he had not only heard the condemned sermons preached in Newgate, but spent many hours in the gloomy cells with the persons who had been executed in London during that period. He passed much time with Fauntleroy, and was with him a considerable part of the day previous to his execution. With Corder, too, of Red Barn notoriety, he contracted a friendship : immediately on the discovery of the murder of Maria Marten, he hastened to the scene, and remained there till Corder's execution. He afterwards wrote the "Memoirs of Corder," which were published by Alderman Kelly, Lord Mayor in 1837—8. The work had portraits of Corder and Maria Marten, and of Curtis, and nothing pleased him better than to be called the biographer of Corder.

By some unaccountable fatality, Curtis, where he was unknown, often had the mortification of being mistaken under very awkward circumstances for other persons. At Dover he was once locked up all night on suspicion of being a spy. When he went to Chelmsford to be present at Captain Moir's execution, he engaged a bed at the Three Cups inn ; on returning thither in the evening the servants rushed out of his sight, or stared suspiciously at him, he knew not why, till at length the landlady, keeping some yards distant from him, said, in tremulous accents, "We cannot give you a bed here ; when I promised you one, I did not know the house was full." " Ma'am," replied Curtis, indignantly, " I have taken my bed, and I insist on having it." " I am very sorry for it, but you cannot sleep here to-night," was the reply. " I *will* sleep here to-night ; I 've engaged my bed, and refuse me at your peril," reiterated Curtis. The landlady then offered him the price of a bed in another place, to which Curtis replied, resenting the affront, " No, ma'am ; I insist upon my rights as a *public* man ; I have a duty to perform to-morrow." " It 's all true. He says he 's a public man, and that he has a duty to perform," were words which every person in the room exchanged in suppressed whispers with each other. The waiter now stepped up to Mr. Curtis, and taking him aside, said, " The reason why mistress will not give you a bed is because you 're the executioner." Curtis was astounded, but in a few minutes laughed heartily at the mistake. " I 'll soon convince you of your error, ma'am," said Curtis, walking out of the house. He returned in a few minutes with a gentleman of the place, who having testified to his identity being different from that supposed, the landlady apologized for the mistake, and, as some reparation, gave him the best bed in the inn.

However, a still more awkward mistake occurred. After passing night after night with Corder in prison, Curtis accompanied him to his trial, and stood up close behind him at the bar. An artist had been sent from Ipswich to sketch a portrait of Corder for one of the newspapers of that town ; but the sketcher mistook Curtis for Corder, and in the next number of the journal Mr. Curtis figured in full length as the murderer of Maria Marten ! He bore the mistake with good humour, and regarded this as one of the most amusing incidents of his life.

It is not generally known that Dr. Maginn wrote for Knight and Lacey, the publishers in Paternoster Row, a novel embodying the strange story of the Polstead murder, in 1828, under the title of the " Red Barn." The work was published anonymously, in numbers, and by its sale the publishers cleared many hundreds of pounds.*

The case of Joseph Hunton, executed for forgery, excited considerable attention from the circumstance of his having been long known in the City of London as a person of good repute, and also from the fact of his being a Quaker.

At the Old Bailey sessions, on the 28th of October, 1828, he was put upon his trial, and found *Guilty* upon a charge of forging—amongst many others—a bill for £162 9s., with intent to defraud Sir William Curtis and Co., and notwithstanding the recommendation of the jury to mercy, he received sentence of death.

The execution of a man who moved in so respectable a sphere of life failed not to attract an immense crowd. He was, on Sunday, visited by several of the Society of Friends, who were accommodated with an apartment, in which they remained in their peculiar devotions for several hours. Afterwards he was attended by two gentlemen, Elders of the Congregation, who sat up with him in the press-room all night, and on the morning of the 8th of December, 1828, he, with three others, viz., James Abbott, aged 28, who resided in Fetter Lane, convicted of cutting his wife's throat, with intent to kill and murder her. John James, 19, for burglary in the house of Mr. Witham, solicitor, Boswell Court. Joseph Mahoney, 26, for burglary in the house of Mr. Barton, in the parish of St. Martin-in-the-Fields, suffered the extreme penalty of the law.

---

* CORDER'S SKELETON.—The bones of Corder having been cleared of the flesh, have been re-united by Mr. S. Dalton, and the skeleton is now placed in the Suffolk General Hospital. A great portion of the skin has been tanned, and a gentleman connected with the hospital intends to have the Trial and Memoirs of Corder bound in it. The heart has been preserved in spirits.—*Bell's Life in London*, 24th May, 1829.

Hunton commenced business at Yarmouth* as a slop-seller ; he opened a concern of some magnitude at Bury St. Edmunds, and was also engaged in business as a sugar baker in the metropolis. He had previously married a lady, a member of the Society of Friends, possessed of property to the amount of £30,000. Relinquishing these concerns, he entered into partnership with Messrs. Dickson and Co., of Ironmonger Lane, who soon discovered that he was engaged in speculations on the Stock Exchange, in which, as it turned out, he was particularly unsuccessful. A dissolution of partnership was the consequence, and then the unhappy man, driven to want and despair, committed those frauds which cost him his life.†

On Wednesday evening, January 14th, 1829, an inquiry of a singular and mysterious nature took place at St. Thomas's Hospital, before Thomas Shelton, Esq., Coroner, relating to the death of an individual styled James Allen, aged 42. The unfortunate deceased, who passed for, and assumed the dress of a man, was killed by a large piece of timber falling on the head while working at the bottom of a pit, as a sawyer, at the yard of Mr. Crisp, shipwright and builder, Mill Street, Dockhead. Death occurred on the way to the hospital. An examination of the body took place, when it was found to be of the female sex. It was

---

* It is somewhat singular and worth recording that at the time Hunton resided at Yarmouth, John Tawell, the Quaker, who was executed at Aylesbury, 28th March, 1845, for poisoning Sarah Hart, his concubine, and he, attended worship in the Friends' Meeting-house in that town. Here the young men frequently met, and thus an intimacy sprang up between two persons whose subsequent career in vice ultimately procured for both an undesirable notoriety, and an ignominious death on the scaffold.

† Thomas Maynard was the last person executed for forgery, 31st December, 1829.

proved before the Coroner that the deceased, who always lived, worked, and dressed as a man, had been married for upwards of twenty-one years, and that the wife—an honest and industrious woman—was still living, and that the deceased had left the wife several times on account of jealousy.   Both the coroner and the jury expressed their astonishment at· so extraordinary a circumstance as· two females living together as man and wife for so long a period. It certainly was both unprecedented and mysterious.

The jury expressed a wish to have the female who lived with the deceased before them, but the coroner said that it was unnecessary, they had only to inquire how deceased—immaterial, male or female—came to her death.   A verdict of "Accidental Death" was returned.

THE FEMALE HUSBAND!

This case of "The Female Husband" took the whole town by storm, and the writers and the "Seven Dials Press" were busy on the subject with "The True Particulars," "Extraordinary Adventures," "Life and Confession of the

Virgin Wife," &c., &c., together with ballads out of number, one from the press of T. Birt, No. 10, Great St. Andrew Street, Seven Dials, is entitled "The Female Husband, who had been married to another Female for Twenty-one Years." It is in form known as a "dialogue song." But from its suggestive character, with *mots à double entente*, we can only venture to quote one verse, while the dialogue between three old married women must be passed by *sub silentio*.

> "What wonders now have I to pen, sir,
> Women turning into men, sir,
> For twenty-one long years, or more, sir,
> She wore the breeches, we are told, sir,
> A smart and active handsome groom, sir,
> She then got married very soon, sir,
> A shipwright's trade she after took, sir,
> And of this wife, she made a fool, sir."

Soho Bazaar, the first of its kind in England, was established by John Trotter, Esq., to whose family it still belongs. The building covers a space of 300 feet by 150, and extends from the Square to Dean Street on the one hand, and to Oxford Street on the other. The bazaar occupies two floors, and has counter accommodation for upwards of 160 tenants. The two principal rooms in the building are about ninety feet long, and in them the visitor may find almost every trade represented. One large room is set apart for the sale of books, another for furniture, and another for birds, cages, &c.; and at one end of the latter room is a large recess, occupied with a rustic aviary, through which runs a stream of water. Connected with the bazaar are offices for the registration of governesses and the hire of servants, &c.; and the scene that here presents itself during business hours is one well worthy of a visit. The bazaar has been frequently patronised by royalty.

THE SOHO BAZAAR.

LADIES in furs, and gemmen in spurs,
   Who lollop and lounge about all day :
The Bazaar in Soho is completely the go—
   Walk into the shop of Grimaldi !
     Come from afar, here's the Bazaar !—
     But if you won't deal with us, stay where you are.

Here's rouge to give grace to an old woman's face,
   Trowsers of check for a sailor ;
Here's a cold ice, if you pay for it twice,
   And here's a hot goose for a tailor.
     Soho Bazaar, come from afar :
     Sing ri fal de riddle, and tal de ral la.

Here's a cock'd hat, for an opera flat—
   Here's a broad brim for a Quaker ;
Here's a white wig for a Chancery prig,
   And here's a light weight for a baker.
       Soho Bazaar, &c.

A fringed parasol, or a toad-in-the-hole,
   A box of japan to hold backy ;
Here's a relief for a widow in grief—
   A quartern of Hodges's jacky.
       Soho Bazaar, &c.

Here, long enough, is a lottery puff
   (I was half-drunk when it caught me) ;
It promised, my eyes ! what a capital prize :
   And here's all the rhino it brought me.
       Soho Bazaar, &c.

"Put it down to the bill," is the fountain of ill ;
   This has the shopkeepers undone ;
Bazaars never trust—so down with your dust,
   And help us to diddle all London.
       Soho Bazaar, &c.

Printed by J. Catnach, 2 & 3, Monmouth Court, 7 Dials.

The first pair of London omnibuses started from the Yorkshire Stingo, public-house, in the New Road, to the Bank of England and back, on Saturday, July 4th, 1829. They were constructed to carry twenty-two passengers, all inside, and were drawn by three horses abreast. The fare was one shilling, or sixpence for half the distance, together with the luxury of a newspaper. A Mr. J. Shillibeer was the owner of these carriages, and in order that the introduction might have every chance of success and the full prestige of respectability, he brought over with him from Paris two youths, both the sons of British naval officers, and these young gentlemen were his "conductors." They were smartly dressed in blue cloth, after the Parisian fashion. Their addressing any foreign passenger in French, and the French style of the affair, gave rise to an opinion that Mr. Shillibeer was a Frenchman, and that the English were indebted to a foreigner for the improvement of their vehicular transit, whereas Mr. Shillibeer had served in the British navy, and was born in Tottenham Court Road ; yet he had afterwards carried on the business of a coach builder both in London and Paris. His speculation was particularly and at once successful, for he insured punctuality and civility ; and the cheapness, cleanliness, and smartness of his omnibuses were in most advantageous contrast with the high charges, dirt, dinginess, and rudeness of the drivers of many of the "short stages" and Hackney coaches, who were loud in their railings against what they were pleased to describe as a French innovation, and many were the street-papers and ballads issued on the subject both for and against the "Shillibeer's" and "French Hearses."

THE 'Buss, the 'Buss, the Omnibus !
    That welcomes all without a fuss ;
And wafts us on, with joyous sound,
Through crowded streets on our busy round,
Reckless of cold and gloomy skies,
Or the driving storm as it downward hies :
Stow'd snug in thee ! stow'd snug in thee !
I am where I would wish to be,
While the rain above and the mud below
Affect me not where'er I go ——
Though the sleet and the slush be ankle deep,
What matters ? while I can ride so cheap !
                    What matters ? &c.

I love, oh how I love to ride
In cozy converse, side by side,
With some sweet sly enchanting one,
Who lets her little 'larum run
Till scarcely can the listener know
If that or Time more swiftly go !
Henceforth I 'll know the terrible bore
Of " padding the hoof " no more, no more ;
But back to the seat I so oft have press'd
I 'll spring, to be wafted the while I rest :
For thou, dear 'Buss ! art a home to me,
While I am snugly seated in thee.
                    While I am, &c.

Jarvey ! Here am I, ye'r honour.

MARCH OF THE TIMES.

New Omnibuses now are beating coaches out of time, sir,
But 'tis a word to which I can't contrive to make a rhyme, sir;
The sight to me is something new, and something rather droll, sir,
Of twenty spooneys bolt upright, all sitting cheek by jowl, sir.

THE HACKNEY COACHMAN.

MY name 's honest Jarvey, I come unto you
    To tell all my woes, for I 've nothing to do,
The cab chaps all calls me a crusty old file,
Because I von't take folks at eight-pence a mile.
Them omnibus fellers makes 'emselves busy,
From Paddington down to the Bank for a *tizzy*,
'Fore they vere invented I show'd 'em the trick,
And for every sich job charged two bob and a kick.
    Then pity poor Jarvey, kind gentlefolks, pray,
        For he 's sadly in debt vithout money to pay.

Vonce I used to yearn a guinea a day,
And at night drove the folks to Woxhall or the play;
But them days are gone by, and the people tells me
As the play-houses now isn't vorth going to see,
'Cause a chap they calls Bunn's made a stable of Drury,
And Macready in *Hion* you 'll *see*, I assure ye,
By paying a sixpence; and I 'll bet a farden
That 's the reason they calls t' other house *Common Garden.*

> Then pity, &c.

*   *   *   *   *

One vould think the fair ladies vould all make a fuss
At being placed face to face vith the men in a *'buss;*
Yet some ladies there are, who, betwixt you and I,
Are fond of a *'buss* when a sweetheart is nigh.
Now, I 'll ask you the question, what can there be vorse
Then to clap twenty passengers into a hearse?
I peep'd into one t' other day, and I saw
'Twere crammed full of ladies, who *were all in the straw.*

> Then pity, &c.

Printed by J. Pitts, Wholesale Toy Warehouse, Great St. Andrew
Street, Seven Dials.

APPEAL TO THE PUBLIC

FROM THE PADDINGTON COACHMEN.

" Nemo mortalium omnibus horis sapit."

WE humbly beg to make our bow to gentry and nobility,
With that which we are noted for—our uniform civility;
For Paddington has long been fam'd for werry quiet lads,
And all agree that none excel the Coachman and their Cads.

We 've always sarv'd the public well—we always kept our time;
Our fares was werry moderate, our cattle werry prime;
To think how we 've been wilified our tender feelings shocks,
For sartainly genteeler men ne'er got upon a box.

Politeness, we are griev'd to say, is of no sort of sarvice,
And werry groundless prejudice prevails against the Jarveys;
And now a clumsy vehicle as started on the road,
To carry twenty souls inside—a pretty tidy load.

Look at the three old hacks abreast, and at its rum dimensions,
The Devil fetch the omnibus, and all these French inventions;
We soon may see if sich machines are us'd by folks of rank—
The Colosseum perch'd on wheels a rolling to the Bank.

The cove that started this machine has made a dang'rous move,
The *Omnibus* in little time a *blunderbuss* may prove.
To us the public must be staunch, and then what will it end in?
With Gemmen he will soon find out the folly of contending.

But if the public are content to see us so ill-used,
And chuse to sanction the *affair* our *fare* must be reduc'd,
Tho' if a taste for such machines continues to increase,
Some folks may fancy riding in the wan of the police.

But still we hope for better things, and while we guide the rein,
We trust that this appeal, in werse, will not be made in wain ;
The Man wot drives the Sovereign every British heart engages,
But we're the lads of Paddington wot always drives the stages.

Then bad luck to the Omnibus, whosever the consarn is,
We still will drive as pretty tits as ever went in harness ;
To do the trick in bang-up style shall still be our endeavour,
As civil, as obliging, and as sober lads as ever.

None will deny our nobs were always screw'd on the right way ;
No other favour we require than clear stage and fair play ;
And when the Omnibus is dead, we'll make the beer and gin go,
And celebrate its obsequies in triumph at the Stingo.

THE STAGE-COACHMAN'S LAMENT.

FAREWELL to my tight little cutch !
    'Farewell to my neat four inside !
Like a shabby old crack'd rabbit-hutch
    They have treated the pet of my pride.

How she stood on her rollers so clean !
    How she scuttled along like a doe,
Or a bowl on a close-shaven green !
    Ah ! warn't she a rum 'un to go !

But now all her claims are forgot,
 And they 've pull'd out her in'ards so soft,
And they 've laid up her carcass to rot
 In a hole of a cutch-maker's loft.

Farewell to my four iron greys,
 And the rest of the prads that I drive !
In these selfish and steam sniffing days,
 'Tisn't fit for good hosses to live.

Your prime fast machiners in lots
 To the hammer are shamefully led :
'Twere better, like so many stots,
 To knock 'em at once on the head.

My face from such deeds turns awry—
 Not so with your change-hunting swarm :
Here 's times for the knackers, says I ;
 'Tis the spirit, says they, of Reform.

Some pretended to pity my case,
 And they told me—the govenor chaps,
I might have in the railway a place,
 To look arter the luggage and traps.

But I bowed, and I grabbed up my hat,
 And shied off, as though stung by a bee ;
Only think of an offer like that
 To a slap-up swell dragsman like me !

   * * *

A plague on them leaders, the Whigs !
 I 'm a given to think very much
That in runnin' their rascally rigs,
 They'll upset, by-and-by, the State-cutch.

THE CHARLEY'S TEAR.

UPON his beat he stood,
   . To take a last farewell
Of his lantern and his little box,
Wherein he oft did dwell.
He listen'd to the clock,
So familiar to his ear,
And with the tail of his drab coat
He wiped away a tear.

Beside that watchouse door
A girl was standing close,
Who held a pocket handkerchief,
With which she blew her nose.
She rated well the police man,
Which made poor Charley queer,
Who once more took his old drab coat,
To wipe away a tear.

He turn'd and left the spot,
Oh ! do not deem him weak ;
A sly old chap this Charley was,
Though tears were on his cheek.
Go, watch the lads in Fetter Lane,
Where oft you 've made them fear ;
The hand, you know, that takes a bribe,
Can wipe away a tear.

The London police grew out of the London watch,
instituted about 1253; the whole system was remodelled
by Mr., afterwards Sir Robert Peel, by 10 Geo. IV., 19th
June, and the New Police commenced duty 29th September,
1829. Sir Richard Mayne was appointed Chief Commissioner of the Metropolitan district. The new system was not
popular with the people, nor with those who deemed they

had "vested rights," and the constables were considered as a target that every one might fire off their chaff and witticisms at with impunity. The term "Bobby"—after Robert Peel, immediately became the cant word, together with "Blue Bottles," "Blue Devils," the "Royal Blues; or, the Cook's Own," and other opprobrious terms. Within a month of the establishing of the New Police—viz., on the 14th of October, 1829, one of the members, named John Jones, was charged, at the Hatton Garden Police-station, with stealing a scrag of mutton from the stall-board of a butcher, named Sommer, in Skinner Street, Somers Town. The circumstance having been witnessed by a neighbour, he pursued the policeman, and took him into custody. He had fifteen shillings and sixpence in his pocket. In his defence, he said he was going to take the mutton to show his wife. This was a circumstance that could not be lost sight of by the Seven Dials printers, and several street-papers and ballads were immediately issued on the subject, and continued to find a ready sale for some months; while "Who stole the mutton?" became the by-word. Following is one of the many ballads that appeared :—

THE NEW POLICEMAN,

AND THE SOMERS TOWN BUTCHER.

Air—"*Bob and Joan.*"

HOLLO! New Police,
 Who in blue coats strut on,
Your fame you won't increase
 By stealing joints of mutton.
Who would e'er suppose,
 In such handsome rigging,
Spick and span new clothes,
 Men would go a prigging?
  Hollo! New Police, &c., &c.

At very little cost
  Jones wished to have a luncheon;
But now the blade has lost
  His uniform and truncheon.
Alas! the worthy soul,
  While the victuals bagging,
Tho' a *scrag* he stole,
  Never dreamt of *scragging.*   Hollo! &c., &c.

Off he made to move,
  And mutter'd in retreating,
" D——, this will prove
  Very pretty eating!"
With this bit of meat,
  Doubtless quite enraptur'd;
But joy is very fleet,
  And Mr. Jones was captur'd. Hollo! &c., &c.

"Oh!" cried Mr. Jones,
  "This is inconvenient!
Curse the mutton bones—
  Gentlemen, be lenient.
This joint, you will remark
  (The truth I won't conceal it),
I *borrowed* for a lark—
  I never meant to steal it."   Hollo! &c., &c.

Here's a pretty prig,
  Thus went Somers Sam on,
First my meat to prig,
  And then to pitch his gammon.
Borrow'd! blow me tight,
  Seeing is believing;
I loves the thing vot's right,
  And always hated thieving.   Hollo! &c., &c.

Peel's new plan, I say,
  Ought to be rejected,
If this here's the way
  We're to be protected.
These coves parade the street
  In dashing dark blue habit ;
But when they eye our meat,
  'Tis ten to one they grab it. Hollo ! &c., &c.

'Twas droll to hear the chaff
  When they were embodied ;
Now it makes me laugh
  To see so many quodded.
Thieves may feel secure,
  Whate'er thé hour or weather,
For Sam is very sure
  They are all rogues together.

-     Hollo ! &c., &c.

The City of London successfully rejected the introduction of the New Police within their territories. "They vorn't a going to hav' no new French Police Spy system in their ancient and honourable City," said Aldermen Cute-Grub-Bub-Turtle-and-Soup, "not if ve knows it." Therefore, no one will be surprised at frequently reading in the newspapers of the period paragraphs like the following :—

EFFECTS OF THE NEW POLICE.

At Guildhall, on Monday, October 12th, 1829, after Sir Peter Laurie had admonished and discharged a disorderly woman, who had been accused of being noisy in the street, he asked her accuser, a watchman, named Livingstone, where his beat was ? The watchman said it was from St. Dunstan's Church to Temple Bar. Do you find any increase of bad characters on your beat? Watchman (smiling) : Yes, I believes I do; the New Policeman drives 'em into the City. Sir Peter : Then you should drive them back again ; it would be better than taking them up. Watchman : When there was a quarrel among them the other night, a policeman came up and drove them through the Bar, saying, "Ye shan't stand here ; go into the City with your rows." Sir Peter

Laurie said that he had heard that a police magistrate had directed the policemen to drive all bad characters into the City. If there was any truth in this, it was an imprudent—an improper observation. He desired the watchman present to drive all the bad characters out of the City. The thing must be put down. Subsequently, some vagrants were brought up, and Sir Peter told them to drive them out of the City instead of apprehending them in future. "We can play at tennis-ball," said the Alderman, in an under tone.

"Who stole the Mutton?" together with many other words and phrases in reference to the supposed partiality of the police to *The Cook ! The Kitchen !! and The Cold Mutton !!!* have clung to the service from the day of its formation to the present time, while comic writers of all degrees, in farces, burlesques, songs, and pantomimes, have never failed to make capital out of the New Police, Peel's Raw-Lobsters, Peelers, Blue Bottles, &c., &c.

I 'M ONE OF THE NEW POLICE.

I 'M one of the New Police—egad,
   The servant maids declare
There is not a lout in all the Force,
   Can strut with such an air.

My gloves of white, my coat of blue,
　My dignity increase—
My every gesture shows to you
　I 'm one of the New Police.
　　　　The New Police—ha, ha !
　　　　　I 'm one of the New Police !

I 'm partial to an outside beat,
　'Cause there I feels secure,
When with the servant girls I romp
　And play at some back door.
I love to loll in kitchens, too,
　Rough mutton joints to fleece,
I'm now in want of prog,
　I 'm one of the New Police.
　　　　　The New Police, &c.

'Tis pleasant, when I peckish feel,
　With Moll or Bess to stop,
And coax them till they go below,
　And broil a mutton chop.
Large rounds of beef I gaze upon,
　Just wink and earn a piece,
I 'd rather than a borough lout
　Be one of the New police.
　　　　　The New Police, &c.

I 'd us'd to live on low lobscouse,
　'Twas foolish—I'd no sense—
I now live like a fighting-cock,
　With little or no expence.
I was a journeyman tailor once,
　But now I 'm in the peace ;
I lie—swear false—break heads—egad !
　I 'm one of the New Police ?
　　　　　The New Police, &c.

Now, then, Sir, I 'll trouble you to move on !

THE LOBSTERS' CLAUSE ; OR, THE NEW POLICE BILL.

I SING, I sing, of the new bill, sir,
　　That to the people seems a pill, sir,
And shortly I 'll relate its clauses,
That you may know what the police law is.
First and foremost, in a straight line running,
For fifteen miles it will stop your funning,
From Charing Cross, which ever way you turn, sir,
If you infringe, your fingers you 'll burn, sir.
Oh, dear, oh, dear ! they 're better off in Greece, sir,
Free from this Metropolis Police, sir.

All the people who used to shew, sir,
Traps on the pavement, will find it no go, sir,
And now within their shop or dwelling,
Their oddcum shorts they must be selling,
If maids after eight their mats should beat, sir,
At the treadmill they 'll have a treat.
And, if little boys roll hoops, or fly kites, sir,
They 'll be lock'd up seven days and nights, sir.
　　　　　　　　Oh, dear, &c.

THE FLOWER OF THE NEW POLICE.

By Sally Spriggins, Spinster.

OH! do not say of womankind,
    That a scarlet coat will enthral 'em ;
If rags could enchant the fair ones thus,
    Rag fair ones you might call 'em.
I never was fond of the garb of war,
    Give me the robe of peace—
The deep, deep blue of X 41,
    The Flower of the New Police.

    *   *   *   *

I know I 'se many rivals, love ——
    There 's three as lives next door,
And caps, I hear, are set at you,
    At number 44 ;
And I wish the maid at three-and-a-half
    Would please to hold her peace,
And not go telling lies of me
    To the Flower of the New Police.

She says I love you, single X,
    And double X, beside,
But that 's all for to hinder you
    From making me your bride.
Whate'er they say, my love for you
    Will never, never cease,
So come to my arms, 'X 41,
    Thou Flower of the New Police.

THE RIGHTEOUS PEELER.

THAT I 'm a righteous cove,
    To you I 'd not be boasting,
Throughout my life I 've strove
    Of money to bring most in ;
I am now in the Police,
    Of course then to be witty,
I make folks keep the peace,
    So listen to my ditty.   Rum tum, &c.

By prigs I am well-known,
    Because I make 'em step hard,
I 'm christened well, I own,
    For they all call me " Jack Sheppard."
Housebreakers, too, I hook,
    And with 'em I makes slaughter,
With my false-swearing look,
    They 're dragged across the water.
                                Rum tum, &c.

The New Policeman.

BLOOD and ouns, faith, and why do you laugh?
  I 'm a gentleman that knows how to fleece man,
Ye spalpeens now stow all your chaff,
    Don't you see I 'm a new policeman,
I 'm created by great Mr. Peel,
    Your morality, faith, to decrease man,
And by the powers I 'll make you feel,
    Because I 'm a new policeman.
                    Hubboboo wack, fal de, &c.

From Lim'rick's sweet city I came,
    Without a shoe to my back, sir,
I carried a hod—what a shame !
    But now I 'm a gentleman, oh, wack, sir !
I 'm dress'd in a neat suit of blue,
    I 'm so pleased that it never will cease, man,
And a shillelah I sport, too,
    Because I 'm a new policeman.

Och ! once if I kicked up a row,
    In a shake I was walked before a beak, sir ;
And the great big son of a sow,
    Would send me to quod for one week, sir ;
But now things are alter'd you see,
    • If you hit 'tis a breach of the peace, man,
So I kick up a row for a spree,
    Because I 'm a new policeman.

George IV., after a long and painful illness, expired at Windsor on the 26th of June, 1830, in the sixty-eight year of his age. He was succeeded by his brother, the Duke of Clarence, who ascended the throne as William IV. He was received by the people with that popular enthusiasm which his frank and manly bearing, characteristic of his profession as a British sailor, was so calculated to excite. The Sailor King, and even Billy, the Sailor King, at once became popular words. Of the many street-ballads written on the subject we select the following :—

Our King is a True British Sailor.

TOO long out of sight have been kept Jolly Tars,
    In the ground-tiers, like huts stow'd away,
Despis'd and contemn'd were their honour'd scars,
    And Red Coats were Lords of the day.
But Britannia now moves as a gallant first-rate,
    And with transports the Blue Jackets hail her ;
For William's right hand steers the helm of the State,
    And our King is a true British Sailor.

No danger the heart of a seaman appals,
    To fight or to fall he is ready,
The safeguard of Britain is her wooden walls,   •
    And the Helmsman cries, "Steady ! boys, steady !"
Cheer up, my brave boys, give the wheel a new spoke,
    If a foe is in view we will hail her,
For William the Fourth is a sound heart of oak, true Blue,
    and a bold British Sailor.

The wild winds around us may furiously whistle,
    And tempest the ocean deform,
But unite the red rose, the shamrock and thistle,
    With King William we 'll weather the storm ;

Hard up with the helm, Britannia's sheet flows,
　Magna Charta on board will avail her,
And better she sails, as the harder it blows,
　For her Pilot's a King and a Sailor.

Co-equal with red be the gallant true blue,
　And nought can their glories o'erwhelm,
Whilst Sydney and Freemen direct the brave crew,
　And William presides at the helm ;
Then fill up a bumper, Britannia appears
　New rigg'd, and with joy we all hail her,
Here's a health to the King, with three times three cheers,
　And long life to the first British Sailor.

Printed by T. BIRT, No. 10, Great St. Andrew Street, 7 Dials.

The late Duke of Wellington was, from the entering upon his life as a statesman, in 1822, until his death, in 1852, considered as a common target whereat caricaturists, political, satirical, comic writers of every degree, and ballad-mongers might shoot at with impunity, while familiar titles, as "Nosey," the "Iron Duke," and a dozen others, were applied with the greatest freedom by the people. According to his biographer, the Rev. George Robert Gleig, the latter sobriquet arose out of the building of an iron steamboat, which plied between Liverpool and Dublin, and which its owners called the "Duke of Wellington." The term "Iron Duke," was first applied to the vessel ; and by-and-by, rather in jest than in earnest, it was transferred to the Duke himself. From the close intimacy existing between William IV. and the Duke, the latter was generally spoken and written of as :—

THE MAN WOT DRIVES THE SOVEREIGN.

The Act, 1st William, commonly called *The Beer Bill ;*
or, the three B. B. B.'s—*i.e.,* " Billy's Beer Bill"—was passed
with the mistaken view of enabling the humble classes to
obtain a necessary beverage, better and cheaper than at the
public-houses, for home consumption. That was the aver-
ment ; but, as a matter of fact, the practice of private brewing
has rapidly declined ; nevertheless, the passing of the Bill
proved to be an unexpected piece of good fortune for the
Seven Dials poets and printers. Songs, dialogues, cate-
chisms, &c., were written and printed off daily, the gist of
all being that both the people and the beer would be ——

ALLOWED TO BE DRUNK ON THE PREMISES.

HEAVY WET.

King William and Reform, I say,
　　In such a case who can be neuter?
Just let me blow the froth away,
　　And see how I will drain the pewter.

Another tankard, landlord, fill,
　　And let us drink to that ere chap, Broom ;
And·then we 'll chaunt God save King Bill,
　　And send the echoes thro' the tap-room.

I Likes a Drop of Good Beer.

COME, one and all, both great and small,
   With voices loud and clear,
And let us sing, bless Billy our king,
Who 'bated the tax upon beer.

Chorus.—For I likes a drop of good beer, I do,
   I likes a drop of good beer,
    And —— his eyes whoever tries
    To rob a poor man of his beer.

Let ministers shape the duty on cape,
   And cause port wine to be dear,
So that they keep the bread and meat cheap,
   And give us a drop of good beer.
      For I likes, &c.

My wife and I feel always dry,
   At market on Saturday night,
Then a muggin of beer I never need fear,
   For my wife always says it is right.
         For she likes, &c.

In farmers' field there's nothing can yield
   The labouring man such good cheer
To reap and sow, and make barley grow,
   And to give 'em a skin full of beer.
         For they like, &c.

Long may King Billy reign,
   And be to his subjects dear,
And wherever he goes we'll wollop his foes,
   Only give us a skin full of beer.
         For we like, &c.

Ballooning, by means of steam, aërial screw machines, with sails, rudders, and a variety of other ill-devised contrivances, were, at this period, *floated* by *flighty* individuals, and afforded a never failing source for comic and satirical writers, from St. Giles' to St. James', and back again, to exercise their good, bad, and indifferent talents upon.

THE ÆRIAL SHIP.

WONDERS, sure, will never cease, at least so people say,
But always keep on the increase, and very well they may,
Since multiplying's all the go, and getting on a head,
We are making wonders now—how shall we get our bread?

The Ærial ship seems all the go, that's if she'll go at all;
Some think she'll make a wondrous hit, some think she'll make a fall.
'Tis certain if she makes a hit, at the rate she's going to go,
To all things standing in her way she'll give a sure death blow.

Railways, then, need be no more, balloons no more be seen—
The wonders of the Great Nassau will then look very *green*.
All the shipping may lie up, and the seamen, in despair,
Must sleep on board of boilers, and live on smoke and air.

*　　　*　　　ト　　　*　　　*　　　*　　　ト　　ィ

But though these things may come to pass, they have not yet appear'd,
And dangers, when they're out of sight, they never should be fear'd.
And all our dread and doubt of this may only be a joke,
For projects which we build in air most often end in smoke.

ÆROSTATION! OR, THE GREAT BALLOON.

WHAT wonders spring up every day, sirs,
Surely they will never stay, sirs;
The march of intellect is blooming,
And the mania now is all ballooning.
There's Mr. Green, so æromantick,
Has built a balloon—in size, gigantic—
Which, when of gas there is a plenty,
Instead of one, will *take up twenty!*
The folks now talk both night and noon, sirs,
Of the wonders of this great balloon, sirs.

Steam carriages by land are now the order of the day, sir,
But why they haven't started yet, 'tis not for me to say, sir ;
Some people hint 'tis *uphill* work—that loose they find a screw, sir,
Such novelties, as Pat would say, of *old* they never *knew*, sir.

                        Bow, wow, &c.

SONG OF THE STEAM COACHMAN THAT DRIVES THE OMNIBUS TO THE MOON.

NOW is the time for a sly trip to *the Moon*, sir,
    There's a new RAIL ROAD just made through *the Sky*,
Or if you prefer it, we have a *prime* BALLOON, sir,
    In which you can ascend with me *up sky-high.*
Travelling the rage is—in the tying of a Sandal,
We take our *tea* in *Tartary,* or *chop* at *Coromandel,*
Then when *blazing hot* we get with *India's gums* and *spices,*
We take a *stroll* towards the *Pole,* and *cool our-selves with ices.*
    ·Now is the time for a sly trip to *the Moon,* sir, &c.

Our HORSES they never tire, for they 're *coal* and *coke*, sir,
  With *jolly lots* of *water* boiling hot,
We *cut along like bricks* among the *fire* and *smoke*, sir,
  Never *blowing no one up*, nor *going to pot*.

Our COACHMAN nice and steady is, not like the *old fat soaker*,
For 'stead of *passing* GLASSES *round*, he *passes round* THE POKER :
Our GUARDS, too, are a quiet set of *fire-blowing* FELLOWS,
Who 'stead of *blowing noisy* HORNS, *now blow a* PAIR OF BELLOWS!

  Now is the time for a sly trip to *the Moon*, sir,
    There 's a new RAIL ROAD just made through *the Sky*,
  Or if you prefer it, we have a *prime* BALLOON, sir,
    In which you can ascend with me *up sky-high*.

The practicability of running steam carriages upon common roads now occupied the attention of scientific men, and experiments were made with various degrees of success.

The Select Committee appointed to inquire into the power, &c., of Steam Carriages, concluded their report with the following summary :—1. That carriages can be propelled by steam on common roads at an average rate of ten miles per hour. 2. That at this rate they have conveyed upwards of fourteen passengers. 3. That their weight, including engine, fuel, water, and attendants, may be under three tons. 4. That they can ascend and descend hills of considerable inclination with facility and ease. 5. That they are perfectly safe for passengers. 6. That they are not (or need not be, if properly constructed) nuisances to the public. 7. That they will become a speedier and cheaper mode of conveyance than carriages drawn by horses. 8. That, as they admit of greater breadth of tire than other carriages, and as the roads are not acted on so injuriously as by the feet of horses in common draught, such carriages will cause less wear of roads than coaches drawn by horses. 9. That rates of toll have been imposed on steam carriages which would prohibit their being used on several lines of road were such charges permitted to remain unaltered.

THE ODDS AND ENDS OF THE YEAR 1830.

COME listen awhile, I'll sing you a song
    Concerning the times, and I will not keep you long,
To please you right well I mean to prevail,
I will begin at the head, and leave off at the tail.

> *Chorus.*—And they are all chaffing,
>   Chaff, chaff, chaffing,
>   And they are all chaffing,
>   In country and in town.

Pray what do you think of the new King and Queen?
Why they tell me in Brighton they are to be seen,
Where lots of nobility do follow, you are sure,
And I hope before long they'll do something for the poor.

And what do you think of my Lords Broom and Grey?
They are Whigs, and they frightened all the Tories, they say,
They have promised very fair, but at present they are still,
And I hope all their promises they mean to fulfil.

What do you think of old Arthur and Bob?
Why I think they're in a mess, for they can't get a job;
May Bobby[1] sell his trap, and old Nosey[2] to the sod.
Oh, how I should laugh if they both went to quod.

What do you think of the new Lord Mayor?[3]
Why a short time ago he made thousands to stare,
He kept them from a dinner, oh! he was mighty civil,
And the bellies of the citizens did groan like the devil.

What do you think of the ex-King of France?
Why I think he done well off to Scotland to dance,
When he'd caused a disturbance from the nation he flew,
And his Ministers are in dungeons, singing parlableu.

What do you think of Saint John Long?[4]
Them that think him a Doctor must be great in the wrong;
From Justice he has flew, and if he does come back,
To the devil they'll send him, singing quack! quack!

What do you think of bold Captain Swing?[5]
I think through the country he has done a wicked thing,
He has caused great destruction in England and France,
If Justice o'ertakes him on nothing he'll dance.

1.—In allusion to the political "Ratting" of the 2nd Sir Robert Peel. 1788—1850.

2.—The late Duke of Wellington. 1769—1852.

3.—Alderman Key, Mayor, 1830. Invitation declined by King William IV.; and the show and inauguration dinner omitted, from apprehension of riot and outrage.

4.—A notorious quack doctor. 1798—1834.

5.—A fictitious and much-dreaded name signed to incendiary threats in the rural districts at the time of the introduction of agricultural machinery.

LEX TALIONIS.

As " Swing's " wild justice is to Burn,
    It is but to reverse the thing,
And tell the culprit in his turn—
    It is " Burn's Justice " he should " Swing."

What do you think of bold Henry Hunt ?
I think he is a man that will speak his mind blunt,
He is chosen M.P., he is clever and cute,
He will polish up the Commons like a Wellington boot.

What do you think of Ireland's Dan ?
I think that O'Connell is a valiant man,
For the Union of Erin he loudly does call,
And he says he is determined to agitate them all.

What do you think of the new Policemen now ?
At Union Hall Police Office there has been a row,
One thought to get promoted, oh ! wasn't he a flat,
To take a loaded pistol and fire at his hat.

What do you think of the new London Bridge grand,
And of the improvements they are making in the Strand ?
Why it will be very handsome, I 'm certain and sure,
But the money would look better, feeding the poor.

Printed by T. BIRT,   **10,**   Great St. Andrew Street,
(wholesale and retail,)   Seven Dials, London.
Country Orders punctually attended to.
Every description of Printing on the most reasonable terms.
Children's Books, Battledores, Pictures, &c.

THE DOGS'-MEAT MAN.

Founded on Fact.

IN Gray's Inn, not long ago,
    An old maid lived a life of woe ;
She was fifty-three, with a face like tan,
And she fell in love with a dogs'-meat man.
Much she loved this dogs'-meat man,
He was a good-looking dogs'-meat man ;
Her roses and lilies were turn'd to tan,
When she fell in love wi' the dogs'-meat man.

Every morning when he went by,
Whether the weather was wet or dry,
And right opposite her door he 'd stand,
And cry " dogs' meat," did this dogs'-meat man.
Then her cat would run out to the dogs'-meat man,
And rub against the barrow of the dogs'-meat man,
As right opposite to her door he 'd stand,
And cry "Dogs' Meat," did this dogs'-meat man.

Q

One morn she kept him at the door,
Talking, half-an-hour or more ;
For, you must know, that was her plan,
To have a good look at the dogs'-meat man.
"Times are hard," says the dogs'-meat man ;
"Folks get in my debt," says the dogs'-meat man ;
Then he took up his barrow, and away he ran,
And cried "Dogs' Meat," did this dogs'-meat man.

He soon saw which way the cat did jump,
And his company he offered plump ;
She couldn't blush, 'cause she 'd no fan,
So she *sot* and grinned at the dogs'-meat man.
"If you 'll marry me," says the dogs'-meat man,
"I 'll have you," says the dogs'-meat man ;
For a quartern of peppermint then he ran,
And she drink'd a good health to the dogs'-meat man.

That very evening he was seen,
In a jacket and breeches of velveteen,
To Bagnigge-Wells, then, in a bran
New gown, she went with the dogs'-meat man :
She 'd biscuits and ale with the dogs'-meat man,
And walked arm-in-arm with the dogs'-meat man ;
And the people all said, what round-did stan'
He was quite a dandy dogs'-meat man.

He said his customers, good lord !
Owed him a matter of two pound odd ;
And she replied, it was quite scan- .
Dalous to cheat such a dogs'-meat man.
"If I had but the money," says the dogs'-meat man,
"I 'd open a tripe-shop," says the dogs'-meat man,
"And I 'd marry you to-morrow."—She admired his plan,
And she lent a *five-pound note* to the dogs'-meat man.

He pocketed the money and went away,
She waited for him all next day,
But he never com'd ; and then she began
To think she was diddled by the dogs'-meat man ;
She went to seek this dogs'-meat man,
But she couldn 't find the dogs'-meat man ;
Some friend gave her to understan'
He 'd got a wife and seven children—this dogs'-meat man.

So home she went, with sighs and tears,
As her hopes were all transformed to fears,
And her hungry cat to mew began,
As much as to say,—"Where's the dogs'-meat man?"
She couldn't help thinking of the dogs'-meat man,
The handsome, swindling, dogs'-meat man;
So you see, just in one day's short span,
She lost her heart, a five-pound note, and the dogs'-meat man.

Printed by J. Catnach, 2, Monmouth Court, 7 Dials.

. Mr. Hunt, the great political firebrand of the day— Radical Hunt—made a public entry into London on January 11th, 1831, in honour of his return as M.P. for Preston.   He was met at Islington Green by a large body of persons, flags, &c., who attended him from that place to his house in Stamford Street, Blackfriars.   The procession— in which the hon. member's " MATCHLESS BLACKING " car formed a conspicuous object—passed down the City Road, across Finsbury Square, through the City, the Strand, Parliament Street, across Westminster Bridge, and thence to Mr. Hunt's residence.   The circumstance caused several street-papers and ballads to be produced.   In fact, Hunt was very popular with the mob, and anything in respect to him found a ready sale, in the streets of the metropolis, while he, with his red-hot Radicalism and his " Matchless Blacking" game, worked the oracle to his own profit and self aggrandizement, and had the blessings of many a street-patterer heaped upon him !   " Yes, sir, ' Old Blacking Pot,' as ' *Peterloo Jack*' (who was a Manchester man, and had one of his legs broken in the Peterloo Massacre, in 1819, and who was a sort of a captain of a school, or companionship, of patterers), used to call him, was an out-and-out friend to the poets, printers, and patterers of the Seven Dials quarter. Yes, sir, he was a very good sort to all us people, sir."

In the month of April, 1831, Mr. F. Lewis introduced in the House of Commons a Bill for the better regulation of the delivery of coals in London and Westminster.   The hon. member explained the evils and exposed the absurdity of the sale by measure.   Solid coals were sent to London, but there broken to fill the measure easier.   He would have sacks to hold a certain weight, and a machine to each wharf to weigh them.   The following street-ballad was published at the period :—

THE NEW COAL ACT.

SEE how the people through the streets
　　On New Year's Day did roll,
All think with wonder and surprise
　　To buy their coke and coal :
It is a fact, this New Coal Act
　　Strikes wonder through the nation,
Some look with scorn, saying "Here's Reform
Complete in operation."
Chorus.—So list awhile unto my song,
　　　　All you that are at leisure,
　　　　I'll tell you how they sell the coals,
　　　　By weight instead of measure.

I say, Mr. Short Weight, I want a peck of coals. We
don't make a quarter of a peck, half-bushel, nor bushel, our
coals is 7 lbs. $1\frac{1}{2}$d. Why, lawk! I never heard of such a
thing. Well, you hear it now, madam. Well, how many
am I to have for a penny? Why, 2 lbs. 2 oz. If that is
all, I can carry them in a teacup. Ten pounds and a
half of coals, if you please, and no cinders among them,
the last I had were all slates.

So now the new year has arrived,
　　Mark well what I do say,
We may expect continually
　　Something new start every day.
Something always to oppress the poor,
　　And keep them all forlorn,
I wonder when King William means
　　This nation to Reform ?

A quarter of a peck of coals, and a half-peck of coke.
Confound the people, they are all mad ; our coals and coke
are all sold by weight. Are yours Newcastle or Sunderland
coals? Why, both, they come from Penzance. Arrah ! bad

luck to you, you sheating humbug; by St. Patrick! I will
pull you and your coke over the coals, you sheated my little
Paddy this morning out of a quarter of a pound of coke,
you spalpeen, you. I say, Mr. Smuttyface, that aint veight,
put in another little nub; la! look mother, here is three
pieces of stones in my hat among the coals. Well, if this
is all the Reform the poor are to get, I wish their Reform
was among the Turks in the West Indies.

> Then off goes little Bob for coals,
>   Off goes Bet, and then her mother,
> A weighing of the coals and coke,
>   Oh! what a fuss and bother.
> One cries out this is not weight,
>   I swear by this and that,
> Bet puts them in her apron,
>   And Jemmy in his hat.

What weight do you call this? That is a seven pound
weight ma'am. I don't think it is above three; why, what
a small bit of coals for $1\frac{1}{2}$d.! Plenty for the money. I
say, Mr. Smut, is the Cholera Morbus among your coals?
Why, sir? Why, because in the fourteen pounds of coals
I bought of you last night there was just $13\frac{1}{2}$ lbs. of slates,
dirt, stones, cinders, and all manner of things, and I thought
that might have been the Cholera Morbus. I say, Mrs.
Speedwell, what have you got in your apron? Nothing, sir.
You have, you have just stole them two nubs of coal while
I have been weighing the coals for my customers; is it not
a very hard thing that people is to be robbed before their
own eyes? Here's another chap putting a piece of coal in
his breeches pocket. My coals aint veight. My coals is
all coke. My coals are all dirt and cinders, and two pounds
short.

> One begins to pocket a lump of coal,
>   Oh! what a pretty joke,

One swears it is slates and cinders,
   And another vows it is coke.
They will keep them busy weighing,
   And little be at leisure.
What a fuss there is in selling coals,
   By weight instead of measure.

Printed by T. BIRT, No. 39, Great St. Andrew Street, Seven Dials.

THE WASHERWOMAN VERSUS THE STEAM WASHING COMPANY.

A DIEU ! my weekly wash, adieu !
   A weeping heart thy loss bewails ;
Perhaps I never more may view
   Thy stiffen'd collars, draggled tails ; ·
No, thou art fled—my only hope,
   Thy smoke and dirt are lost to me ;
Adieu to pearlash, farewell soap,
   Oh, base Steam Washing Company !
         Adieu, my weekly wash, &c.

No more I 'll be a laundress gay,
   And get a lunch and cheerful sup,
Or rub for half-a-crown a day !
   My broken bits, my snuff 's knock'd 'up.
No more with jokes the hours I 'll cheer,
   Fled, fled 's my darling cup of tea,
For Fate has taken all, oh dear,
   To the Steam Washing Company !
         Adieu, my weekly wash, &c.

  * * * * *

Oh, how I wish there ne'er was smoke,
   And I should then not live on air ;
I 'd keep my tub, I 'd crack my joke,
   And in my *boils* I 'd drown despair.
For Fortune looks just like *stone blue*,
   And poverty is *wringing* me,
But every joy has left my view
   For thee—Steam Washing Company !
         Adieu, my weekly wash, &c.

* Printed by J Catnach, 2 and 3, Monmouth Court, 7 Dials
   Battledores, Lotteries, and Primers sold cheap.

THE TRIAL, SENTENCE, FULL CONFESSION, AND EXECUTION OF
BISHOP & WILLIAMS,
THE BURKERS.

BURKING AND BURKERS.

The month of November, 1831, will be recorded in the annals of crimes and cruelties as particularly pre-eminent, for it will prove to posterity that other wretches could be found base enough to follow the horrid example of Burke and his accomplice Hare, to entice the unprotected and friendless to the den of death for sordid gain.

The horrible crime of "Burking," or murdering the unwary with the intention of selling their bodies at a high price to the anatomical schools, for the purpose of dissection, has unfortunately obtained a notoriety which will not be soon or easily forgotten. It took its horrifying appellation from the circumstances which were disclosed on the trial of the inhuman wretch Burke, who was executed at Edinburgh in 1829, for having wilfully and deliberately murdered several persons for the sole purpose of profiting by the sale of their dead bodies.

APPREHENSION OF THE BURKERS.

On Tuesday, November 8th, four persons, viz., John Bishop, Thomas Williams, James May, and Michael Shield, were examined at Bow Street Police Office on the charge of being concerned in the wilful murder of an unknown Italian boy. From the evidence adduced, it appeared that May, *alias* Jack Stirabout, a known resurrection-man; and Bishop, a body-snatcher, offered at King's College a subject for sale, Shield and Williams having charge of the body in a hamper, for which they demanded twelve guineas. Mr Partridge, demonstrator of anatomy, who, although not in absolute want of a subject, offered nine guineas, but being struck with its freshness sent a messenger to the police station, and the fellows were then taken into custody, examined before the magistrates, when Shield was discharged and the others ultimately committed for trial.

THE TRIAL.

Friday, December 2nd, having been fixed for the trial of the prisoners charged with the murder of the Italian boy, the Court was crowded to excess so early as eight o'clock in the morning.

At nine o'clock the Deputy Recorder, Mr Serjeant

Arden, came into the court, when the prisoner severally pleaded "Not Guilty."

† The Jury were then sworn, and at ten o'clock Chief Justice Tindal, Mr Baron Vaughan, and Mr Justice Littledale entered the Court, with the Lord Mayor and Sheriffs. The Bench was crowded with persons of rank, amongst whom was the Duke of Sussex.

Mr Bodkin having opened the case, Mr Adolphus proceeded to state to the Jury the leading facts, as they were afterwards stated in the evidence produced. The case for the prosecution having closed, the prisoners were called upon for their defence.

The prisoner Bishop in his defence stated that he was thirty-three years of age, and had followed the occupation of carrier till the last five years, during which he had occasionally obtained a livelihood by supplying surgeons with subjects. He most solemnly declared that he had never disposed of any body that had not died a natural death.

Williams' defence briefly stated that he had never been engaged in the calling of a resurrectionist, but had only by accident accompanied Bishop on the sale of the Italian boy's body.

May, in his defence, admitted that for the last six years he had followed the occupation of supplying the medical schools with anatomical subjects, but disclaimed ever having had anything to do with the sale of bodies which had not died a natural death. That he had accidentally met with Bishop at the Fortune of War public house on the Friday on which the body was taken up for sale to Guy's Hospital.

At eight o'clock the jury retired to consider their verdict, and on their return they found the prisoners were Guilty of Murder.

The Recorder then passed the awful sentence upon them, "That each of them be hanged on Monday morning, and their bodies be delivered over for dissection and anatomization."

The prisoners heard the sentence as they had the verdict, without any visible alteration. May raised his voice, and in a firm tone said, "I am a murdered man, gentlemen."

THE FULL CONFESSION OF BISHOP AND WILLIAMS.

On Saturday morning Williams addressed a note to Mr Wontner, stating that he and Bishop wanted particularly to see him and Dr Cotton, the Ordinary. In the course of the interview which immediately followed, both prisoners made a full confession of their guilt, both exculpating May altogether from being party to any of the murders. Having received the confessions, Mr Wontner immediately waited upon Mr Justice Littledale and Baron Vaughan, and upon communicating to them the statements, they said they would at once see the Home Secretary on the subject.

On Sunday morning the Sheriffs visited all three of the prisoners in succession, and with the Under-Sheriffs were engaged between three and four hours in taking down the statements of the convicts. The result of all these investigations was that the same afternoon a respite during his Majesty's pleasure arrived at Newgate for May, and his sentence will be commuted to transportation for life.

THE EXECUTION.

During the whole of Sunday crowds of persons congregated in the Old Bailey, and the spot on which the scaffold was to be erected was covered with individuals conversing on the horrid crimes of the convicts, and in the course of the day strong posts were erected in the Old Bailey and at the ends of Newgate street Giltspur street, and Skinner street, for the purpose of forming barriers to break the pressure of the crowd.

At half-past twelve o'clock the gallows was brought out from the yard, and drawn to its usual station opposite the Debtor's door. The crowd, as early as one o'clock amounting to several thousand persons, continued rapidly increasing.

By some overnight three chains had been suspended from the fatal beam, and this led the crowd to suppose that May had not been respited. Mr. Wontner, on hearing of the mistake, directed that one of the chains should be removed. The moment this was done, an exclamation of "May is respited," ran through the crowd, and, contrary to the expected tokens of indignation, distinct cheers were heard amongst the crowd on witnessing this token that mercy had been shown to May.

At half-past seven the Sheriffs arrived in their carriage, and in a short time the press-yard was thronged with gentlemen. The unhappy convicts were now led from their cells. Bishop came out first, and after he was pinioned he was conducted to a seat, and the Rev Mr. Williams sat alongside of him, and they conversed together in a low tone of voice.

Williams was next introduced, and the wonderful alteration two days had effected in his appearance astonished everyone who was present at the trial. All the bold confidence he exhibited then had completely forsaken him, and he looked the most miserable wretch it is possible to conceive. He entered the room with a very faltering step, and when the ceremony of pinioning him commenced, he was so weak as to be scarcely able to stand.

Everything being ready, the melancholy procession moved forward. Bishop was then conducted to the scaffold, and the moment he made his appearance the most dreadful yells and hootings were heard among the crowd. The executioner proceeded at once to the performance of his duty, and having put the rope round his neck and affixed it to a chain, placed him under the fatal beam. Williams was then taken out, and the groans and hisses were renewed. The dreadful preparations were soon completed, and in less than five minutes after the wretched men appeared on the scaffold the usual signal was given. the drop fell, and they were launched into eternity. Bishop appeared to die very soon, but Williams struggled hard. Thus died

THE DREADFUL BURKERS OF 1831.

It may be remarked, *en passant*, that Mr. Corder, with Paragalli and Colla, the two Italian witnesses, who gave evidence as to the identity of the body, said to be that of the Italian boy, at the trial of Bishop, Williams, and May, appeared at Bow Street, in consequence of doubts being entertained by a portion of the public as to the body being that of Carlo Ferrari, to re-assert their former evidence. Mr. Corder afterwards published a statement in the " Times " newspaper, which gave scarcely the possibility of doubt that the body offered at King's College *must have been* that of Ferrari, notwithstanding the murderer's assertion to the contrary. On December the 10th, a *Post-obit* prosecution of Williams, the Burkite murderer, took place in the Court of Excise, where he was charged, on information, with having carried on an illicit factory for making glass at No. 2, Nova Scotia Gardens, Bethnal Green. An officer proved the seizure of goods used in the manufacture of glass, at the house of the person charged, and that Bishop was at the time in company. The Court condemned the goods seized.

A drama on the subject of the " Burkers " was produced at an unlicensed theatre, designated THE SHAKESPEARE, in the neighbourhood of the Curtain Road, Shoreditch, and for a time was specially attractive. In the young actor, who played Carlo Ferrari, the Italian boy, might now be recognised an eminent tragedian.*

---

* E. L. Blanchard, in an article entitled, "Vanished Theatres," in the *Era Almanack*, 1877.

That the murder of Celia Holloway by her husband, John William Holloway, at Brighton, in the year 1831, created a profound sensation in its immediate neighbourhood, and throughout the country generally, there can be no doubt. There are many circumstances in connection with the foul deed that would lead to that end. The somewhat romantic manner of finding the trunk of the murdered woman, imperfectly buried, in such a peaceful and retired spot as the "Lover's Walk," and under such peculiar circumstances, by the Brighton fisherman, Maskell, had the effect of causing thousands from day to day to visit, not only the plantation, but also the pretty and sweet Auburn-like village of Preston, adjoining Brighton. Subsequently, the other portions of the remains were found in a cesspool common to four or five houses in Margaret Street, in one of which Holloway had resided; and, when the whole were placed together by the surgeon, they were identified, not only by Celia Holloway's sister, but also by several of the neighbours.

The examinations before the magistrates and the charging the prisoner's paramour, Ann Kennett, as an accomplice, tended very materially to keep up the excitement, and even after the two prisoners were committed for trial, new and sensational statements continued to crop up; and, in the absence of any fresh and authentic news on the all-absorbing topic, there were plenty of manufactured tales afloat on the subject, and we are credibly informed that there were several "Cocks"—*i.e.*, Catchpennies, sold about the streets of Brighton, Horsham, and Lewes. The following piece of doggerel was published by Catnach, who sent two first-class patterers down to the scene of the circumstance, where they lived from August until the December following, receiving, almost weekly, fresh supplies of street-papers. While many others of the same stamp were printed at Brighton by Phillips, the local Catnach, at that period carrying on business at 9, Poplar Place, Meeting House Lane.

LAMENTATION AND CONFESSION
OF
JOHN WILLIAM HOLLOWAY,
WHO NOW LIES IN HORSHAM GAOL, AWAITING HIS TRIAL FOR
THE CRUEL MURDER OF HIS WIFE,
CELIA HOLLOWAY.

YOU tender-hearted Christians, I pray you now draw near, ·
    And listen unto these few lines you quickly soon shall hear ;
My name it is John Holloway, the truth I will unfold,
And when I think on what I 've done it makes my blood run cold.

In Donkey Row I took a house, and there enticed my wife,
'Twas there by strangulation I took away her life :
An innocent babe all in her womb I murdered with my wife,
In pieces then I cut her up all with my bloody knife.

When I cut the body up—Oh ! what a shocking sight
Then on a barrow I wheel'd her to Preston in the night
Her head and arms, her legs and thighs, from her body I cut off,
Two thighs with her body I then buried in the Lover's Walk.

John Gillam, a fisherman belonging to Brighton town,
And a constable from Preston soon the body found ;
Oh ! when the body was dug up, what a shocking sight to see,
Her head and arms, her legs and thighs, were cut from her body.

And when the body was dug up some thousands flocked around,
Then my wife's sister came and swore to her new stays and gown ;
Then taken was Ann Kennett, and put in close confined,
And out of Brighton I did go, trying to ease my mind.

When back to Brighton I returned, thinking it was all right,
But the God above was watching me and brought the deed to light,
Then taken was John Holloway and put in close confine—
I am the wretched murderer, and must answer for my crime.

In these dark cells of Horsham gaol I cry both day and night,
For the bleeding corpse of my poor wife is always in my sight :
When I hope her soul is in heaven at rest when tormented I shall be,
I deserve nothing but the Burning Flames for my sad cruelty.

Now young and old, pray beware of my unhappy fate,
Pray let your Parsons comfort you before it is too late ;
Hark ! hark ! I hear the dismal bell, how harsh it tolls—
May the Lord have mercy on me and all poor unhappy souls !

J. Catnach, Printer, 2 & 3, Monmouth Court, 7 Dials.

From day to day the copse in Lover's Walk, where the mutilated body was found, became a great object of attraction. The Chain Pier, the Devil's Dyke, then kept by Mr. Peter Berkshire, and all the customary places of resort were forsaken, and hundreds were seen wending their steps towards the copse, to obtain a view of the unconsecrated grave of the unfortunate Celia. Branches of the trees which overhung it were broken off, and carried away with the same enthusiasm as a pilgrim would bear away a relic of the Cross from the Holy Land. On the surrounding trees the name of Holloway was carved in every direction ;

himself suspended on a gallows, and in some instances accompanied by epithets too coarse and indecent to be inserted. It is not to be here supposed that the Brighton poets could lose sight of so favourable an opportunity of displaying their poetical abilities. Thus on one tree might be read—

> Here lay poor Celia,
> Curses be on Holloway,
> He 'll wish himself away
> On the great judgment day.

On another

> Here lay a wife, a mother, and a child,
> D——n him who placed them in a place in so wild.

Even the witling could not allow so grave a subject to escape him without exercising his talent upon it, and thus on one tree was cut—

> Women are bad—not so was Celia dead;
> You 'll ask me why—Celia wants her head.

We here insert an engraving of the interior and exterior of the house in Donkey Row where the fatal act was committed, and the cupboard in which Ann Kennett was concealed is that under the stairs, where the chaff on the floor and the head on the shelf are represented.

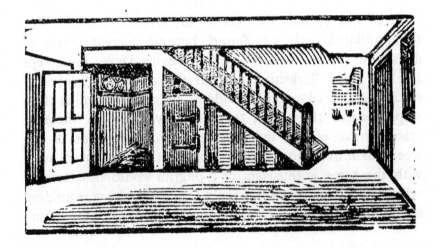

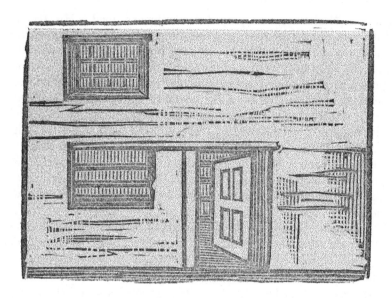

The Brighton magistrates committed Holloway and his paramour to take their trial, at the Lewes Assizes, which were held on Wednesday, December 14th, before Mr. Justice Pattison, when the jury found Holloway guilty, but acquitted the female prisoner. The execution took place at Horsham, on December 16th, 1831, thus described in a local print—

Long before day-break on Friday morning, a number of people, many on foot, went from Brighton to Horsham, a distance of 22 miles, to see the last of the murderer, Holloway. The morning was exceedingly bright, and on the road, from an early hour till twelve o'clock, were seen a great many country people going towards the place of execution. At about half-past eleven o'clock, the under-sheriff and his officers arrived, by which time the crowd had greatly increased, amounting probably to 2,000 persons. Among those who came to witness the scene were the two sisters and brother of the murdered Celia Holloway; the former requested permission to see Holloway, but in consequence of some levity of conduct were refused admittance. They remained, however, till the drop fell.

As early as four o'clock in the morning Holloway had again been visited by the chaplain (the Rev. Mr. Witherby) who continued his pious exertions till within a short time of the culprit being led forth to be pinioned. The exhortations of the rev. gentleman worked a visible change in Holloway, who prayed fervently and loud. His reckless spirit was evidently subdued, and he listened attentively to his spiritual instructor and responded to his exhortations, ejaculating, repeatedly, "May the Lord have mercy on my soul," "Thou hast paid the debt." A person named Nute, was also with him for twelve hours previous to his execution. The mother of the wretched culprit was also present, and Mr. Robert Huish, a literary gentleman, engaged by Mr., Alderman Kelly, the great "number-book" trade publisher, of London, to collect materials for the Life, Trial, and Execution of Holloway. Mr. Nute, the Ranter and local agent for the sale of Kelly's publications, who improved the occasion of the execution by doing a little preaching and bookselling on his own account, was on the drop when Holloway was turned off.

The hour had now arrived, and Holloway manifested no reluctance when the turnkey came for him. At ten minutes before twelve o'clock the culprit left his cell, accompanied by Mr. Nute and the gaoler, and walked with a firm step through the yard into the kitchen, where about twenty persons, namely : sheriffs, officers, reporters, &c., were waiting. The executioner was also at hand, ready to pinion him. Holloway appeared in a blue jacket and waistcoat, brown trousers, and low shoes. His hair was rough. Before him he carried a Bible. He regarded those around him with silent attention, and they in turn silently fixed their eyes upon him. The executioner beckoned him to advance. For a moment he cast a hurried glance towards Mr. Nute, and, turning round, caught hold of his hand, which he squeezed apparently in agonizing despair. Still holding the Bible, he followed the executioner, when the latter rather unceremoniously went up to him and took off his handkerchief, which, as usual, he was about to thrust into the culprit's bosom, when Holloway said, "No! no! keep it." The executioner then motioned him to advance into the press-room, where the implements for pinioning were prepared. Holloway had several times previously kissed the Bible, exclaiming repeatedly, "Blessed Word!" Mr. Nute asked him if he died in peace with all men. He replied, "I do die in peace ; no one has injured me ; if they have, I forgive them. I die justly ; to Thee I commend my soul ; Lord support me ; Thou hast paid the debt ; Lord, receive my spirit !" The last sentence he repeated four times with solemn earnestness. Mr. Nute asked him one or two other questions, namely, whether he felt that God had forgiven him his sins ; and whether he found God Almighty ready to save ; to which he replied, "Yes, yes." Holloway then fell upon his knees on the rugged floor, and offered up a prayer to Heaven. He said, "Be with me at this moment, Lord God of Heaven. Through the merits of a merciful Saviour, I hope for mercy." The culprit had to wait two or three minutes after being pinioned before the necessary arrangements were completed, during which time he said to the executioner, "Mind, you have promised that I shall have time to speak; and the executioner replied, "You shall!" The chaplain then approached; the massive bolts were withdrawn, and the great doors were thrown open. The assembled multitude gazed with eager curiosity on the awful procession.

The chaplain then walked towards the scaffold, reading the burial service; and the culprit followed with a firm and quick step, praying as he advanced. He ascended the steps of the drop rather quickly, and placed himself immediately under the fatal rope. The executioner then proceeded to put on the cap, and make fast the rope about the culprit's neck. While he was doing this, Holloway said in a low whisper, "Give me a good fall," and the executioner, in consequence, gave him rather more than the usual length of rope for the fall. Holloway then knelt down and prayed fervently for about half-a-minute, repeatedly calling on the Lord to receive his spirit. When he arose, he advanced suddenly to address the crowd, which he did in the following terms :—
"My dear friends, I need not tell you that sin brought me to this untimely end, and I would entreat you to be aware that he who follows a life of sin is as likely to be brought to the same condition ; I tell you, if you trifle with sin and folly, you know not where it will end. I justly suffer ; I have spilt innocent blood, but I hope God will have mercy upon me ; He has said to those who repent, 'All your sins and blasphemies shall be forgiven you.' Therefore, turn from sin, and the Lord will show you forgiveness. All I have to say is, take warning by my unhappy fate, and if you prize life, sin not. Reflect on my dying words, for in a very short time the eye that sees you now will see you no more, and in a few short years you will all be in eternity. Now, may the Lord bless you and keep you from sin, by which I am brought to this untimely end ; and may the God of Mercy, through Jesus Christ, receive my spirit."

These words were spoken in a rapid, firm, and audible voice ; and, as he went on, Holloway gradually rose to so high a tone that he might have been heard at a great distance. He then stepped back ; the executioner drew the cap over his eyes ; and the chaplain continued to pray, concluding with the Lord's Prayer, during which Holloway, with great solemnity, repeatedly ejaculated, "Lord receive my spirit !" until the signal, when the bolt was withdrawn and the wretched culprit's life was at an end. He appeared to suffer but little. There was no manifestation of feeling in the crowd, nor could we perceive any tokens of commiseration.

The subjoined incident is illustrative of a popular superstition regarding the bodies of murderers—

About a quarter of an hour after Holloway was turned off, a countryman, who was said to come from Cowfold, bargained with the hangman to have his wen rubbed by the hands of the deceased. The superstitious fellow mounted the scaffold with the hangman, who untied the rope which bound Holloway's wrist, and placed the hands of the deceased on the forehead of the countryman, who sat trembling in that position upwards of five minutes. The executioner then took the man's handkerchief from his neck and thrust it into Holloway's bosom, till he had made it warm by the heat of the body, and then put it to the wen; the man dismounted, and held the handkerchief to it for several minutes, at the same time expressing his "faith" in the remedy. This scene excited the disgust of every one present, and when two women advanced for a similar purpose, the undersheriff refused to permit it, and ordered them away.

After the body had hung the usual time, the executioner lowered it into the hands of the turnkey beneath. They then carried it into the press-room, where it was stripped, and for a few minutes lay exposed. A young phrenologist was present, who examined the head for scientific purposes, and several casts were taken of the features. The rope with which Holloway had been hung was purchased of the executioner by some person from Lewes, for half-a-crown. The body was then given over to Mr. Lawrence, for the County Hospital; Mr. Lawrence, jun., with Police Superintendent Penfold, and one or two others from Brighton, arrived with a chariot containing a large trunk, to convey the body to that place. By this time the crowd had dispersed, and there were scarcely twenty persons present when the party drove off to Brighton.

On the following day the body of the murderer Holloway was exposed to public gaze in the magistrates' room at the Town Hall, and so great was the curiosity of the public that it is calculated upwards of 23,000 persons were admitted in the course of the day, from ten in the morning till a little after four o'clock in the afternoon. The body was subsequently removed to the County Hospital, where on Monday morning the dissection was commenced by Mr. Lawrence and Mr. Taylor. The skeleton, properly adjusted, is now in the museum in connection with the Brighton and Sussex County Hospital.

Ann Kennett, Holloway's paramour, having been acquitted on the capital charge, was subsequently indicted at the Lewes Assizes, in March, 1832, for "concealing and harbouring" Holloway, in other words, of assisting him in the commission of the crime he committed, but the jury returned a verdict of *Not Guilty*.

During the many solitary hours which Holloway passed in the gloom of his prison, he frequently amused himself with writing poetical epistles to Ann Kennett, one of which we subjoin as characteristic of the man, and indicative of the strong affection which he bore for that woman. We have retained his own orthography, as illustrative of his style of writing, and his skill in the art of tagging rhymes.

MY dearest life when this you see
    pray look and read and think on me
who gladly gives my life to screane
my darling from the smalest paine
pray love my Child and fondle over
that as you have done hits father
I know that you have loved me so
you have sacrificed your peace for woe
then can I you sweat love look cooly on
the life that I myselfe undone
that action I for ever scorn
I love the ground that you walk on
that lovly babe of myne when bornd
early teach it to love and fear the Lord.
and may we all in glory meet
to praise Immanuel at his feet
O could I be alowed that pleasure
to live to see my darling treasure

O that lovly babe my flesh and blood
let it be taught to serve its God.
may your love for me my dearest wife
be as myne is to you true thoough life
was I to live and you to die
I never would marry wilse time doeth flye
I would be true below my love
thought your spirit be goane above
and look forward to the time when we
shall meet againe in unity
for if your love you to another give
how can you love me while you live
but now I leave you to your choice
and hope that you regard my joice
you cannot love two men together
for if you love the one you must forget the other
and as through life we have boath loved so truely
let your love be fixed on me and not on cash or beuty
could I know a nouther would know you
I nere could let you live to proove untrue
O do not proove untrue proove faithful Ann
and I shall die in peace with God and man

An individual, passing under the name of Eliza Edwards, died on the 18th of January, 1832, in Union Court, Orchard Street, Westminster. There were no claimants for the body, which was therefore taken for dissection to Guy's Hospital, under the Anatomy Act. There, to the astonishment of all, the body was discovered to be that of a man. The principal Secretary of State (with very bad taste) ordered a public investigation. The jury visited St. Margaret's workhouse, where the body lay. It appeared that of a youth of seventeen, very effeminate, the whiskers having been plucked out by tweezers, and the chin without a beard. Dr. Clutterbuck proved that he visited the deceased as his patient, Miss Edwards, and had no idea of her being a man. Maria Edwards said she was sister to the deceased; they had constantly lived together for ten years, and only knew each other as sisters. The deceased was an actress; had played in the country—last at Leatherhead; had been three years in London, living less reputably. She had been visited and *kept* by several men; but she died in great distress, and had received a small relief from the parish. Miss Edwards was introduced to the stage by Talma; had acted under the name of Walstein, and played the first characters in Tragedy., Mary Mortimer had known the deceased for eleven years, and never suspected her sex. She appeared a most lady-like woman; witness saw her act at Norwich. The body was satisfactorily identified, and the jury adjourned. On Thursday the jury met again and received further evidence. The room was ordered to be cleared of strangers, but this was found impossible; the jury retired to an adjoining room, and, after a 'few minutes' consultation, the verdict was returned—"That the deceased died by visitation of God; and, in returning this verdict, the jury are compelled to express their horror at the conduct of the deceased, and strongly recommend to the proper authorities that some means may be adopted for the disposal of the body, which will mark the ignominy of that conduct."

The above scandal created a great sensation in the metropolis at the time, and afforded a golden opportunity to all connected with street-literature to captivate the masses by their effusions, both in prose and verse.

Street-ballads on political subjects, though not regarded as of great interest by the whole body of the people, are still eventful among certain classes, and for such the street author and ballad singer cater. The measure of Reform by Earl Grey's administration, was proposed in the House of Commons by Lord John Russell, 1st March, 1831. On the first division, *second* reading, 22nd March, there stood for it, 302; against it, 301. Ultimately, the Bill for that session was abandoned, and Parliament dissolved. The Reform Bill of 1832 was read for the *third* time on the 23rd of March, when the numbers stood thus :—for the Bill, 355; against it,

239—majority for it, 116.   In the Lords, the Bill was carried
through the Committee on the 30th of May, and read a *third*
time on the 4th of June.   For the Bill, 106 ; against, 22
—majority, 84.   Received the Royal Assent, 7th of
June, 1832.

The Reform Bill.

As William and *Bill* are the same,
　Our King, if he "weathers the storm,"
Shall be called in the annals of fame,
　The *Glorious* BILL *of Reform !*

During the whole of the time the Reform Bills of 1831–2
were before the Houses of Parliament, the "Catnach Press,"
in common with other printing offices that produced street-
literature, was very busy in publishing, almost daily, songs
and papers in ridicule of borough-mongering and of the
various rotten boroughs then in existence, but which were
entirely swept away by the passing of this Bill ; fifty-six
boroughs in England being disfranchised, while thirty were
reduced to one member only ; twenty-two new boroughs
were created to send two members, and twenty to send one
member ; other important changes were also made.   Songs
upon the subject were sung at every corner of the streets, to
the great delight of the multitude.

　　　" Little Johnny, bless the darling boy,
　　　　Loves Reform ! Reform !
　　　Long time he has nursed his favourite toy;
　　　Reform ! Reform ! "

KING WILLIAM IV. AND HIS MINISTERS FOR EVER!

TUNE.—"*All Nodding, nid, nid, Nodding.*"

YOU heroes of England draw near awhile,
The Isle of Great Britain will ne'er fail to smile,
For William and his Ministers will never look with scorn,
They are every one determin'd to struggle for Reform.
  And they are all conversing about Parliament Reform.

Pray what do you think of William and his Queen?
A better in Great Britain there never can be seen,
Conquered by the Tories, they'll never be, we're told,
For the rights of the people they'll fight like heroes bold.
  And they're all struggling to obtain the nation's rights.

What do you think of brave Russell, Brougham, and Grey,
They have boldly beat the Tories now they have got fair play,
To fight for your liberties they eager do resolve,.
And his Majesty on Friday last did Parliament dissolve.
  And they're all trembling, they'll not get in again.

What do you think of the Blacking man, of Wilson, and others?
Why like a set of turn-coats they'll go to h—— like brothers
Into the House of Commons they will never go again,
They may cry and pray, lord! lack-a-day, it will surely be in vain.
  And they're all lamenting because their seats they must resign.

What do you think of Hobhouse and Sir Frank?
I think they're men of honour, and can play a pretty prank.
They've done the best you must allow to crush a desperate evil,
While Blacking men and Soldiers both will ramble to the Devil.
  And they're all conversing about Parliament Reform.

What do you think of the agitator Dan ?
For the rights of Great Britain he stuck up like a man.
The state of the nation he told the Tories blunt,
And if I may be believ'd, he's not deceived, like foolish Harry Hunt.
 And they're all conversing about Parliament Reform.

What do you think of Waithman and of Wood?
They've done their best endeavours to do the people good,
They stuck to William and his Ministers, rumours could not be afloat,
That they like many others will never turn their coat.
 So we're all rejoicing the Dissolution's taken place.

What do you think of the Rat-catcher Bob?
I think he had a sneaking to get into a job,
Along with the old Soldier, but mark what I do say,
The King will never part with Russell, Brougham, or Grey.
 So they're all praying, the Tories are praying for the death of
  all the three.

Now what do you think about the Dissolution?
If William had not closed the House, there'd have been a revolution.
In every part of England there's been some funny stories ;
So success to Russell and to Grey, the Devil take the Tories, .
 Who are all lamenting the places they have lost.

Pray what do you think of the Borough-mongers now?
Each day and every hour they've been kicking up a row.
They've endeavoured the whole nation to fill with discontent,
But they never more will have a chance to get into Parliament.
 So they're all lamenting because they are turned out.

I'm certain every Briton owns it was to gain their right
King William and his Ministers did so boldly fight ;
Turn-coats, Borough-mongers, and Tories you will see
King William take by the heels and drown them in the sea.
 So we're all laughing at the Borough-mongers' fall.

Here's a health to King William and his Ministers so true,
We are certain they will never flinch, their courage is True Blue ;
Turn-coats, Borough-mongers, and Tories too may grunt,
But the Devil will drive them in a van, with Wilson and with Hunt.
 And they're all lamenting.

Printed by T. BIRT, No. 39, Great St. Andrew Street, Seven Dials.

' ATTACK on KING WILLIAM IV. at ASCOT HEATH,

On Tuesday, the 19th of June, 1832.

The Ascot Races for 1832 will be rendered memorable in the history of this country by reason of a stone thrown at his Majesty while on the grand stand at Ascot Races, which hit him on the forehead. The man by whom it was thrown was immediately secured, and proved to be Denis Collins, a seaman with only one leg, formerly a pensioner of Greenwich Hospital, from whence he had been dismissed for ill-conduct. On his examination he confessed he committed the outrage in revenge because no notice had been taken of petitions which he had sent to the Lords of the Admiralty and the King. He was committed to Reading gaol to take his trial, which took place at Abingdon, on August 22nd. The jury returned a verdict of guilty on the fifth count, that

of intending some bodily harm to his Majesty, but not guilty
of the intent to kill.

Mr. Baron Gurney passed sentence on the prisoner, that
he *be drawn on a hurdle to the place of execution*, and being
hung by his *neck* until dead, his *head* be afterwards *severed
from his body*, and his body *divided into four pieces*, and
disposed of as his Majesty should think fit. His sentence
was afterwards respited.

Nothing better than the above circumstance could have
suited the producers and workers of street-literature. King
William and Queen Adelaide were very popular at the time.
" Yes, sir, we all did well out of that job of the wooden-legged
sailor and old King Billy. It lasted out for months. We
had something fresh nearly every day. We killed old Billy
five or six times; then we made out that the sailor-chap was
a love-child of the Sailor· King and Madame Vestris ; then,
that he was an old sweetheart of Queen Adelaide's, and that
he was jealous and annoyed at her a-jilting of him and
a-marrying of old King Billy, and so on. But it was an
awful sell, and a robbery to us all, because they didn't hang
and cut the chap up into four quarters—that would have
been a regular Godsend to us chaps, sir. But I think old
Jemmy Catnach, as it was, must have cleared pretty nigh
or quite a fifty pounds for himself out of the job. A-talking
about Madame Vestris, sir, reminds me that once we had a
song about her, and the chorus was :—

> " 'A hundred pounds reward
> For the man that cut the legs above the knees
> Belonging to Madame Vestris.' "

THE CROWN AND HORSE SHOES INN, ENFIELD CHASE SIDE.

On Thursday, December 20, 1832, information was given at the various metropolitan police-offices of a horrible murder, committed near the pleasant little village of Enfield, which is situate about ten miles from town. It appears that a little boy, named Ellis, was going from Enfield Chase towards Enfield town, down Holt-White's-Lane, when he observed something in the ditch, which appeared to him a human body. He called to a man, named Wheeler, who was going to his work at a farm, occupied by Mr. Poiser, who went with him to the edge of the ditch, in which they found the body of a man. The face was in the ditch, but on turning the body face upwards, a most awful and horrible sight presented itself. The face was cut and slashed in a most dreadful manner; the flesh was *scored out*, as it were in five places, and the right whisker cut away; and in the throat of the murdered man there was a deep stab, right through, as a butcher would kill a sheep, and as if the knife had been turned round in the throat. The body was instantly recognised as that of a young man, named Benjamin Crouch Danby, about twenty-seven years of age, and the son of the late Mr. Danby, the well-known forensic wig-maker, of the Temple. When very young he adopted the seafaring profession, and had only just returned from a long voyage. On landing he started off at once to Mr. Addington, a master baker, of Enfield, who was a near relation. He met with a very kind reception, and his joyous spirits, and free, sailor-like manner, attracted the notice of the inhabitants. He appeared to enjoy himself, and spent his money with great freedom. On Wednesday afternoon, about four o'clock, he left Mr. Addington's house, promising to return at ten at night, but he did not make his appearance at the time specified. This created alarm, and Mr. Addington was out until a late hour in search of him. The next morning the family received intelligence of the situation in which the unfortunate man had been discovered. Speedy inquiries were set on foot, and it soon transpired that the deceased had been displaying his money, treating the company, drinking freely, tossing for liquor, and later in the evening playing at dominoes at the Crown and Horse Shoes inn, situate by the side of the New River, and near Chase-side.

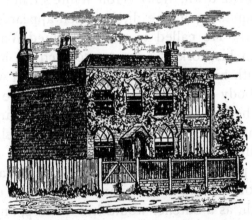

CHARLES LAMB'S HOUSE AT ENFIELD.

It so happened that on the day of the murder Charles Lamb, the celebrated English essayist, who, with his demented sister Mary, was then residing in a pleasantly situated house* at Enfield Chase-side, had received a visit from some friends living at Edmonton, distant three miles. In the afternoon Charles accompanied them part of the way home, and on his return journey strolled into the Crown and Horse Shoes inn, then kept by one Joseph Perry, and called for some refreshment. And if the truth must be spoken, Charles Lamb was very fond of "a drop of good beer," and a roadside hostel where he could at once unbend himself, study English character in its working attire, moisten his discourse and his clay from unsophisticated pewter, and hum :—

> "Charley loves good ale and wine,
> Charley loves good brandy,
> Charley loves a pot and pipe
> As children sugar candy."

For each host or hostess Charles Lamb had his salutation, his joke, or his *lamb-pun !* and was an honoured and familiar guest, and well known as the "funny little old gentleman in black" at nearly all the humble and wayside "Pubs" in and about the Green Lanes and ways between Enfield and Edmonton, Southgate, South Lodge, Trent Place, Potter's Bar, and Waltham Cross, wherein he could take his leisure

---

* Lamb, writing to Thomas Hood, the poet, Tuesday, September 18, 1827, says :—

"DEAR HOOD,— * * * —Our new domicile is no manor-house; but new, and externally not inviting, but furnish'd within with every convenience : capital new locks to every door, capital grates to every room ; with nothing to pay for incoming; and the rent £10 less than the Islington one. It was built, a few years since, at £1,100 expense, they tell me—and I perfectly believe it. And I get it for £35, exclusive of moderate taxes. We think ourselves most lucky."

at his pleasure and realize to the fullest extent Shenston's lines on an inn :—

"Whoe'er has travell'd life's dull round,
    Where'er his stages may have been, .
May sigh to think he still has found
    The warmest welcome at an inn."

That Charles Lamb drank freely, can be no matter of question. " This failing," says one of his biographers, "has often been greatly exaggerated, but there is no doubt it existed. The fact seems to be that he had a constitutional craving for exhilarating drinks, and the relief they gave him from the dreadful anxiety and depression caused by his sister's precarious health and often recurring illness, tempted him to indulge in them to an extent which—while it would have been moderation to a stronger man—to his delicate and sensitive organization was excess. It was not the mere excitement of drinking that fascinated him : it was the relaxation, the forgetfulness of care, the confidence, the ready flow of words to embody the conceptions of his ever-fruitful fancy, that gave an almost irresistible charm—to porter in bright pewter pots at wayside inns, and to brandy, with or without water, at home." He wrote in his Essay " On the Artificial Comedy of the last Century ":—

" I confess for myself that—with no great delinquencies to answer for —I am for a season to take an airing beyond the diocese of the strict conscience,—not to live always in the precincts of the law-courts,—but now and then, for a dream-while or so, to imagine a world with no meddling restrictions—to get into recesses whither the hunter cannot follow me—

.   Secret shades
Of woody Ida's inmost grove
    While yet there was no fear of Jove.

I come back to my cage and my restraint the fresher and more healthy for it. I wear my shackles more contentedly for having respired the breath of an imaginary freedom. I do not know how it is with others, but I feel the better always for a perusal of one of Congreve's—nay, why should I not add even of Wycherley's?—Comedies, I am the gayer at least for it."

At one time Lamb and his sister resolved to give up alcoholic drinks altogether. "As for Mary," he informed Miss Wordsworth, "she has taken to water like a hungry otter. I, too, limp after her in lame imitation, but it goes against me a little at first. I have been an acquaintance with it now for full four days, and it seems a moon. I am full of cramps and rheumatisms, and cold internally, so that fire won't warm me; yet I bear all for virtue's sake." Total abstinence plainly did not agree with him, and was soon given up.*

Now, as before mentioned, on this particular occasion— viz., Wednesday, the 19th December, 1832, Charles Lamb finished his early afternoon walk by a visit to the Crown and Horse Shoes inn; after awhile he got into conversation—for company's sake—with the persons there assembled, who, like himself, were drinking and enjoying themselves after their own manner. At length the mirth, like the company, getting a little too fast and furious, Lamb, who was well known to the landlord as a customer and a near neighbour, paid his reckoning and went away as straight as he conveniently could, under existing circumstances, to his sister Mary, who is said to have kept too jealous ward over him, and was a little too severe upon his peccadilloes in this direction; so much so that there were times when he was glad to escape from her peevish temperament and seek retirement and forgetfulness in the village or wayside alehouses of the surrounding neighbourhood.

The following morning the Enfield constables, Mead and Watkins, were on the alert, and, "from information received,"

---

* A Biographical Essay on Elia, by H. S., Bell and Daldy, Fleet Street, 1867.

apprehended John Cooper, the son of a poor man in the town, Samuel Sleath, *alias* Fare, William Johnson, the son of a gardener of that name in Enfield, on suspicion of being the murderers of Mr. Benjaman C. Danby, and, in consequence of being seen in their company on the previous evening at the Crown and Horse Shoes, the—*the*—*the* gentle-minded and genial-hearted Charles Lamb—the distinguished author of " Essays of Elia," and intimate friend and companion of Coleridge, Wordsworth, Hazlitt, Leigh Hunt, Godwin, Talfourd, Thelwall, and a host of other literary men of the day—*as being an accomplice!*

The parties thus charged were taken before Mr. Cresswell, a magistrate in the neighbourhood, when, after a long private examination, the three first-named men were remanded to await the result of the Coroner's inquest. The matter, of course as regarded Charles Lamb, was soon explained, and he was at once set at liberty.

The Coroner, and a jury composed of the most respectable inhabitants of Enfield, were engaged from six on Thursday night to one on Friday morning. The inquest was then adjourned till the evening ; and so interesting were the circumstances brought before their notice, that they would have continued the inquiry to a later hour, had it not been for the sudden illness of the foreman, brought on by exhaustion. Under such circumstances the inquest was adjourned to the following Monday morning. The inquiry was held at the sign of the Old Serjeant (since demolished), in Parsonage Lane, Enfield, before Henry Sawyer, Esq., Coroner for the Duchy of Lancaster, in the jurisdiction of which Enfield Wash is situated. The jury returned a verdict —" That Benjamin Crouch Danby was wilfully murdered by William Johnson, and John Cooper, at ; or about midnight of Wednesday, December the 19th, and that Samuel Fare aided and assisted in the commission of the crime."

At the Old Bailey Sessions, held January 4, 1833, William Johnson and Samuel Fare were arraigned on two indictments. The first, charging Johnson with the murder of Benjamin Crouch Danby, and Fare as an accessory : the second, charging both prisoners with robbing Danby. John Cooper—the greatest delinquent—was admitted as an approver. Johnson was found guilty of the murder, and Fare with robbing the deceased of a tobacco-pipe bowl, of peculiar form, which he used for measuring shot, and eleven shillings. Johnson was executed January 7. The "Lamentation and Confessional Verses," printed and pub—lish—ed on the occasion, informed the public that Johnson was a diabolical murderer, and of the deepest dye, and, in reference to the victim, that :—

> " This young man he was a sailor,
> And just returned from sea,
> And down to Enfield Chase he went
> His cousin for to see ;
> Little thinking that ere night—
> Would prove his destiny."

The lane or road in which the atrocious murder took place is called Batches Road, but is better known as Holt-White's-Lane, and leads from Enfield to Barnet. Since the dreadful occurrence, the site has been well preserved to the present date. Immediately opposite where the body was found was an oak tree, on which Mr. Richard C. Farr, then carrying on business as a builder in Enfield, cut out with a set of chisels on the morning of the discovery of the murder the following :—

B. C. DANBY

MURDERED HERE.

Dec. 19th,

1832.

• Only the stump of that tree now remains : a few years ago the body was cut down just below the inscription, but the mark of the spot where the murdered man laid is still kept fresh to the view."*

HOUSE AT EDMONTON WHERE CHARLES LAMB DIED.

About Midsummer of 1833, Charles Lamb and his sister gave up their lodgings at Enfield and removed to Bay Cottage, Church Street, Edmonton, kept by Mr. Walden, whose wife acted as a professional nurse. Lamb's death

---

* In June, 1877, in company with Mr. R. L. Farr, Photographer, Raleigh Road, Enfield, and Mr. Richard Searle, blacksmith, a very old and respected inhabitant, we visited Enfield ; and our thanks being due, are hereby given to those two gentlemen for their kindness in showing us all the places in and about the good old town that had any reference to the murder of B. C. Danby, and to the walks and haunts of Charles Lamb, the author of "Essays of Elia." We have also been in communication with the Rev. H. G. Hodson, M.A., Vicar of Enfield. *Ex nihilo nihil fit.*

was the consequence of what at first was thought but a slight accident. He stumbled against a stone when returning home one afternoon from a visit to the Bell, at Edmonton —*the* BELL, from which Mrs. John Gilpin witnessed her husband ride by—and fell, very much injuring his nose and face, thereby getting the *gravel-rash !** He was immediately picked up by Mr. Robert Gosset, still carrying on the business of an auctioneer and surveyor, who, with the assistance of two others passing at the time, conveyed Lamb to his residence ; in a few days erysipelas set in, and the result was fatal.

EDMONTON CHURCH.

Charles Lamb lies buried in Edmonton churchyard : over his grave is placed an ordinary—very ordinary—grave-stone, on which is inscribed the following cock-and-bull-yarn by Mr. Henry Francis Cary—" Dante Cary." It is a pity one

---

* GRAVEL RASH, a scratched face,—telling its tale of a drunken fall. A person subject to this is called a GRAVEL GRINDER, " Hotten's Slang Dictionary "

of the Seven Poëts of the Seven Dials was not employed for the *job !* But; however, " Its never too late to mend." A proposal for erecting a more suitable monument, and setting the grave in order, was announced a few years ago. Is it not time that something in that way was done? Our mitè is ready on application.

TO THE MEMORY

of

CHARLES LAMB,

Died 27th Dec[r.] 1834, Aged 59.

Farewell dear friend, That smile, that harmless mirth,
No more shall gladden our domestic hearth ;
That rising tear, with pain forbid to flow,
Better than words, no more assuage our woe ;
That hand outstretched, from small but well-earned store,
Yields succour to the destitute no more.
Yet art thou not all lost ; Thro' many an age
With sterling sense and humour shall thy page
Win many an English bosom, pleased to see
That old and happier vein revived in thee.
This for our earth, and if with friends we share
Our joys in heaven, we hope to meet thee there.

ALSO,

MARY ANNE LAMB,

SISTER TO THE ABOVE,

Born 3rd Dec[r.] 1767. Died 20th May, 1847.

Furthermore, the gravestone is made to perpetuate the name—a most unusual circumstance—of the Sexton of the parish, who has cut on the edge of the stone, thus :—

H I O R N S,

SEXTON.

On May 30th, 1833, a prize-fight took place between Simon Byrne and Deaf Burke, in which the former was killed. The fight lasted three hours and six minutes, and extended to ninety-nine rounds. Burke was the victor, and the unfortunate Simon Byrne was conveyed, in a state of complete exhaustion, to the Woolpack inn, St. Alban's. Medical assistance was immediately called in ; but at twenty minutes past eight on Sunday he breathed his last. He was about thirty-two years of age, and left a wife and four children. The Coroner's jury recorded the following verdict: "Manslaughter against Deaf Burke, principal in the first degree, and Thomas Spring, James Ward, Richard Curtis, and Thomas Gaynor, as seconds ; also against the umpire or umpires, referee or referees, and the time-keeper, all then and there aiding and abetting, whose names are unknown to us, as principals in the second degree." On the 11th of July, James Burke, better known as Deaf Burke, and Richard Curtis, having surrendered themselves, were tried for manslaughter. The indictment charged Burke with having inflicted divers mortal bruises, in a pugilistic contest at No Man's Land, on Simon Byrne, whereof death ensued ; and Richard Curtis, with having aided and abetted him in the felony by acting as his second. Evidence was produced to show that the deceased appeared to have a former disease on the lungs, and that there was no external injury answering to the internal appearances which could have caused death. Mr. Justice Park, after hearing this statement, addressed the jury and said, "Gentlemen, that makes an end of the case ; the prisoners must be acquitted." Spring, Ward, and Gaynor immediately surrendered, but no evidence being offered against them, they were found "Not guilty."

THE DEATH OF SIMON BYRNE!

MOURN, Erin's sons, your hero brave; his loss all may deplore,
Brave Simon Byrne, that hero bold, alas! he is no more;
For courage true and science good he never was afraid,
Of Larkins, Sampson, Ward, Mc Kay, could ne'er be dismayed.

CHORUS.

Mourn! Erin mourn, your loss deplore; poor Simon's dead and gone,
An hero brave laid in the grave as ever the sun shone on.

On Thursday, May the 30th day, brave Simon took the ring,
Back'd by Jem Ward the champion, likewise by gallant Spring,
To fight Burke for two hundred pounds, a man of courage bold,
To stop reports that with Ward the battle he had sold.

Both men stript, then shook hands, when began a great display,
For thirty rounds shouts did resound, brave Byrne will win the day,
But Burke, as hard as beaten steel, and deaf to all their cries,
When all thought he was beaten dead, time call'd, he up did rise.

It's knock down for knock down they fought till the ninety-ninth round,
When Burke gave a tremendous blow, which fell'd him to the ground,
And time being call'd, Simon's backers found it was in vain,
Brave Byrne he fell his last that time, he could not rise again.

To St. Alban's he was convey'd, assistance came with speed.
The sufferings that he did undergo would make a heart to bleed,
He sigh'd and said—"It's not the blow distresses me so sore,
I did my best, I've lost!" he sigh'd; brave Byrne was then no more.

Few hours before brave Simon died, these words he was heard to say,
" Three years ago, this very day, I fought Sandy Mc Kay,
I caused his death, I meet the same, farewell my infants all,
Dear wife, farewell, in heaven again to meet I hope we shall."

The solemn bell, its awful knell did call our hero brave,
Hundreds did cry as he pass'd by unto the silent grave,
And now the green sod covers o'er that once manly frame,
Say, was there e'er his like before, or will there be again ?

When Burke and seconds of brave Byrne did hear that he was dead,
To France and other parts for safety off they quickly fled,
And may the contributions which these valiant men have made,
Be followed up with spirit for his wife and children's aid.

J. Catnach, Printer, 2 and 3, Monmouth Court, 7 Dials.

During the Parliamentary Sessions of 1833, Sir Andrew Agnew, who sat for Wigtonshire, 1830—8, a strict Scottish Sabbatarian, with a long line of ancestry, having for their motto, CONSILIO NON IMPETU—*i.e., By counsel, not by force !!* introduced a very stringent and in every way obnoxious bill for the *Better Observance of the Sabbath*, which called forth a vast quantity of caricatures from George Cruikshank downward, together with squibs in prose and verse and street-ballads by the yard.   In one entitled " The Agony Bill," it was said if it passed the Houses of Parliament that

Not even salts must work on Sunday.

Chorus.—At this you 'll laugh, for it 's meant to gag you ;

This is the Bill of Sir Andrew Agnew.

While another set of rhymes, entitled an " Ode to Sir Andrew Agnew," put this somewhat pertinent question—

Besides, sir, here 's a poser—

At least to *me* it seems a closer,

And shows a shocking lack of legislative skill—

If nothing, Sir 's to work from Saturdays to Mondays,

Pray how 's your Bill

To work on Sundays?

On the day appointed for the second reading of the Bill, Mr. Roebuck said that the Almighty did not require such paltry and unnatural sacrifices from his creatures as the asceticism of this Bill contemplated.   The Bill was thrown out, as was two others of a similar tendency, also introduced by Sir Andrew on other occasions.

THE

WIGTON REPROBATES;

OR THE FATE OF

SIR   ANDREW   AGNEW.

" Those whom God loveth he chasteneth."—Hence poor Sir Andrew Agnew, with his Sunday Bills tied to his tail, flies from the ungodly of Wigton, to hide in oblivion the vexation of his defeat.

ALAS ! tis enough to make Puritans faint,
To hear how the sinners have treated a saint,
Heave a sigh ev'ry heart, let each phiz. be demure,
For the game is all up with Sir Andrew the Pure.

Oh, ye scum of the earth ! did you dare to reject,
So chosen a vessel, a Spirit elect ?
You will find, in the end, 'tis disgrace and not glory,
That *Whig*-town no longer is rul'd by a *Tory*.

Think, think of his zeal and his courage unshrinking,
To keep us on Sabbaths from eating and drinking,
And worldly affairs from our memory casting,
To spend them in sorrow, in praying and fasting.

The heart of a stone it would surely have melted,
To see how unkindly with mud he was pelted :
Drown'd puppies, dead cats, with iniquitous mirth,
Were shower'd down like hail on this saint of the earth.

To Wigton be woe ; may it sink in decay,
For driving a saint like Sir Andrew away ;
For their infidel wish and unholy endeavour,
To sink his proud name in oblivion for ever !

May Providence soon send a suitable man
To finish the work he so nobly began ;
To prove that religion exhibits its power,
In gloom and dejection and visages sour.

To prove our existence is merely a trial,
How far we can exercise sad self-denial,
And denounce, with a frown, all enjoyment and mirth,
As man was created for sorrow on earth.

Then, oh ! 'tis enough to make Puritans faint
To learn how vile sinners have treated the saint ;
Heave a sigh ev'ry heart, let each mug be demure,
For the game is all up with Sir Andrew the Pure.

Printed by J. Catnach, 2 and 3, Monmouth Court, 7 Dials.
Battledores, Lotteries, and Primers sold cheap. Sold by Marshall, Bristol ; Hook,
Market Street, Brighton ; Inkpen, Lewes.

The burning of the old Houses of Parliament, October,, 1834, was made the most of by all connected with the production and distribution of street-literature. The "Houses that Taxes built, all gone to Blazes," became at once a popular term with the running patterers, and one which just tickled the thoughts and ears of the people. The gist of most of the ballads and witticisms, or clap-trap lines and statements of the hawkers, was to the effect of the general regret that the whole of the ministers and members were not burnt with the Houses of Parliament, for then, as they asserted, there would be no more taxes to pay or aristocrats to keep ; while all sorts of causes and motives were attributed to the destruction of the national buildings according to the wit or whim of the patterer.

An action for crim. con.—Birch *v.* Neale—heard in the Court of Common Pleas, June 25th, 1835, before the Chief Justice and a special jury, created a great metropolitan sensation in consequence of the popularity of the parties concerned, the peculiar evidence given by the two female servants,.and the number of street-ballads, all highly-spiced with *mots à double entente* on the "Amorous Curate and the Rector's Wife," "The Parson's Wife and the Spreeish Curate of West Hackney," and "Full Particulars," &c., produced by the writers for the "Seven Dials Press."

The plaintiff, the Rev. Mr. Birch, was the son of the well-known Alderman Birch, the famous cook and confectioner of 15, Cornhill, who was many years a member of the Common Council, and was elected Alderman of the ward of Candlewick. He was also Colonel of the City Militia, and served as Lord Mayor in 1815—the year of the battle of Waterloo. He possessed considerable literary taste, and wrote poems and musical dramas, of which "The Adopted Child" remained a stock piece to our time. Dr. Kitchener, in his "Cook's Oracle," extols the mock turtle soup of Birch, and his skill was long famed in Civic banquets. At the time of this action the son was rector of St. Ann, West Hackney Parish, near London; the defendant, the Rev. Mr. Neale, a very popular preacher, his curate. Mr. Thesiger, Mr. Platt, and Mr. Browne appeared for the plaintiff; Sir Frederick Pollock and Mr. Richards were for the defendant. The jury returned a verdict for the plaintiff with £200 damages. In addition to the usual newspaper reports of the case, and the ballads and fly-sheets written and manufactured exclusively for street sale, the trial *in extenso* was published in pamphlet form.

In 1836, Mr. T. D. Rice, who had previously appeared at the Surrey Theatre, in " Bone Squash Diablo," made his first appearance at the Adelphi, in a farcical Burletta, called " A Flight to America; or, Twelve Hours in New York." The sketch, written for him by Mr. Leman Rede, introduced Rice as a nigger, Yates as a Frenchman, and Mrs. Stirling, Miss Daly, John Reeve, and Buckstone strengthened the cast. " Jump Jim Crow " caught the fancy of the town at once, and the familiar tune was soon to be heard everywhere. Rice stayed through the whole season, playing an engagement of twenty-one weeks, then considered something extraordinary. For a long period he performed at the Adelphi and the Pavilion Theatres the same evening, and it was calculated that in so doing he had travelled considerably more than a thousand miles, while being encored five times at each theatre for 126 nights, it was easy to set down the figure of 1,260 as representing the number of times he had sung " Jim Crow," during that period. Rice cleared by this engagement eleven hundred pounds.* A street-ballad of the day informed the public that it could have :—

---

* History of the Adelphi Theatre, by E. L. Blanchard. "Era Almanack," 1877.

"The Jim Crow rum, the Jim Crow gin,
The Jim Crow needle, and the Jim Crow pin ;
The Jim Crow coat, the Jim Crow cigar ;
The Jim Crow dad, and the Jim Crow ma';
The Jim Crow pipe, the Jim Crow hat.
The Jim Crow this, and the Jim Crow that.

There were a hundred-and-one versions of "Jim Crow,"
fresh stanzas being added from day to day on the passing
events, for the most part written by Leman Rede, and
Buckstone, the *honorarium* offered by Rice being one
shilling per line. We select as follows from the first version
as sung at the Surrey Theatre :

JIM CROW.

HOW are you massa gemmen,
        An de ladies in a row,
All for to tell you whar I 'm from,
        I 'se going for to go !
For I wheel about an turn about, an do just so,
An cbery time I turn about, I jump Jim Crow.

'Twas down in " Ole Wurginny,"
 About thirty years ago,
Dat dis han'sum picaninny
 'Gan to jump Jim Crow,
   So I turn about, &c.

'Twas wid ole massa Jackson,   \
 In de state ob Tennessee,
Dat I fuss larn de rudiments
 Ob trabbling joggrafee.
   When I turn about, &c.

An in de hurry scurry,
 Ob dis lunar world below,
I tought I 'd come to Surrey
 An jump Jim Crow.
   So I turn about, &c.

JIM ALONG JOSEY.

O H, I 'se from Lusiana, as you must all know,
  Dar 's where Jim along Josey 's all de go—
Dem nigger all rise when de bell does ring,
And dis am de song dat dey do sing.
        Hey get along, get along Josey,
          Hey get along, Jim along Joe—
        Hey get along, get along Joe,
          Hey get along, Jim along Joe.

Once old Jim Crow was dare all de go,
'Till he found him rival in Jim along Joe;
Now poor old Jim, dey hab put him to bed,
And Jim along Josey hab come in him stead.
                    Hey get along, &c.

Oh, when I get dat new coat I expects to hab soon,
Likewise de new pair tight knee'd Trousaloon;
I 'll walk up and down Bond Street wid my Susanna,
And in my mout I smoke de real Habannah.
                    Hey get along, &c.

My sissa Rosa de oder night did dream,
Dat she was a floating up and down de stream,
And when she woke she did begin to cry,
" O ! de white cat pick'd out de black cat's eye."
Hey get along &c.

Now away down South, not berry far off,
De bull frog died wid de hooping cough ;
And t 'other side de Mississippi, as you must know,
Dare was whare dey christen me Jim along Joe.
Hey get along, &c.

Dem New York nigger tink dey 're so fine,
Because dey drink noting but de genuine ;
But de poor Kentuck nigger when der day gone by,
Dey sarve dem like an old horse, kicked out to die.
Hey get along &c.

Oh, I 'm de bold nigger dat don't mind my troubles,
Because they 're noting more dan bubbles,
D 'ambition dat such nigger feels,
Is showing de science of him heels.
Hey get along, &c.

De best President we eber had was General Washington,
And de one we 've got now is Massa Van Buren,
But although the old General's long gone dead,
As long's de country stands, him name shall float ahead,
Hey get along, &c.

DANDY JIM, FROM CAROLINE.

I'VE often heard it said ob late,
   Dat Souf Carolina was de state,
Whar a handsome nigga 's bound to shine,
Like Dandy Jim, from Caroline,
     For my ole massa tole me so,
     I was de best looking nigga in de country, O,
     I look in de glass an found 'twas so,
     Just what massa tole me, O.

I drest myself from top to toe,
And down to Dinah I did go,
Wid pantaloons strapped down behind,
Like Dandy Jim, from Caroline.
     For my ole massa, &c.

De bull dog cleared me out ob de yard,
I tought I 'd better leabe my card,
I tied it fast to a piece ob twine,
Signed " Dandy Jim, from Caroline."
     For my ole massa, &c.

She got my card an wrote me a letter,
An ebery word she spelt de better,
For ebery word an ebery line,
Was Dandy Jim, from Caroline.
     For my ole massa, &c.

Oh, beauty is but skin deep,
But wid Miss Dinah none compete,
See changed her name from lubly Dine,
To Mrs. Dandy Jim, from Caroline.
     For my ole massa, &c.

An ebery little nig she had,
Was de berry image ob de dad,
Dar heels stick out three feet behind,
Like Dandy Jim, from Caroline.
     For my ole massa, &c.

I took dem all to church one day,
An hab dem christened widout delay,
De preacher christened eight or nine,
Young Dandy Jims, from Caroline.
     For my ole massa, &c.

An when de preacher took his text,
He seemed to be berry much perplexed,
For nothing cum across his mind,
But Dandy Jims, from Caroline.
  For my ole massa tole me so,
  I was de best looking nigga in de country, O,
  I look in de glass, and found 'twas so,
  Just what ole massa tole me, O !

ALL ROUND THE ROOM.

ALL round the room I waltz'd with Ellen Taylor,
   All round the room I waltz'd till break of day,
And ever since that time I 've done nothing but bewail her,
   Alas ! she 's gone to Margate, the summer months to stay.
'Twas at a ball at Islington I first chanc'd to meet her,
   She really look'd so nice I couldn't keep my eyes away ;
In all my life before I ne'er saw so sweet a creature,
   She danc'd with me three hours, then fainted quite away.

Spoken.—She was such a divine creature ! I fell in love with her the moment I saw her. I looked languishing at her, and she did the same at me ; then she gave such a sigh—such a heavy one !—you might have heard it——

All round the room, &c.

My Ellen 's rather tall, and my Ellen 's rather thin, too,
   Her hair is rather sandy, and at singing she 's *au fait,*
That she should leave me now I think it quite a sin, too,
   I 'm sure I shan't be happy all the time she is away.

Spoken.—She was an *h*angel ! such a natural sort of woman ! She wore a bustle—that wasn't very natural, though—it was rather a largish one ; I suppose, upon a moderate calculation, it would have reached——

All round the room, &c.

For seven long years I 'm apprentic'd in the City,
   But four of them are gone, and I 've only three to stay :
But if Ellen should refuse me, oh, crikey ! what a pity !
   I 'll go and ask her pa, and I think he won't say nay.

Spoken.—No, I don't think he 'll refuse me ; and if he don't, I 'll marry Ellen, and we 'll go into business. We 'll keep a catsmeat shop ; no, we 'll keep a chandler's shop. Ellen would look so nice behind the counter, serving the customers out a ha'p'orth of treacle, a red herring, a half-quartern of butter, &c. Then we 'll keep a one-horse shay, and I 'll drive the children out with us on a Sunday—yes, I'll drive them——

All round the room, &c.

SAM WELLER'S ADVENTURES!

A SONG OF THE PICKWICKIANS.

Who caus'd the smiles of rich and poor ?
Who made a hit so slow, but sure ?
And rose the worth of literature ?
Sam Weller.

I 'M pretty well known about town,
    For to gain a repute is my pride,
Though no vun can doubt my renown,
    I 'm a *covey of polish* beside !
I renovates *cases* for feet,
    Vhether high-lows or tops is the same,
I turns 'em off hand werry neat,
And Samivel Veller's my name.!
Fol lol, &c.

In the Borough my trade I dragged on,
    Vith no vun to envy my sphere ;
I polish'd the *soles* of each don,
    From the cadger bang up to the peer !

Their *understandings* I greatly improv'd,
　Vot happen'd to fall in the way ;
And many a gen'leman mov'd
　To me in the course of the day.
　　　　　Fol lol, &c.

Vun gen'leman—Pickvick, Esquire,
　The head of the noted P. C.
Vun day tumbled in to enquire,
　If I'd had the *fortin* to see
A cove vearing Vellington *kicks*,
　And a Miss Rachel Vardle beside,
Vot the gent. had lugged off by the *nicks*,
　And promis'd to make her his bride,
　　　　　Fol lol, &c.

I knowed by the cut of his boot,
　As the cove had put up at our inn,
So Pickvick, without a dispute,
　Comes tumbling down with the *tin !*
And me arter that he engages,
　To follow him in his career—
Good *togs* and twelve *shiners* for vages,
　Paid every *annual year.*
　　　　　Fol lol, &c.

Some coves when they rises, you know,
　They stick to vulgarity will ;
But that vos my notice below,
　'Cos as how I'm a gen'leman still.
" For riches is nothing to me,
　If ever them I vos among "—
As the gen'leman said, d'ye see,
　At the time he vos goin' to be hung !
　　　　　Fol lol, &c.

I trotted all over the town,
  And *seed* all the pleasures of life—
'Cos being to knowingness *down*,
  I never get into no strife.
" I couldn't see more if I wished,
  So I must be content, I suppose' "—
As the *blind man* said vhen he vas *swished*
  To the lady vithout any nose !
                    Fol lol, &c.

"Now I hopes you're all hearty and *chuff*,
  'Cos I'm now going to take my release "—
As the poulterer said, with a huff,
  Vhile a-killing the *hinnocent* geese !
" But I hopes I shall see you again,
  'Cos I knows you on niceties stand"—
As the *hemperor* dictated, vhen
  The crocodile nipped off his hand !
                    Fol lol, &c.

Sir :—You're an 'umbug : that is—" In a Pickwickian sense."

The year 1837 produced two senational murders and executions. The first case—that of Pegsworth—made a great stir, particularly in the east part of London. It was on the evening of the 9th of January, 1837, that a most atrocious and cold-blooded murder was committed in Ratcliff Highway. The individual who suffered was Mr. John Holliday Ready, who for some time carried on the trade of a tailor, draper, and milliner. John Pegsworth, was a messenger in the tea department of St. Katherine's Docks, he had formerly kept a small tobacconist's shop in the same street, and had contracted a debt of £1 with Mr. Ready, who, being unable to obtain payment, took out a summons against him in the Court of Requests, Osborne Street, Whitechapel. The Court gave judgment against Pegsworth for the full amount and costs, which he was ordered to pay by instalments. On the evening of the same day Pegsworth proceeded to a cutler's shop in Shadwell, where he bought a large pig-knife, armed with which he immediately repaired to the house of Mr. Ready for the purpose of executing his diabolical intention. He entered the shop, and having spoken to Mrs. Ready, passed on to the parlour and got into conversation with Mr. Ready. Pegsworth, although pressingly asked to do so, declined taking a seat, and after he had been talking about ten minutes in a calm and collected manner on the subject of the debt and the misfortunes he had met with in business, he pointedly asked Mr. Ready if he intended to enforce the payment of the debt? Ready said he should be compelled to issue an execution against his goods if the money was not paid. The words had scarcely left the lips of the unfortunate man than Pegsworth uttered some exclamation which is supposed to have been, "Take that!" and plunged the knife with great force into his breast up to the hilt. Ready called out to his wife, "O, I am stabbed!" fell back in his chair, and almost immediately expired. Mrs. Ready,

who saw Pegsworth move his arm, but was not aware her
husband was stabbed until she saw him fall back, screamed
aloud for assistance, and several of her neighbours rushed
into the shop for the purpose of securing the murderer, who
did not make the least attempt to escape, but having completed his purpose, withdrew the knife from the body of his
victim, laid it on the table, and calmly awaited the arrival
of the police.

Pegsworth was tried at the Central Criminal Court of
London on the 12th of February, and found guilty of wilful
murder, and was executed in front of the debtor's door in
the Old Bailey on the 9th of March following.

During the whole of the time that was occupied in the
trial and execution of Pegsworth, a circumstance took place
which excited an extraordinary sensation throughout the
metropolis and its neighbourhood—namely, the discovery
near the Pine Apple Gate, Edgware Road, of the trunk of
a human being, tied up in a sack, dismembered of the arms,
legs, and head,

The utmost vigilance was exercised to trace out the
murderer, but for several days no light was thrown upon
the transaction. At length, on the 6th of January, as a
barge was passing down the Regent's Canal, near Stepney,
one of the eastern environs of London, the bargeman, to
his unspeakable horror, fished up what proved to be a
human head. Proper notice of this circumstance was
forwarded to the police. It was now very generally supposed the head would prove to belong to the body found in
the Edgware Road, although at a distance of nearly five
miles, and this conjecture proved to be correct.

On the second of February the remaining portions of the
human being was discovered in a sack in an osier bed, near
Cold Harbour Lane, Camberwell. These mutilated remains
were carefully matched together, and at length recognised

as those of a Mrs. Brown, and suspicion fell, and justly so, upon James Greenacre and his paramour Sarah Gale.

In the Greenacre tragedy Catnach did a great amount of business, and as it was about the last "popular murder" in which he had any trade concern, we give, on the next page, a facsimile copy of one of the several " Execution Papers " published at the time, and it is estimated that 1,650,000 copies, in all, were sold.

In respect to the last two murders we have cited, Mr. Mayhew received from an old "running patterer" the following statement—"Pegsworth was an out-and-out lot. I did tremendous with him, because it happened in London, down Ratcliff Highway—that's a splendid quarter for working—there's plenty of feeling—but, bless you, some places you go to you can't move nohow, they've hearts like paving stones. They wouldn't have 'the papers' if you'd give them to 'em—especially when they knows you. Greenacre didn't sell so well as might have been expected, for such a diabolical out-and-out crime as he committed; but you see he came close after Pegsworth, and that took the beauty off him. Two murderers together is no good to nobody."

LIFE, TRIAL, CONFESSION, & EXECUTION.

OF

JAMES GREENACRE,

FOR THE

EDGEWARE ROAD MURDER.

On the 22nd of April, James Greenacre was found guilty of the wilful murder of Hannah Brown, and Sarah Gale with being necessary after the fact. A long and connected chain of evidence was produced, which showed, that the sack in which the body was found was the property of Mr. Ward; that it was usually deposited in a part of the premises which led to the workshop, and could without observation have been carried away by him; that the said sack contained several fragments of shavings of mahogany, such as were made in the course of business by Ward; and that it contained some pieces of linen cloth, which had been patched with nankeen; that this linen cloth matched exactly with a frock which was found on Greenacre's premises, and which belonged to the female prisoner. Feltham, a police-officer, deposed, that on the 26th of March he apprehended the prisoners at the lodgings of Greenacre; that on searching the trowsers pockets of that person, he took therefrom a pawnbroker's duplicate for two silk gowns, and from the fingers of the female prisoner two rings, and also a similar duplicate for two veils, and an old-fashioned silver watch, which she was endeavouring to conceal; and it was further proved that these articles were pledged by the prisoners, and that they had been the property of the deceased woman.—Two surgeons were examined, whose evidence was most important, and whose depositions were of the greatest consequence in throwing a clear light on the manner in which the female, Hannah Brown, met with her death. Mr. Birtwhistle deposed, that he had carefully examined the head; that the right eye had been knocked out by a blow inflicted while the person was living; there was also a cut on the cheek, and the jaw was fractured, these two last wounds were, in his opinion, produced after death; there was also a bruise on the head, which had occurred after death; the head had been separated by cutting, and the *bone sawed nearly through*, and then broken off; there were the marks of a saw, which fitted with a saw which was found in Greenacre's box. Mr. Girdwood, a surgeon, very minutely and skilfully described the appearances presented on the head, and showed incontestibly, that the head had been severed from the body *while the person was yet alive;* that this was proved by the retraction, or drawing back, of the muscles at the parts where they were separated by the knife, and further, by the blood-vessels being empty, the body was drained of blood. This part of the

evidence produced a thrill of horror throughout the court, but Greenacre remained quite unmoved.

After a most impressive and impartial summing up by the learned Judge, the jury retired, and, after the absence of a quarter of an hour, returned into court, and pronounced a verdict of "Guilty" against both the prisoners.

The prisoners heard the verdict without evincing the least emotion, or the slightest change of countenance. After an awful silence of a few minutes, the Lord Chief Justice said they might retire, as they would be remanded until the end of the session.

They were then conducted from the bar, and on going down the steps, the unfortunate female prisoner kissed Greenacre with every mark of tenderness and affection.

The crowd outside the court on this day was even greater than on either of the preceding; and when the result of the trial was made known in the street, a sudden and general shout succeeded, and continued huzzas were heard for several minutes.

THE EXECUTION.

At half past seven the sheriff arrived in his carriage, and in a short time the press-yard was thronged with gentlemen who had been admitted by tickets. The unhappy convict was now led from his cell. When he arrived in the press-yard, his whole appearance portrayed the utmost misery and spirit-broken dejection; his countenance haggard, and his whole frame agitated; all that self-possession and fortitude which he displayed in the early part of his imprisonment, had utterly forsaken him, and had left him a victim of hopelessness and despair. He requested the executioner to give him as little pain as possible in the process of pinioning his arms and wrists; he uttered not a word in allusion to his crime; neither did he make any dying request, except that his spectacles might be given to Sarah Gale; he exhibited no sign of hope; he showed no symptom of reconciliation with his offended God! When the venerable ordinary preceded him in the solemn procession through the vaulted passage to the fatal drop, he was so overcome and unmanned, that he could not support himself without the aid of the assistant executioner. At the moment he ascended the faithless floor, from which he was to be launched into eternity, the most terrific yells, groans, and cheers were vociferated by the immense multitude surrounding the place of execution. Greenacre bowed to the sheriff, and begged he might not be allowed to remain long in the concourse; and almost immediately the fatal bolt was withdrawn, and, without a struggle, he became a lifeless corse.—Thus ended the days of Greenacre, a man endowed with more than ordinary talents, respectably connected, and desirably placed in society; but a want of probity, an absolute dearth of principle, led him on from one crime to another, until at length he perpetrated the sanguinary deed which brought his career to an awful and disgraceful period, and which has enrolled his name among the most notorious of those who have expiated their crime on the gallows.

On hearing the death-bell toll, Gale became dreadfully agitated; and when she heard the brutal shouts of the crowd of spectators, she fainted, and remained in a state of alternate mental agony and insensibility throughout the whole day.

After having been suspended the usual time, his body was cut down, and buried in a hole dug in one of the passages of the prison, near the spot where Thistlewood and his associates were deposited.

A NEW

POLITICAL AND REFORM ALPHABET,

WITH

FABLES ON THE TIMES.

A for ATTWOOD. A tough wood of a good grain, grows at Birmingham, and is used as the principal material in building up the Unions.

B for BROUGHAM. A broom worn to a stump, formerly the Queen's own, but now owned by none.

C for CALTHORPE. A word despised by the Whigs, but will ever live in the hearts of the people.

D for DAN. A Patriot of the land of Coercion, where St. Patrick banished the toads, and Stanley the freedom.

E for ELDON. Old Bags; one that shed an abundance of crocodile tears without one drop of pity, and would put down, if he could, Penny Papers.

F   for FRANKY.   A pretended friend of the people, arrived at his second childishness, and plays at Shuttlecock with the Electors of Westminster.

G   for GREY.   A dealer in humbugs : who behaved as a father to the people, by giving them that which they asked for.—The Bill, the whole Bill, and *Nothing but the Bill !*

H   for HOBBY.   A Westminster Rat, who had so often received the favours of the people, that at last they had nothing to give but cabbage stumps, which he received in showers at Covent Garden.

I   for INJURY.   A performance that takes place every day and night, by the Rich against the Poor Man and a Brother.

J   for JUSTICE.   A balance between Might and Right, but always leaning to power and riches.

K   for KING.   A title of Monarchy, an Idol of immense weight.

L   for LOYALTY.   A word nearly threadbare in some countries.

M   for MOUTH.   A part of the human body, padlocked by Law, by which the millions now are oppressed.

N   for NOBLE.   A mad Scottish fool.

O   for O'CONNELL of the Patriot School.

P   for PEELERS.   A body of great Force.   Brave and noble conquerors of an un-armed and peaceable people.

Q   for QUESTION—how long will they last ?

R   for REFORM. A word that filled the mouths of thousands, but the stomachs of few :—A Bill that ·was spoiled in the nursing. A thing without benefits.

S   for STOMACH.—"Apartments Unfurnished," Inquire Within !

T   for TRUNCHEON. A Knock-down argument of Power, an instrument of the Whigs.

U   for UNION. A word despised by all oppressors.

V   for VERDICT. A word lately known as a Terror to the Blues, but the Glory of others.

W   for WHIGS, who'd that Verdict suspend.

X   for the CROSS with which it will end.

Y   for YOUTH. An unbaked and doughy nonentity.

Z   for ZANY. A Tool employed to raise laughter, by his gestures, actions, and speeches. N.B.—A large collection kept in the Houses of Lords and Commons.

TUTOR.—"There's a good boy, now get your new edition of 'Æsop's Fables,' and I will hear you read the 'Fable of the Ministers in Danger.'"

PUPIL.—*(Reading.)* "There was a Ministry in Danger of a Turn-out, and many were their opinions concerning the best plan to be adopted to secure their seats, when a noble Hermit said there was nothing so good as a Coercion Bill; an Ex-Chancellor (called Old Bags) said a Coercion Bill might do very well, but there was nothing so good, nor so essential, as the suppression of the Penny Press ; but their

Wise and Grey old leader being present said, 'Gentlemen, you can do as you please, but take my word there is nothing like the Destruction of the Unions.'"

T.—"There's a good boy, now read me the Fable of 'The Mountain and the Mouse.'"

P.—"Yes, Sir. There was a Bill which made a great noise in a certain country for many years, and they said it was in Labour, and the People looked with hopes for the Production of great Benefits, and great was their joy at the thoughts, when after many months' pain and anxiety, it produced a mouse."

T.—" I hope, my children, this will be a warning to you, never build your hopes on the promises of those who are reaping the harvest of your labour, for they will take away your Substance, and leave you the Shadow to feed upon.

'You trusted to the Whigs, and the Tories turn'd out,
Now which of the two is the best, there's a doubt;
For the Tories and Whigs are all birds of a feather,
May the D——l come soon and take both together.'"

J. Catnach, Printer, 2 & 3, Monmouth Court, 7 Dials. Cards, Bills, &c., Printed on very reasonable terms.

From time immemorial the ballad singer, with his rough and ready broad-sheet, has travelled over the whole surface of the country in all seasons and weathers, yet there was one time of the year, however, when he went out of his every-day path and touched on deeper matters than accidents, politics, prize fights, sporting matches, murders, battles, royalty, famous men and women. Christmas time brought, both to him and his audience, its witness of the unity of the great family in heaven and earth, its story of the life and death of Him in whom that unity stands. Several examples, of Christmas carols and Scripture-sheets, bearing Catnach's imprint lie before us, thanks to the kindness of Mr. W. S. Fortey, Catnach's successor; these broadsides bear several distinctive marks which show that it was an object of more than ordinary care to publishers and ballad singers. In the first place, these Christmas sheets are double the size of the ordinary broad-sheet, and contain four or five carols—generally one long narrative ballad, and three or four short pieces. Each of them having two or three large woodcuts and several of smaller sizes. One sheet is entitled "The Trial of Christ," another, "Faith, Hope, and Charity," "Our Saviour's Love," a fourth "The Tree of Life," the next "A Copy of a Letter written by our Blessed Jesus Christ, and found eighteen miles from Iconium, sixty-three years after our Blessed Saviour's Crucifiction.—Transmitted from the Holy City by a converted Jew. Faithfully Translated from the Original Hebrew Copy, now in possession of Lady Cubas's family, in Mesopotamia. This letter was found under a great stone, round and large, at the foot of the Cross. Upon the stone was graven, 'Blessed is he that shall turn me over.' All people that saw it prayed to God earnestly, and desired that he would make the writing known unto them, that they might not attempt in vain to turn the stone over."

Another entitled "THE STAGES OF LIFE: or, The various Ages and Degrees of Human Life explained by these Twelve different Stages, from our Birth to our Graves."

INFANCY
To 10 *Years old.*

" HIS vain delusive thoughts are fill'd
    With vain delusive joys—
The empty bubble of a dream,
    Which waking change to toys."

From 10 *to* 20 *Years old.*

" HIS heart is now puff'd up,
    He scorns the tutor's hand ;
He hates to meet the least control
    And glories to command."

From 20 *to* 30 *Years old.*

" THERE 's naught here that can withstand
    The rage of his desire,
His wanton flames are now blown up,
    His mind is all on fire."

From 30 to 40 Years old.

"LOOK forward and repent
  Of all thy errors past,
That so thereby thou may'st attain
 True happiness at last."

From 40 to 50 Years old.

"AT fifty years he is
  Like the declining sun,
For now his better half of life,
 Man seemeth to have run."

From 50 to 60 Years old.

"HIS wasted taper now
  Begins to lose its light,
His sparkling flames doth plainly show
 'Tis growing towards night."

From 60 to 70 Years old.

"PERPLEX'D with slavish fear
  And unavailing woe,
He travels on life's rugged way
 With locks as white as snow."

From 70 to 80 Years old.

"INFIRMITY is great,
  At this advanced age,
And ceaseless grief and weakness leagued,
 Now vent their bitter. rage."

From 80 to 90 Years old.

"LIFE'S ' Vital Spark '—the soul,
  Is hovering on the verge
Of an eternal world above,
 And waiting to emerge."

From 90 *to* 100 *Years old.*

"THE sun is sinking fast
　　Behind the clouds of earth,
' Oh may it shine with brighter beams,
　Where light receiv'd her birth."

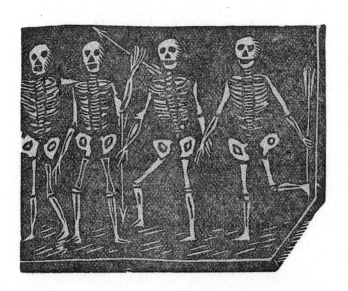

"Looking at these Christmas broad-sheets," says the writer of an article on street-ballads, in the "National Review," for October, 1861, "it would really seem as if the poorest of our brethren claimed their right to higher nourishment than common for their minds and souls, as well as for their bodies, at the time of year when all Christendom should rejoice. And this first impression is confirmed when we examine their contents. In all those which we have seen, the only piece familiar to us is that noble old carol 'While shepherds watched their flocks by night,' where the rest come from, we cannot even conjecture ; but in the whole of them there is not one which we should wish were not there. We have been unable to detect in them even a coarse expression ; and of the hateful narrowness and intolerance, the namby-pamhy, the meaningless cant, the undue familiarity with holy things, which makes us turn with a shudder from so many modern collections of hymns, there is simply nothing.

"Account for it how we will, there is the simple fact. Perhaps it may lead us to think somewhat differently of those whom we are in the habit of setting down in the mass as little better than heathens. We cannot conclude this article better than by giving an extract or two from these Christmas broad-sheets."

"The Saviour's Garland, a choice Collection of the most esteemed Carols," has the usual long narrative ballad, which begins:

"Come, all you faithful Christians
That dwell upon the earth,—
Come, celebrate the morning
Of our dear Saviour's birth:
This is the happy morning,—
This is the happy morn
Whereon, to save our ruined race,
The Son of God was born."

And after telling simply the well-known story, it ends:

"Now to him up ascended,
Then let your praises be,
That we His steps may follow,
And He our pattern be;
That when our lives are ended
We may hear His blessed call:
'Come, souls, receive the kingdom
Prepared for you all.'"

Another, " The Star of Bethlehem, a collection of esteemed Carols for the present year," opens its narrative thus :

> " Let all that are to mirth inclined
> Consider well and bear in mind
> What our good God for us has done,
> In sending His beloved Son.
>
> Let all our songs and praises be
> Unto His heavenly Majesty ;
> And evermore amongst our mirth
> Remember Christ our Saviour's birth.
>
> The twenty-fifth day of December
> We have great reason to remember ;
> In Bethlehem, upon that morn,
> There was a blessed Saviour born," &c.

One of the short pieces, by no means the best, we give whole:

" With one consent let all the earth
    The praise of God proclaim,
Who sent the Saviour, by whose birth
    To man salvation came.

All nations join and magnify
    The great and wondrous love
Of Him who left for us the sky,
    And all the joys above.

But vainly thus in hymns of praise
    We bear a joyful part,
If while our voices loud we raise,
    We lift not up our heart.

We, by a holy life alone,
    Our Saviour's laws fulfil ;
By those His glory is best shown
    Who best perform His will.

May we to all His words attend
    With humble, pious care ;
Then shall our praise to heaven ascend,
    And find acceptance there."

We do not suppose that the contents of these Christmas broad-sheets are supplied by the same persons who write the murder-ballads, or the attacks on crinoline. They may be borrowed from well-known hymn books for anything we know. But if they are borrowed, we must still think it much to the credit of the selectors, that, where they might have found so much that is objectionable and offensive, they should have chosen as they have done. We only hope that their successors, whoever they may be who will become the caterers for their audiences, will set nothing worse before them.

Christmas broad-sheets formed an important item in the office of the "Catnach Press," as the sale was enormous, and Catnach always looked forward for a large return of capital, and a "good clearance" immediately following the spurt for Guy Fawkes' speeches, in October of each year. But although the sale was very large, it only occupied one "short month." This enabled them to make Carols a stock job, so that when trade in the Ballad, Sensational, "Gallows," or any other line of business was dull, they used to fill up every spare hour in the working off or colouring them, so as to be ready to meet the extraordinary demand which was sure to be made at the fall of the year,

Like most of the old English customs, Christmas-carol singing is fast dying out. Old peripatetic stationers well remember the rich harvest they once obtained at Christmas times by carol selling. Now there are very few who care to invest more than a shilling or two at a time on the venture; whereas in times long past, all available capital was readily embarked in the highly-coloured and plain sheets of the birth of our Saviour, with the carol of "Christians, awake," or "The Seven Good Joys of Mary:"—

" The first good joy our Mary had,   ·
    It was the joy of one,
To see her own Son, Jesus,
    To suck at her breast-bone.
To suck at her breast-bone, God-man,
    And blessed may He be,
Both Father, Son, and Holy Ghost,
    To all eternity."

Now, whether carol singing has degenerated with carol
poetry, and consequently the sale of Christmas carols
diminished, is a question we need not enter upon; but
when we turn to the fine old carols of our forefathers, we
cannot help regretting that many of these are buried in the
records of the long past.

Here are a couple of verses of one, said to be the first
carol or drinking-song composed in England.   The original
is in Anglo-Norman French :—

"Lordlings, from a distant home,
To seek old Christmas are we come;
    Who loves our minstrelsy—
And here, unless report mis-say,
The greybeard dwells ; and on this day
Keeps yearly wassail, ever gay
    With festive mirth and glee.

ʇ   *   *   *   *

Lordlings, it is our host's command,
And Christmas joins him hand in hand,
    To drain the brimming bowl ;
And I 'll be foremost to obey,
Then pledge we, sirs, and drink away,
For Christmas revels here to day,
    And sways without control.

Now *wassail* to you all ! and merry may you be,
And foul that wight befall, who drinks not health to me."

One can well imagine the hearty feeling which would greet
a party of minstrels carolling out such a song as the above
in Christmas days of yore ; and then contrast the picture
with a *troupe* from St. Giles's or Whitechapel bawling out
" God Rest you Merry Gentlemen !"   The very thought of
the contrast sends a shudder through the whole human
system ; and no wonder the first were received with welcome
feasting, and the latter driven "with more kicks than half-
pence" from the doors.

In an old book of "Christmasse Carolles newely emprinted
at London, in the fletestrete at the sygne of the Sonne by
Wynkyn de Worde.   The yere of our Lorde, m.d.xxi.
Quarto."   Is a carol on " Bryngyng in the Bore's Head ":—

"The bore's head in hande bring I,
With garlandes gay and rosemary,
I pray you all synge merely,
    Qui estis in convivio.

The bore's head, I understande
Is the chiefe servyce in this lande,
Loke wherever it be fande,
    Servite cum Cantico.

Be gladdë, lordes, both more and lasse,
    For this hath ordayned our stewarde,
To chere you all this Christmasse,
    The bore's head with mustarde."

With certain alterations, this carol is still, or at least was
very recently, retained at Queen's College, Oxford, and
sung to a cathedral chant of the psalms.

It would occupy too much space to search into the origin
of Christmas carols. They are doubtless coeval with the
original celebrations of Christmas, first as a strictly Romish
sacred ceremony, and afterwards as one of joyous festivity.

Some idea of the present market value of Catnatch literature may be formed from the two items here following, taken from the catalogue of a second-hand bookseller:—

"BROADSIDES.—A Collection of 9 Curious Old Broadsides and Christmas Carols, printed at Seven Dials and elsewhere. On rough folio paper, *and illustrated with quaint and rude woodcuts, in their original condition, with rough edges, neatly mounted on white paper and bound in half Roxburghe.* Contents :—Letter written by Jesus Christ —6 Carols for Christmas—Messenger of Mortality, or Life and Death Contrasted—Massacre of the French King, by which the unfortunate Louis XVI. suffered on the scaffold, with a large woodcut of his exe- cution—£1 11s. 6d.

"OLD SONGS AND BALLADS.—A Collection of 35 most Curious Old Songs and Ballads, printed at Seven Dials, on rough old straw paper, and *illustrated with quaint and rude woodcuts or engravings.* In their original condition with rough edges, *very neatly mounted on fine paper, and bound in half Roxburghe—*£2 2s."

In the British Museum there is a large collection of popular ballads—upwards of 4,000—printed by Catnach and many other printers of street literature throughout the kingdom. The title in the Catalogue is " COLLECTION OF SONGS," 2 vols., folio ; the press mark 1,876. *d.* They were acquired in 1868, and contain the book-plate of R. F. Baker.

Catnach was now at the height of his fame as a printer of ballads, Christmas-pieces, carols, lotteries, execution papers, dying speeches, catchpennies, primers and battle- dores, and his stock of type and woodcuts had very con- siderably increased to meet his business demands. And it may be said that he was the very Napoleon of buyers at sales by auction of "printers' stock." On one occasion, when lot after lot was being knocked down to him, one of the " Littlejohn crew " of "knock-out-men" of the period, observed to the auctioneer, "Why, sir, Mr. Catnach is buying up all the lots." "Yes," replied the auctioneer, "And what's more, Mr. Catnach will pay for them and

clear away all his lots in the morning;" then adding, somewhat pointedly, "which is a thing I can't say of all parties
who attend my sales."

But although we are informed, *vivâ voce* of a contemporary,
that Jemmy Catnach was so large a buyer at sales by auction
of "printers' stock," we may, with some degree of safety,
come to the conclusion that he could have only bought such
lots that would be considered by other master printers as
worthless, and that it was the apparent cheapness that would
be the incentive for his buying up all the worn-out and
battered letter, for Jemmy was a man who hated "innowa-
tions" as he used to call improvements, and he, therefore,
had a great horror in laying out his money in new and improved manufactured type, because, as he observed, he kept
so many standing formes, and when certain sorts ran short
he was not particular, and would tell the boys to use anything which would make a good shift. For instance, he
never considered a compositor could be aground for a
lowercase "l" while he had a figure "1" or a cap. "I" to
fall back upon; by the same rule, the cap. "O" and
figure "0" were synonymous with "Jemmy;" the lowercase "p," "b," "d," and "q," would all do duty for each other
in *turn*, and if they could not always find Roman letters to
finish a word with, why the compositor knew very well that
the "reader" would not mark out Ita*lic*, nor wrong founts.

From a small beginning in the world, Catnach was soon
able to see his way clear to amass a fortune. He had now
established his reputation as a man of enterprise, and he
was very sensitive to maintain a sort of shabby-genteel
appearance. It was amusing, especially when over his
glass, to hear him describe the effect the "awfuls" had on
the public. The proprietor of any of our leading journals
could not have felt prouder than did Catnach, as he saw
drafted from his press the many thousands of varied productions. His staff was never a large one. At ordinary

times it seldom exceeded four. A gentleman, still a resident in Alnwick, informs us that he called upon Catnach in Monmouth Court in the latter part of 1830. "I found him," he says, "not only to be a humane, but also a very benevolent man, and when I parted with him he gave me several sums of money, some amounting to £5, which I was to give to several of Jemmy's old friends in *Canny Alnwick.*

The accession of Princess Victoria to the Throne of England at the death of her uncle, William IV., in June, 1837, and subsequently her Coronation at Westminster Abbey, in June of the next year, set poets of all degrees, from St. James's to St. Giles's, at work eulogising the "Maiden Queen," and the "Seven Bards of the Seven Dials," were not a whit behind their more fortunate and highly-favoured brother " paper stainers " in odes and panegyrics in all manner of length of stanzas and number of harmonic disposition of syllables. All the printers of street literature pressed forward, with Catnach well to the front, and street-ballad after street-ballad followed in rapid succession. The following is entitled—

MAY THE QUEEN LIVE FOR EVER!

WHEN William, the Sailor, belov'd by us all,
    Was brought to his moorings by death ;
Then ensigns of Britain were struck one and all,
    And a nation sigh'd o'er his last breath.
But he's gone ! and as Providence still to provide
    For the good of Old England is seen ;   .
An angel is sent o'er fates to preside ;
    And Victoria reigns Albion's Queen.
            Then huzza ! huzza !
        May the Queen live for ever !
        The glory, the pride of our land !

When Elizabeth guardian of Britain was hail'd,
 Not an enemy frown'd on our isle ;
But her genius and patriot spirit prevail'd
 Over threats that but call'd forth a smile ;
And our Sovereign, Victoria, will equally prove
 That no foe can that armour withstand,
Which is form'd and fenc'd round by her people's firm love,
 Who 'd defend her with heart and with hand.
Then huzza ! &c.

QUEEN VICTORIA,

The Royal Queen of Britain's isle,
Soon will make the people smile,
Her heart none can the least defile,
 Victoria, Queen of England.
Although she is of early years, .
She is possessed of tender cares,
To wipe away the orphan's tears,
 Now she is Queen of England.
Chorus—Of all the flowers in full bloom,
 Adorn'd with beauty and perfume,
 The fairest is the rose in June,
 Victoria, Queen of England.

From the LORD MAYOR : Sir John Cowan, Wax Chandler
 to Her Majesty.

*Wick*toria, all hail ! may thy bonny blue eye
 Ne'er with tears of dull sorrow be *dripping*.
May thy *stores* all increase, and thy country's *mould*
 For ever in riches be *dipping*.

May you never *wax* warm in debate, my dear Queen,
 Nor care a *rush-light* for the faction ;
For they who 'd oppose thy wise councils, I ween,
 Are *taper* in thought and in action.
The Town, Dec. 9, 1837.

SAILOR JACK AND QUEEN VICTORIA.

YOU 'VE heard of Sailor Jack, no doubt,
  Who found our good King William out.
To Windsor Castle, too, he 'd been,
A visiting the King and Queen.
                    Ri tooral, &c.

Now Jack, who 'd travell'd far away,
Returned to port the other day.
He turn'd his bacca o'er and o'er,
For he found the Sailor King no more.
                    Ri tooral, &c.

" Shiver my timbers ! here 's a breeze !
We 've got a woman now to please ;
So straight to London I must go,
To see who 's got the craft in tow."
                    Ri tooral, &c.

Then to the palace soon he came—
He 'd got no card, but sent his name.
"Go back," said they, "she won't see you!"
Said Jack—"No, damme, if I do!"

      Ri tooral, &c.

"Stand back, you lubbers! not see me—
The friend of his late Majesty?"
He floor'd them all, sprung o'er the stair,
And got where the Court assembled were.

      Ri tooral, &c.

They, in amazement, view'd the scene.
Says Jack, "I want to see the Queen!"
When, smiling, seated from afar,
Says she—"Well, here I am, old tar."

      Ri tooral, &c.

"All right!" says Jack, on hearing this,
"I 've come here just to warn you, miss,
Don't you by courtier sharks be led—
For, d'ye see, I likes your *Figure Head.*"

      Ri tooral, &c.

"Don't fear me, Jack—it's true, indeed,
But I 'm British-born, and take good heed;
And if against my peace they strike,
I 'll give 'em, Jack, what they won't like."

      Ri tooral, &c.

"Hurrah!" says Jack, "your Majesty—
Just like your noble family!
You knows what 's what, and I 'll repeat
What you have said to all the fleet."

      Ri tooral, &c.

"I like your manners," answered she,
"An admiral you soon shall be."
The lords in waiting there, said "No !"
The Queen—"Why, can't I make him so?"

Ri tooral, &c.

"You jealous swabs, what are you at?
I knows I am too old for that—
So one request instead I'll make,
Off pigtail you'll the duty take."

Ri tooral, &c.

The Queen, who quite enjoyed the fun,
Soon promised Jack it should be done,
Says he, "I've one thing more, and 'tis
To ax you how your mother is?"

Ri tooral, &c.

"Why, hark ye, Jack," the Queen replied,
"The old 'un's still her country's pride."
"She is—and if you'll view my ship,"
Says Jack, "for both I'll stand some flip."

Ri tooral, &c.

Then to his messmates soon he hied,
"I've seen her—it's all right," he cried,
"I'll prove to you she's wide awake—
She's a trim-built craft, and no mistake."

Ri tooral, &c.

They ordered grog to crown the scene,
And drank—"The Navy and the Queen !"
Says Jack—"Our toast shall ever be,
'God bless her gracious Majesty !'"

Ri tooral, &c.

Printed by J. Catnach, 2, Monmouth Court, 7 Dials.
Cards, Bills, &c., Printed on Low Terms.

VICTORIA THE QUEEN.

I 'LL drink "Success to Freedom's cause,"
   Where'er it meets my view,
I 'll drink—" The Church, the State, and Laws,"
   The " Tri-colour" and " Blue,"
I 'll drink—" Old England "—she 's our boast,
   What nation 's like her seen ;
But when I 'm ask'd, be mine the toast—
   " VICTORIA !—THE QUEEN ! "

I 'll drink—" The People," may each heart
   In unity be twin'd,
And Fortune's smiles bid care depart
   The bosom of mankind.
I 'll drink—" The Press "—itself a host,
   Since ever it has been ;
But when I 'm ask'd, be mine the toast—
   " VICTORIA—THE QUEEN ! "

I 'll drink—" The Ministers that guide
   The helm of our affairs,"
I 'll drink—" The Thistle, Scotland's pride"—
   " The Plough, and its repairs."
I 'll drink—" The Health of our good host,"
   The various healths between ;
But when I 'm ask'd, be mine the toast—
   " VICTORIA—THE QUEEN ! "

VICTORIA 'S THE TOAST.

FILL the glass, boys, trim it well,
   Then each true Briton to his post,
With heart and soul in every bowl,
   To pledge old England's boast.
Hurrah ! hurrah !! hurrah !!!
   For VICTORIA 's ! the Toast.

MR. FERGUSON AND QUEEN VICTORIA.

Tune—"*Jim Crow.*"

COME all you Britons, high and low,
    And banish grief and care,
There's a proclamation issued out,
    "You don't lodge here!"

CHORUS.

    They ran away without delay,
        To the Queen to banish fear,
        But she said, "My chaps, it's very fine,
        But you don't lodge here."

There was an Orange merchant,
    As you shall understand,
So she started him to Hanover,
    To cumber up the land.

The next, it was a soldier,
    And he wore scarlet clothes,
So the Queen took up the poker,
    And hit him on the nose.

The next was Bobby Orange Peel,
    She thought he was a flat,
In his right hand was a truncheon,
    And in his left a trap.

The next was Frank, from Wiltshire,
  She put him to the rout,
She wopp'd him all round Windsor Park,
  And cured him of the gout.

The next it was a leg of Lamb,
  He thought to make things right,
Says the Queen, " My lord, it's very fine,
  But you don't lodge here to-night."

The next man was from Bedford,
  A little chap that's never still,
" You don't lodge here to-night," says she,
  "Till you have burnt the Poor Law Bill."

There Springed a little man from Cambridge,
  Rice was his name, you know,
So she made him dance and wheel about,
  And jump Jim Crow.

The next was Mr. Broomstick,·
  With him she play'd a rig,
She wopp'd him with the Poor Law Bill,
  And choked him with his wig.

Then up came Dan O'Connell,
  Saying, " I'll befriend the people,"
With a great shillaly in his hand,
  As big as Salisbury steeple.

Old women, three hundred and ninety-five,
  To petition her did begin,
Crying, " Please your gracious Majesty,
  · Take the duty off the gin."

Says the Queen, " To do old women good,
  I'll strive with great delight ;
It's all right Mrs. Ferguson,
  But you don't lodge here to-night."

Then toddled up old Joey Hume,
   Saying "Sufferings I have had many,
The villains knock'd me all the way
   From Brentford to Kilkenny."

Says the Queen, "I am going to Brighton,
   So quiet let me be,
For if you come to trouble me,
   I'll drown you in the sea.

"And when I open Parliament,
   Then you'll find I'll do enough,
I'll take the duty off the tea,
   Tobacco, gin, and snuff.

"I'll make some alterations,
   I'll gain the people's right,
I will have a Radical Parliament,
   Or, they don't lodge here to-night

"I must tell both Whigs and Tories,
   Their tricks I do not fear,
Their sayings all are very fine,
   But they don't lodge here.

"About the Whigs and Tories,
   There has been a pretty bother,
I think I'll give the Devil one
   To run away with the other."

· Birt, Printer, 39, Great St. Andrew Street, Seven Dials.
Printing of every description done cheap.

The next ballad is on the Coronation of her Majesty Queen Victoria, 28th June, 1838.

IMPERIAL

A ROUSE ! arouse ! all Britain's isle,
    This day shall all the nation smile,
And blessings await on us the while,
    Nów she 's crown'd Queen of England.

Victoria, star of the Brunswick line,
    Long may she like a meteor shine,
And bless her subjects with a smile,
    Victoria, Queen of England.

Then let England, Ireland, Scotland join,
And bless thy name in every clime,
In unison we all combine
    To hail thee Queen of England.

CHORUS.

Then hail, Victoria ! Royal Maid,
For it never shall be said,
Thy subjects ever were afraid
To guard the Queen of England.

The Queen's marriage with Prince Albert, 10th February, 1840, produced another crop of ballads for halls, parlours, and the streets. The following punning one, from which we select three of the stanzas, was very popular :—

MANY suitors the Queen's had—of class, clime and creed,
But each failed to make an impression, indeed ;
For, for Albert of Coburg the rest off she packs—
Thus "giving the *bag* each " and keeping the "Saxe !"
A fortunate fellow is he, all must say,
And right well his *cards* he has managed to play ;
The *game* he has won, and no wonder, I ween,
When he play'd "speculation and turned up *the Queen*."

> Our cups to the dregs, &c., &c.

"Those will now wed who ne'er wedded before,
Those who always wedded will now wed no more ;"
Clerks will no time have to lunch, dine, or sup,
And parsons just now will begin to *look up!*
To churches, indeed, this will be a God-send,
Goldsmiths be selling off *rings without end ;*
For now, you'll not find from castle to cot
A *single* man living who *married* is not !

> Our cups to the dregs, &c., &c.

But hence with all quibbling, for now I'll have done,
Though all I have said has been purely in fun ;
May the Queen and the King shine like Venus and Mars,
And heaven *preserve* them without any *jars.*
Like *Danæ* of old, may we see it plain,
Till time is no more, these bright *sovereigns rain ;*
May pleasure and joy through their lives know no bounds
So let's give them a *toast,* and make it *three rounds.*

> Our cups to the dregs in a health let us drain,
> And wish them a long and a prosperous reign ;
> Like good loyal subjects in loud chorus sing,
> Victoria's wedding with Albert her King.

THE ROYAL NUPTIALS.

COME, blythe or sad, or with gin half mad,
 I 'll not detain you long, sirs,
While I relate some affairs of State
 I 've worked into a song, sirs.
'Twas t' other day, with my "fake away!"
 I in a crowd did mingle,
When a snob did sing, "God save the King,
 The Keveen vill not live single!"

CHORUS.

Prince Halbert 's come from Germanii
 For to change his sitivation;
Then may the House of Hanover last
 For many a generation.

Spoken—Well, do you know, Mrs. Tomkins, hour little Keveen, 'eaven
bless her seveet face !—has the nicest taste as iver I knowed.   Well, I
never, if she hasn't chuz for her husband the comeliest youth you 'd
meet in a 'ole day's walk.   Oh, crikey ! you only go take a sqevint at
his likeness in the picter-shops.   I 'm blest if 'e a'nt got the seveetest
lookin' heyes, the bussabelest lips, the roundest chin, and bloominest
cheeks, and the reapin' hookinest Romian nose I ever seed upon a man.
My heyes ! vot a race of little kings and keveens ve shall 'ave.   Oh,
bless the little 'arts of the dear little hangels ! I 'm told, Mrs. Knowall,
she 'ad hall the great dooks hand princes of Europe—'ad hour dear
little keveen, makin' love to her, and trying to come round her.   You
may well say that, Mrs. Tomkins ; there vos the Count of Stras*bug*—
the Prince of Vitten*bug*—the 'Al of 'Am*bug*—the Dook of 'Um*bug*,
and that dear fellow, Halbert of Co*bug*, but hout of them hall, she
fixes 'er heyes upon Halbert of Co*bug*, an' sings hout—"There 's the
man for my money !"

> In the council there the Keveen did swear,
>   "Prince Hal, my German cousin—
> Stop, Mel. [bourne] I pray—you 're much too grey,
>   I 'd choose out of fifty dozen.
> It don't suit me to *singular* be,
>   These cold nights lying alone, sirs.
> Pray, where 's my fan ?   In short, he 's the man
>   To share Victoria's throne, sirs !"

Spoken—Oh, tunder an' ages, Mrs. Thumpkin's ! may be St. Giles's
won't be alive the day the Queen's married ! I 'm tould the prince has
promised for to sind a shipful ,of barrins, tin ·cart loads of murphies,
*Gar*man sassages widout *ind*, an' a full kevotten, imparial mizzur—av
the pure craytur, to iviry mother's son av us, that we will all toast his
most gracious majesty's imparial highness's health, and may he live a
thousand years after he 's dead and buried ! and may they be surrounded
to all etarnity wid a score or more av her princes and princeasses, to
the honour and glory av the queen, long life to her !   And here 's good
luck till the pair av them, say I, Mrs. Flaherty—Dan O'Connell, Prince
Albert, and Erin-go-bragh ! Amin, sweet vargin !

> Och, may be all Ireland won't rejoice,
>   The day our Queen is married,

And many a lass will tipple the glass,
    And say—" Too long I 've tarried.".
The day she weds, faith ! nuptial beds
    Will swarm in exuberance glorious ;
The hint they will take, ànd loyally make
    Young Alberts and Victorias !

Spoken—Weel, I 'm oot-an'-oot puzzlit to mak' it oot hoo they maw-nages rile meeridges. I sispecks it 's a' done by protocolin, an' deeplo-mawtic ceercumveention. But this Albert 's a braw bairn, if he 's only lak till his lakness, an' if there 's jeest eneuch o' saxpences distreebited, I 'm sure I 'll be setisfied. I trist the rile boonty 'll fa' doon upon us a' in showers o' siller. I 've heerd tell—thof I dinna ken whather it 'll be geenuine or no—there 'll be a bullick roasted whole in Clare-mawrket, an' anither in Smathfiel', wi' lots o' pegs, an' ither powltry, an' a' the streets is to be paved that day wi' reedy-fried polonies. An' I 'm sure I dinna care to fash mysel' aboot it, if there 's onny planty o' sma' still Heeland whosky, an' a feestfu' o' saxpences for every puir bodie like mysel', that 's scant o' cash.

    Knees firmly built 'neath Highland kilt,
        That day shall charm each vrow, sir,
    Each canny Scot shall pay his shot
        By stripping off his trousers ;
    And shanks, I ween, shall then be seen,
        With loyalty to bristle—
    If whoskey bathes the shamrock green,
        I' faith 'twill drown the thistle.

Spoken—Py G—t ! it shall pring town a plessing on the brincibality. If a poy shall be porn, shall it not be christened Brince of Wales ? If a peautiful girl, shall she not be brincess of the same ? Leeks shall flourish on that tay, and be eaten with the pest of peef. May all their poys be like Harry of Monmouth, that pest of England's kings ! May they have blenty of prains, and pe pig poys too, and goot ! May the face of a Chartist be never more seen in Wales. If I caught one now, I 'd plow out his prains py a plunder puss. Leeks for ever ! and when a brince is porn, I peg and bray that none of us may want, either in mouse or pelly.

Long live the Queen, with joyous mien,
　On Albert smiling blandly,
Through England may their wedding day
　Be celebrated grandly.
That forehead fair—oh, may it ne'er
　Be wrinkled with a frown, sirs,
And may the pair have soon a heir
　To wear old England's crown, sirs.

Printed and Published by John *Duncombe* & Co.,
10, Middle Row, Holborn.

OLD ENGLAND'S ROYAL BRIDE.

Unfurl the banners to the breeze,
　And bid the cannon roar,
Let Britain, mistress of the seas,
　Her loudest plaudits pour ;
From shore to shore the shout shall run,
　Upborn upon the tide,
To welcome with the morrow's sun,
　Old England's Royal bride.

THE WISH.

May ever blessings o'er thee smile
Most happy Queen of England's Isle,
　When at the altar thou
To him who owns thy heart and hand,
Fair monarch of a favour'd land,
　Perform thy nuptial vow.

THE QUEEN AND PRINCE ALBERT GOD BLESS THEM.

W E'RE met round the board, and pleasures light up
The eye that day's cares have been dimming !
And friendship invites us to drink of the cup
In bumpers as bright as they're brimming !
A toast I'll propose, and man never rose
With feelings more glad to express 'em,
Then pass round the wine, I'll give you with mine,
" The Queen and Prince Albert, God bless 'em ! "

We're met round the board, and while each man grows warm,
And sinks party feeling and quarrel,
So bind round our crown, we'll a triple wreath form
Of vine-leaf, myrtle, and laurel !
May joy light their way to life's latest day,
A nation's smiles have to caress 'em—
Then pass round the wine, I'll give you with mine,
" The Queen and Prince Albert, God bless 'em ! "

We're met round the board, and let's hope as time runs,
Should foemen compel us to slaughter,
A sample of our age I'll show to our sons,
And she of sweet peace to our daughters !
The loving, the brave, quite ready to save,
Our birthright, our wrongs to redress 'em !
Then pass round the wine, I'll give you with mine,
" The Queen and Prince Albert, God bless 'em ! "

THE QUEEN OF THE NICE LITTLE ISLANDS.

Tune—The King of the Cannibal Islands.

OH, here I am, both fair and young,
    A maiden scarcely twenty-one,
And a German Prince before 'tis long,
    Will marry the Queen of England.
He is my fancy, I declare,
A buxom youth as you shall hear,
All hardships for him I will bear,
He is worth one hundred pounds a-year;
My German Prince I will nobly treat,
And feed him with good pudding and beef,
I will put new shoes upon his feet,
    When he marries the Queen of England.

CHORUS.

Don't ax 'em, tax 'em, merrily be,
Sausages and skillygolee,
Won't Prince Albert have a spree,
    When he marries the Queen of England?

The other day, with good intent,
Victoria went to Parliament,
Saying, "I have for Prince Albert sent,
    To marry the Queen of England."

And now, my Lords and Gentlemen,
Attend to what I say, and then
I am going to marry, you may depend,
And you must your assistance lend,
To grant my Albert young and fair
(Deny it you will not dare),
One hundred thousand pounds a-year.
    When he marries the Queen of England.
                  Don't ax 'em, &c.

My Albert he is handsome made,
A sausage-maker by his trade,
No one shall ever him degrade,
    When he marries the Queen of England.
I have sent my servants off, you see,
Unto the land of Germany,
To fetch Prince Albert home to me,
And when he comes I will happy be.
Soon as he lands on Britain's Isle,
I'll tog him out in such a style,
With a shirt and a four-and-ninepenny tile,
    When he marries the Queen of England.
                  Don't ax 'em, &c.

I will my loving Albert treat
With a handsome dandy coat so neat,
And a pair of breeches from Monmouth Street,
    When he marries the Queen of England.
If I don't get married I will kick up a row,
I am in a comical way, I vow;
O, dear, I feel—I can't tell how,
The marriage fit comes on me now;
It is Prince Albert I adore,
And I am rich if he is poor—
No one in the world but him, I'm sure,
    Shall marry the Queen of England.
                  Don't ax 'em, &c.

I can make my husband's family thrive,
I have thousands three hundred and ninety-five,
I will make my German Prince alive,
    When he marries the Queen of England.
Oh, when that he has married me,
In a very short time you sure will see,
If with John Bull he can agree,
He 'll be able to buy all Germany ;
My mother she has often said,
'Tis a burning shame to die a maid,
Prince Albert, I am not afraid,
    Will marry the Queen of England.
                    Don't ax 'em, &c.

I have found a husband to my mind,
And I will be a wile so kind—
You must for him some money find
    When he marries the Queen of England.
I have a little cash in store,
But none to spare, I 'm certain sure,
And when I 'm married I shall want some more,
As my intended is very poor.
If short of cash, then tax away,
Salt and pepper, curds and whey—
O, won't young Albert sport and play
    When he marries the Queen of England.

Printed by John Duncombe & Co., 10, Middle Row, Holborn.

VICTORIA'S WEDDING DAY.

Let the merry bells be ringing,
    Let the jocund music play—
Let the nation's voice be singing,
    'Tis Victoria's wedding day.

HERE'S A HEALTH TO VICTORIA THE PRIDE OF OUR LAND.

Air.—*"Here's a health bonnie Scotland to thee."*

HERE'S a health to Victoria, the Pride of our land,
    Bright hope-star of Albion's Isle ;
All will answer the summons, with heart and with hand,
    And welcome thy name with a smile.
Green Erin shall dash the sad tears from her brow,
    And shout from the lakes in her glee,
And Scotland come down from her Mountains of snow
    With a blessing, dear Princess, to thee.
    Here's a health to Victoria, the pride of our land,
    Bright hope-star of Albion's Isle,
    All will answer the summons, with heart and with hand,
    And welcome thy name with a smile.

To Prince Albert a health ! Who will not, with acclaim,
    Quaff a cup to the choice of the Queen?
The young children, too, be they worthy the name,
    And that worth "keep their memory green."
Let our wars e'er be just, and our navies ride free,
    With honour all over the wide main,
Here's the Press, pure, untaxed, as all knowledge should be—
    Come, with three cheers, pledge a bumper again.
                Here's a health to Victoria, &c.

'Tis our festive night now, and each heart wakens up
    To the joy-stirring sound of good cheer,
Be the healths we now quaff o'er brimming wine cup
    Like heart-vows, held fervent and dear.
Victoria, the Queen ! like a beautiful flower,
    May thy virtues so gently unclose,
May we hail thee, as now, in life's latest hour,
    Queen of hearts, and our own British Rose.
                Here's a health to Victoria, &c.

THE QUEEN'S MARRIAGE.

YOUNG and old pray attend,
        To these lines I have penn'd,
To amuse you I am going to try,
        About England's Queen,
        Who long single has been,
But a husband's now got in her eye.

        Prince Albert's the man
        Who will do what he can—
That he'll please her will quickly be seen ;
        He is now on his passage
        With a cargo of sausage,
As a dowry for our young Queen.

        Now on Saturday last,
        Being neither feast nor a fast,
The Queen called a Council, they say,
        When she enter'd the room,
        She gave a loud groan,
And very near fainted away.

Melbourne rose and looked blue,
Saying, "What's here to do,
That our Queen does so sigh and moan?"
"But," says Nosey, quite pat,
"I now smell a rat,
She is tired of laying alone."

Says the Queen "Duke, you are right,
I am dreaming each night
Of Prince Albert, of the famed German nation—
And as my cousins before,
Have had Germans by score,
I'll enjoy the same recreation.

"So John Bull he may laugh,
And the Radicals chaff,
For Prince Albert to me is a treat—
Him I'll have in a crack,
With no shirt to his back,
Or stockings or shoes to his feet.

"Now there's Portugal's Queen,
Who is just turned nineteen,
Two husbands she's had, it is known—
To his country's joy,
She has a beautiful boy—
A heir unto Portugal's throne.

"And just over the main,
There's the young Queen of Spain,
Who for playthings ought to be crying—
And though only ten,
She winks at the men,
And for a husband she soon will be trying.

"There's the boasted Queen Bess,
Must have been in the mess,
On a dark winter's night was afraid—
Though often she sighed
For Essex, her pride,
But I am told she died an old maid.

"I should lose the blessing of life,
If I am not made a wife—
My mother has oft said the same—
Soon you I will call,
Privy councillors all,
For to die an old maid is a shame."

Says a councillor grave,
"My leige you shall have
A husband, who will you be greeting—
So for Albert quick send,
And bid him attend,
We'll examine him this present meeting."

Then Albert came in
With a bow and a grin,
And speaking with humble submission—
"Good gentlemen all,
What for me you call?"
"Why, to give you a colonel's commission."

"If she has you for a mate,
What is your estate?
And what cash have you got in your banks?
Now if that is your best,
You are queerly drest,
And badly shod is your shanks."

"Oh, my togs have been tried,
  But I have family pride,
And a garden of crout and fine cabbages—
  And I can bring to you,
  And that annually, too,
A ship load of fine German sausages."

  Then the Queen she arose,
  Crying, " Don't speak of his clothes,
But give me a partner for life.
  My lords, don't dispute
  About his ragged suit,
For I wish to be made Albert's wife.

"Shall it ever be said
  England's Queen died an old maid ?
Let your council forbid it, I pray—
  To the nation's great joy,
  They shall have a fine boy,
Aye, in less than nine months and a day."

J. Catnach, Printer, 2, Monmouth Court, 7 Dials. The Largest Stock
    of Songs, Old and New, in the Trade.

The license enjoyed by the Court jesters, and, in some respects by the minstrels of old, is certainly enjoyed, undiminished, by the street-writers and singers of " Ballads on a Subject." They are aspiring satirists who, with a rare impartiality, lash all classes and creeds, as well as any individual. " One man, upon whose information I can rely," writes Mr. Henry Mayhew, " told me that he himself had ' worked,' in town and country, twenty-three different songs on the marriage of the Queen. They all ' sold,' but the most profitable was one commencing :—

> " ' Here I am in rags,
>   From the land of all dirt,
>   To marry England's Queen,
>   And my name it is Prince Albert.'

' And what's more, sir,' continued the ballad-singer, ' not long after the honeymoon a duchess drove up in her carriage to the printers, and bought all the songs in honour of Victoria's wedding, and gave a sovereign for them, and wouldn't take the change, and didn't the printer, like an honest man, when he 'd stopped the price of the papers, hand to us chaps the balance to drink, and *didn't* we drink it ! There can't be a mistake about that.' "

The Queen was now married to the husband of her choice. " It is that," said Lord Melbourne to her, " which makes your Majesty's marriage so popular, as they know it is, not for State reasons." A few months after the wedding-day, the Prince wrote to an old college associate—" I am very happy and contented." After the wedding, the young couple stayed for four days at Windsor, reading, riding, walking together, and giving small dinner parties in the evening. They then returned to Buckingham Palace, where a large crowd had collected to welcome them, and fairly commenced the common duties of their married life. At first it would appear that jealousies, in quarters which need not be specified, prevented the Prince taking his proper position as the head of his home and household. He wrote to his friend, Prince Löwenstein, in May, 1840—" I am only the husband, not the master of the house." But the common sense of the Queen, and the dignity of the Prince, soon set this matter to rights. When urged that she, as being Sovereign, must be the head of the house, she quietly rejoined that she had sworn to obey, as well as love and honour her husband, and that she was determined to keep all her bridal troth. She communicated all foreign despatches to him, and frequently he made annotations on them, which were communicated to the Minister whose department they affected. ' He had often the satisfaction of discovering that the Minister, though he might say nothing on the subject, nevertheless acted upon his suggestions. His correspondence to Germany soon bore a very different tone and complexion. To use his own words, and slightly expand them, he " endeavoured to be of as much use to Victoria as possible." The Queen now, having received the approval of the Duke of Wellington, whom she consulted as a confidential friend, for the first time put her husband in his proper place, by giving him, by Royal Letters Patent, to which Parliamentary sanction is not required, rank and precedence next to herself, except in Parliament and the Privy Council.

Frequent levées, and " dinners followed by little dances," formed the chief amusements of the young couple in the earliest stage of their married life. They went much, too, to the play, both having an especial relish for and admiration of Shakespeare. The Queen, although now a married woman, by no means neglected useful or solacing and refining studies. She took singing lessons from Lablache, and frequently sang and played with the Prince, sometimes using the piano, sometimes the organ as accompaniment. They went to Claremont, the Queen's favourite youthful haunt, to celebrate her birthday, and continued to do so, even after the purchase of Osborne. Both Queen and Prince were extremely glad to get away from the smoke and grime of London ; in fact, these constituted a peculiar source of physical oppression to both, and they were always glad to retire to the rural quiet and seclusion of Claremont.

The first alarming incident of the Queen's wedded life occurred on the 10th of June, 1840. In her first early days of maiden Queenhood, she had been annoyed by madmen wanting to marry her. On more than one occasion her saddle horse was attempted to be stopped in the Park by one of such maniacs, as she was attended by an equerry; and in two or three instances similar attempts were made by innocent lunatics to force their way into Windsor Castle, in each case armed with nothing more deadly than a proposal of marriage :—notably was the " Boy Jones," in respect to whom there was a street-saying much in vogue, of "That Boy Jones again," which was used to cover or account for all petty delinquencies in public or domestic life.

The " Boy Jones," like a Lord Byron before him, "awoke one morning and found himself famous," and rather liked it, for all England rang with his name and fame ; he was written up—and down—by ballad-mongers, newspaper and magazine contributors ; while from the cheap and nasty presses of E. Lloyd, 62, Broad Street, Bloomsbury —a fellow who published pirated editions of Charles Dickens's early works, in penny numbers, as " Penny Pickwick," by " Bos," " Oliver Twiss," by " Bos," &c., &c. ; Cleave, Shoe Lane ; Hetherington and Marks, of Long Lane. There was issued a vast quantity of squibs and cartoons for street sale of " Her Majesty's Chimney Sweep," " The Royal *Sooter*," " The Buckingham Palace Hero," " The Royal Flue Faker," &c.

THE BOY THAT WAS FOUND IN THE PALACE.

Tune—" The Very Identical Flute."

YOU have heard of the chap that they found t'other day
    In Buckingham Palace, I tell you the truth—
'Twas in the next chamber to where the Queen lay,
    They found me, this very identical youth.
At first, they all thought I had come there to plunder,
    But I had no notion of stealing, not I—
Pages, nurses, and officers, pulled me from under
    The very identical couch where she lay.
                                    Ri tol, &c.

    *   *   *   *   *   *

Prince Albert, you all know, is in a decline, sirs,
    And the young Queen must look out again, it is clear—
So I wanted to ask her if she would be mine, sirs,
    I should like the identical thousands a-year.
Now what do you think, just to shorten my tail, sirs,
    They called me a madman, and what is worse still,
For my second appearance refused to take bail,
    But sent me to tread the identical mill.
                                    Ri tol, &c.

J. Catnach, Printer, 2 & 3, Monmouth Court, 7 Dials, where all sorts
    of Ballads are continually on sale.

But what we are about to narrate was a much more serious matter. A youth named Edward Oxford, some seventeen or eighteen years of age, either a fool or a madman, fired two pistol-shots at her, as she and her husband were driving in a phæton up Constitution Hill. He was at once arrested, and it being impossible to assign any conceivable cause for the act, he was declared insane, and doomed to incarceration for life. Neither the Queen nor the Prince were injured, and both showed the utmost self-possession.

Perhaps the best proof of her bravery on the occasion of this outrage, as it was an unquestionable proof of her tenderness of heart, was the fact that within a minute or two after the shot of Oxford had been fired, she had the horses' heads turned towards her mother's house, that her mother should see her sound and uninjured, ere an exaggerated or indiscreetly communicated report of the occurrence could reach her. Immediately after, she drove to Hyde Park, whither she had been proceeding before the outrage occurred, to take her usual drive before dinner. An immense concourse of persons of all ranks and both sexes had assembled, and the enthusiasm of her reception almost overpowered her. Prince Albert's face, alternately pale and flushed, betrayed the strength of his emotions. They returned to Buckingham Palace attended by a most magnificent escort of the rank and beauty of London, on horseback and in carriages. A great crowd of a humbler sort was at the Palace gates to greet her, and it was said that she did not lose her composure until a flood of tears relieved her pent-up excitement in her own chamber. "God save the Queen" was demanded at all the theatres in the evening, and in the immediately succeeding days the Queen received, seated on her throne, loyal and con-gratulatory addresses from the Peers in their robes, and wearing all their decorations; from the Commons, from the

City Corporation, and many other public bodies, and caused a profound sensation among all classes of society in the British dominions, and many street papers were published on the subject

O GOD, PRESERVE THE QUEEN.

O GOD ! whose mighty power alone
   Can ward the traitor's blow—
To thee a nation's praise is given,
   To Thee the myriads bow.
We bless thee ; and our prayer shall be,
   As Britons' prayers have been.
" From secret foe and dastard blow,
   O God, preserve the Queen !"

Without thy aid our love is vain ;
   Thy providence we crave—
One reckless hand may take the life,
   Which millions cannot save.
When crime or folly fain would strike,
   Do thou still intervene, .
And for our country's sake, we pray,
   O God, preserve the Queen !

Guard her domestic peace—protect
   The partner of her love ;
And may their coming years be crowned
   With blessings from above.
Give them long life, and health and strength—
   True hearts and minds serene—
His prayer and ours alike shall be,
   O God, preserve the Queen !

ADDITIONAL VERSE TO THE NATIONAL ANTHEM.

O, GRANT our earnest prayer,
Smile on the Royal pair,
  Bless Prince and Queen !
May Albert's name be dear
To every Briton's ear,
The peasant and the peer—
  God save the Queen.

GOD SAVED THE QUEEN.

G OD saved the Queen ! the young and good
      Sheds love around her bright and far.
Joy—joy ! that no dark stain of blood
  Hath dimm'd her star—
That crime grew palsied by a throne,
  Where virtue's spirit sits serene,
And while heav'n watch'd above its own,
  God saved the Queen !

God saved the Queen ! the happy light
  Of marriage bliss was on her brow,
Still in her heart the young delight
  Dwells sweetly now.
The transport of a people's joy
  At its unfading, wild is seen ;
For blessed in its un-alloy—
  God saved the Queen !

God saved the Queen ! all thoughts apart,
  The crowning joy fills every mind !
She sits within the nation's heart,
  An Angel shrined !
There, very happiness to lure,
  To light it yet with glory's sheen—
To glad the rich, to bless the poor—.
  God saved the Queen !

A Funny DIALOGUE*

BETWEEN A  MACKEREL

FAT BUTCHER

In Newport Mar-

And A

ket Yésterday.

BUTCHER.—Well, Mr. Mackerel, pray let me ask you how you come to show your impudent face among those who don't want to see you or any of your crew?

MACKEREL.—That my company is not agreeable to many such as you I very well know ; but here I am, and will keep my place in spite of you. Don't think to frighten me with your lofty looks, Mr. Green. You are an enemy to the poor, I am their true friend, and I will be in spite of you.

BUTCHER.—I will soon see the end of you and your vain boasting. What's the poor to me?

MACKEREL.—I and thousands of my brethren are come to town for the sole good of the industrious poor. We will soon pull down your high prices, your pride and consequence, and Melt your fat off your overgrown Carcass. I am their sworn friend, and although you are biting off your tongue with vexation, yet I am determined they shall have a cheap Meal—good, sweet, and wholesome—put that in your pipe and smoke it.

BUTCHER.—Aye, aye. You are a sancy set, confound you altogether. Oddzbubs, I wish the Devil had the whole of your disagreeable tribe.

MACKEREL.—I would advise you, Mr. Green, not to show your teeth when you can't bite. Millions of my friends are on their way to town to make the poor rejoice. We have had a fine seed time, everything looks promising. Meat must and will come down. The poor will sing for joy, and you may go hang yourself in your garters.

Catnach, Printer, 2, Monmouth Court.
Cards, Bills, &c., Printed on Low Terms.

* See " Hugo's Bewick Collector," Supplement, p. 219.

There was a personage styled " Dando," who acquired a very unenviable name and fame as the " Oyster-Eater ;" his *modus operandi* was to visit hotels and eating-houses, in general, but oyster shops or stalls, in particular, when, after he had eaten to repletion, or had swallowed the last oyster to be had in the establishment, he would tell the proprietor that he might whistle for his money, and that his name was " Dando." " What ! Dando, the oyster-eater ?" would be the reply. " Yes ; I'm Dando, the oyster-eater ; I've no money, but you may kick me, bite me, or punch me, if you like ; or, if you prefer the bother and anxiety of attending the police-court, you can give me into custody." Frequently it happened that his victims were very poor shop, or stall-keepers, and he would, in the most remorseless manner possible, devour the whole of their stock-in-trade. He was several times sent to gaol, but at the expiration of his term of imprisonment, he returned to the town with increased appetite, and immediately commenced his victimising propensities, and so continued until the day of his death, which took place in Clerkenwell prison. He furnished the groundwork for a time serving farce, by Stirling, entitled, " *Dandolo ; or, the last of the Doges,*" produced in 1838, at the New City, *alias* Norton Folgate Theatre, under the management of Mr. Cockerton, in which that merry son of *Momus*, Sam Vale, played the gormandizing oyster-eater with great gusto. Following is one of the very many street-ballads published at the time ; while " Dando astonishing the Natives," formed the subject for several of the comic caricatures of the penny plain and two-pence coloured school, then so much in vogue, and published for the trade by the houses of Fairburn, Hodgson, Skelt, Parks, and Marks.

THE LIFE AND DEATH OF DANDO,
The celebrated Oyster Glutton.

T H E *March of Intellect* announces
    That some live on the *march of bounces :*
So, as *bouncing* now is quite the thing,
A *bounceable* song I 'll try to sing.
Some *bounce about,* with kicks and blows,
And some get *punch'd* upon the *nose ;*
But that 's here nor there—there once did dwell
Dando, the *bouncing* seedy swell—
    So shickery, trickery, rum tum bawl,
    Sponging and lounging on victims all ;
    Death collar'd Dan in Clerkenwell—
    Dando, the *bouncing* seedy swell.

Dando, he had *Long-Acre* limbs,
And many *victimizing* whims.
An old white hat slouch'd over his eyes,
And a *flounder mouth* for *mutton pies.*
His coat was rusty, hole-y and fat,
His hair was like an old door-mat ;
He stepp'd out lofty in Pell Mell—
Dando, the bouncing seedy swell.
    So shickery, &c.

His Sunday dress went *up the spout ;*
His shoes let water in and out ;
His stockings, too, seem'd in despair—
Like *port-holes,* they *let in fresh air.*
For prisons he 'd not care a pin,
He was *no sooner out* than *in,*
For something good he 'd always smell—
Dando, the bouncing seedy swell.
    So shickery, &c.

One day he walk'd up to an oyster stall,
To *punish the natives,* large and small ;
Just *thirty dozen* he managed to bite,
With *ten penny loaves*—what an appetite !
But when he had done, without saying good day,
He *bolted* off, *scot free,* away ;
He *savag'd the oysters,* and left the shell—
Dando, the bouncing seedy swell.
    So shickery, &c.

He once went into a tavern so sly :
Two ducks he devour'd, and six plates of pie,
A large leg of mutton, and part of a trout,
Two bottles of sherry, and then he walked out ;
But when he was stopp'd, says he, with a groan,
"You cannot, you know, get blood from a stone."
To *live on the bounce* why he did very well—
Dando, the bouncing seedy swell.
           So shickery, &c.

Dando, he 's gone ; alas ! poor Dan !
He 'll go no more in the *Police-van ;*
But Dando's name fills some with dread—
I think he was *born in an oyster bed.*
Dando, he 's gone to *feed the worms,*
With him they 'll live on very good terms.
So *Dando oysters* the folks can sell—
Dando, the bouncing seedy swell.
           So shickery, &c.

J. Catnach, Printer, 2 and 3, Monmouth Court, 7 Dials.

The whole metropolis of London, on the 26th of May, 1838, was startled and horrified by the discovery of the murdered body of Eliza Grimwood, a remarkably handsome young woman, one of the gay belles of London of that period. She was found, terribly mutilated, lying on the floor in a house of ill-fame at No. 12, Wellington Terrace, Waterloo Road, near to a district then largely inhabited by that unfortunate class. At the inquest, held at the York Tavern, before Mr. Carter, it was elicited that the unfortunate woman, who was about twenty-five years of age, lived with George Hubbard, a bricklayer, and a married man. He had not, however, lived with his wife for twelve years, and six years since he had seen her. He had cohabited with the deceased for ten years, ever since she was about fifteen, and she was his first cousin and knew that he was a married man. The deceased went out of an evening to the various theatres for the purpose of forming the acquaintance of gentlemen to bring home and pass the night with her, and by this means she not only maintained herself, but also assisted her paramour, who used to sleep in an upper room.

Mary Fisher deposed that she was servant at the house in question, and in the service of William Hubbard, who kept the house. She had lived there two years. Her master came home on Friday night, about six o'clock, and after having had his supper retired to bed, between eight and nine o'clock, and she did not see him again till the next morning. The deceased went out after Hubbard had gone to bed, and she returned home at about one in the morning with a strange man. She opened the door for them, and the strange man, who was behind the deceased on entering, shut it after him, so that witness had not an opportunity of seeing distinctly who he was. Deceased came down into the kitchen and then told her she could go to bed. She did so, and did not hear any noise during the night. In the morning Hubbard came down and awoke her, and told her of the murder. Hubbard and the deceased, on the whole, lived on very good terms, and did not quarrel very often. She had no reason to believe that her master was concerned in the murder of the deceased. Before she opened the street door to let her mistress in, when she last entered the house, she heard a cab come up to the door, and therefore believed that she came home in a cab.

Inspector Field, of the L Division, deposed that he had made every search for the instrument with which the murder was committed, but had failed to find it. From inquiries he had made, he had ascertained that the deceased, on the Friday night, had been to the Strand Theatre, and that on leaving a gentleman pulled her arm, and they both got into a cab together.

The Superintendent of the Police asked the Coroner whether Hubbard ought to be detained in custody.

The Coroner replied that the police might take what course they thought proper. He did not think there was evidence enough to warrant his detention, and he should therefore not make any order. The inquiry was then adjourned.

After several adjournments, the jury said they could not believe most of the witnesses that had been brought forth by the police.

The Coroner then summed up the evidence. He said he considered that Hubbard had maintained the statement throughout, and that statement had been borne out by the other inmates of the house. The only point which had raised suspicion in his mind at first was the fact that it was once thought the chamber utensil had been removed, but it had just transpired that one of the policemen saw it there when he entered the room, so that point was set at rest. The theory, which was to him the most clear, was, that as the deceased was murdered in her own room, and that as she had all her clothes on but her gown, it showed that the

Z 2

monster who accompanied her home did not intend to stay long. He then probably intended to leave the house without paying her, and that she then endeavoured to prevent him. He then turned round and struck her with something at the back of the neck, which rendered her senseless, and finally finished by cutting her throat. That the monster wore a cloak had been proved. It had also been shown that he had just such a weapon as would have produced the injuries found upon her. In reference to there being no blood found on the street-door handle, he thought it was very probable that the assassin wiped his hands on the napkin found under deceased's head. Or he might have put on gloves to let himself out, or have laid hold of the door-handle with his cloak. He thought the fact of the candlestick being found on the door-mat strengthened his theory, and showed that he had taken it there to let himself out with.

The jury then retired, and after a long deliberation returned with a verdict: "That, having examined the evidence adduced in the case, we are satisfied that no charge has been establisedh against any person or persons : and under such circumstances we return a verdict of wilful murder against some person or persons unknown."

The number of letters sent anonymously by persons to the police and coroners is one of the most remarkable features of the public excitement in murder cases. Some of them are written with the evident honest intention of making valuable suggestions for the detection of criminals. A large portion are evidently written by monomaniacs, who evidently fancy they have been in some way connected with the murder. Many of these persons are frequently traced out and found to be really of unsound mind, and ought properly to be in a lunatic asylum. Other letters are written for sheer mischief, and come from that senseless, half-educated class of idle louts who cannot see that, however good a lively joke may be in its proper place, it is exceedingly ill-mannered and mischievous, and calculated to frustrate the ends of justice when so great a crime has been committed as that of taking the life of an unfortunate fellow-being. The Coroner ordered all the letters to be retained, and Hubbard to be liberated.

So great was the excitement in the Waterloo Road and all over the metropolis, that a public meeting was afterwards held, at which it was resolved to offer a reward of fifty pounds for the apprehension of the murderer, and also to memorialise the Secretary of State to offer a still further sum.

On the Sunday following, a letter, signed " John Waters Cavendish, Goswell Street," was received by the Coroner at his house, in which the writer stated "that he was the person who accompanied Eliza Grimwood home, and that whilst in her room, Hubbard came downstairs and assaulted them both, and that a general scuffle ensued, and that he then took up the candlestick and let himself out. They would find a pair of black gloves in the place, which he left behind."

In consequence of this, and also because Hubbard left his house, and first went to sleep at his mother's, and then at his sister's, Inspector Field thought he had better make sure of his not escaping, and so took him into custody.

Finally, the inquiry ended without any satisfactory results, and Hubbard was discharged.

The furniture and effects of the deceased were afterwards sold by auction. Her brother took possession of the things, and instructed the auctioneer. Hubbard threatened him with an action if he dared to sell them. The auctioneer, however, proceeded. The furniture realised £64; her watch and jewellery £80; she had saved £320 in the savings' bank, and insured her life for £300 in the Norwich Union Life Assurance Office.

In the meantime Eliza Grimwood's brother, who administered to the property, met with an accident, by which he broke three of his ribs.   He had to lay by in hospital, but while there Hubbard obtained admission to his bed-side, and behaved so violently that an appeal had to be made to the magistrates to request the authorities of the hospital not to admit him.

The Coroner, however, and magistrates having expressed an opinion that there was no evidence against him, he resumed his place in society again.

The " Forfarshire " steamer, on its passage from Hull to Dundee, on September 6th, 1838, was wrecked in a violent gale, and thirty-eight persons out of fifty-three perished. The Outer Fern Isle Lighthouse-keeper, James, and his heroic daughter

GRACE DARLING,

ventured out in a coble on the overwhelming billows to save her fellow-creatures' lives, or perish in the courageous effort. The circumstance caused many street-ballads to be written and sold, not only in the metropolis but in every town, nook, and cranny of Great Britain.

In Memoriam

OF

GRACE DARLING,

Who departed this life,

OCTOBER 20, 1842,

AGED 27 YEARS.

On the afternoon of the 21st of November, the country was gladdened by the birth of the Queen's first-born, the Princess Royal, now Crown Princess of Prussia. The event occurred considerably before the period anticpated by the Queen's medical and other attendants, and preparations had to be made in a hurry; nevertheless, the news was received with joy by the nation, and removed many doubts that had been freely entertained by the gossips and *sage-femme* of the period, and a ballad states that:—

O F course you've heard the welcome news,
Or you must be a gaby,
That England's glorious Queen has got
At last a little baby?
A boy we wanted—'tis a girl!
Thus all our hopes that were
To have an *heir unto the Throne,*
Are all *thrown to the air.*

How could folks think she'd have a boy?
To me it seemed all fun;
For in a dark November *fog*
We seldom have a *sun!*

Yet after all I 'm wrong myself
  To reason so, perhaps,
For we all know that winter is
  The time for getting *chaps*.

*   *   *   *   *

John Bull must handsomely come down
  With something every year,
And he may truly to the child
  Say, " You 're *a little dear.*"
Sad thoughts will fill his breast whene'er
  He hears the infant rave,   .
Because when hearing a *wight squall*
  It brings *a notion grave !*

Howe'er, let 's give the Princess joy,
  Though now 's her happiest lot ;
For sorrow tends a *palace* more
  Than e'er it does a *cot !*
If in some years a son appears,
  Her claim to rule were vain,
And being near the *Court* she 'll have
  To *stand out of the* REIGN !

THE PRINCESS OF OLD ENGLAND.

HAIL, royal Princess ! welcome be,   ·
  Victoria's first born, child of the free !
May heaven's blessing on thee pour
The manifold gifts it has in store—
May British subjects on thee smile,
Sweet innocent of England's isle.

May thy fame re-echo far and wide,
Child of Britain, England's pride—
And long life may she see—
May it be one of felicity. ʼ
              May British, &c.

And whilst enjoying every pleasure,
May she become Old England's treasure,
Victoria's first-born then shall be,
The child of love and liberty,
May British subjects on thee smile,
Hail, Princess of Old England's isle.

A QUEEN'S WANTS AT CHILD BIRTH;

Or, What a Bother in the Palace.

London, November 21st, 1840.

COME, all good people, list to me,
   I will tell you of a jovial spree,
News from London has come down,
That a young Princess has come to town.

> Chorus—What a bother in the palace,
>   In the month of November,
>   Such a bother in the palace,
>   You never did see.

Now all those things, as I heard say,
The Queen did want upon that day,
Night-caps, gowns, frocks, and frills,
And old John Bull must pay the bills.

*   *   *   *   *

There was such work, I do suppose,
For to put on the baby's clothes.
Oh, nurse, look here, how very silly,
You 've run a pin in the little girl's belly.

God bless the Queen, we wish her joy,
And may the next one be a boy,
And if they both should crave for more,
Let 's hope they will have half a score.

THE OWDHAM CHAP'S VISIT TO TH' QUEEN.

IT happen'd t' other Monday morn, while seated at my
    loom, sirs,
Pickin' th' ends fro' caut o' th' yorn, caur Nan pop'd into
    th' room, sirs.
Hoo shouted eaut, aw tell thee, Dick, aw think thou 'rt actin'
    shabby,
So off to Lunnon cut thy stick, and look at th' royal babby.

Everything wur fun an' glee, they laugh'd at o aw tow'd em,
An' ax'd if th' folk wur o like me, ut happen'd t' come
    fro' Owdham.

Then off aw goes an' never stops, till into th' palace handy,
Th' child wur sucking lollypops, plums, and sugarcandy ;
An 'little Vic. i' th' nook aw spied, a monkey on her lap, mon,
An' Albert sittin' by her side, a mixin' gin an' pap, mon.
                Everything wur, &c.

When Albert seed me, up he jumps, an' reet to me did
    waddle,
An' little Vicky sprung her pumps wi' shakin' o' my daddle ;
They ax'd me to tak' a glass o' wine, for pleasure up it waxes,
O yes, says aw, six, eight, or nine, it o' comes eaut o' th'
    taxes.
                Everything wur, &c.

They took the Prince of Wales up soon, an' gan it me to
    daudle,
Then Albert fotch'd a silver spoon, an' ax'd me to taste at
    t' caudle.
Ecod, says aw, that 's good, awd buck, it's taste aws ne'er
    forget, mon,
An' if my owd mother 'd gan sich suck, 'cod aw 'd been
    suckin' yet, mon.
                Everything wur, &c.

They ax'd me heau aw liked their son, an' prais'd both th'
nose an' eyes on 't,
Aw towd 'em though 't were only fun, 't wur big enough for
th' size on 't.
Says aw your Queenship makes a stir (hoo shapes none like
a dunce, mon,
But if eaur Nan lived as well as her hoo'd breed 'em two
at wonce, mon).

> Everything wur, &c.

They said they'd send their son to school as soon as he
could walk, mon,
And then for fear he'd be a foo', they'd larn him th'
Owdham talk, mon.
·Says aw there's summut else as. well, there's nout loik
· drainin th' whole pit,
For fear he'll ha' for t' keep hissell, aw 'd larn him work
i' th' coal pit.

> Everything wur, &c.

Then up' o' th' slopes we hod a walk, to give our joints
relief, sirs,
And then we sat us deun to talk 'beaut politics and beef,
sirs, ·
Aw towd 'em th' corn laws wur but froth, an' th' taxes must
o drop, mon,
That when eaur Nan wur makin' broath, some fat might get
to th' top, mon.

> Everything wur, &c.

So neau my tale is at an end, but nowt but truth aw tells,
sirs,
If ever we want the times to mend, we'll ha' for t' do 't eaur
sells, sirs.
So neau yo seen aw've towd my sprees, and sure as aw am
wick, mon,
If my owd wife and Albert dees, aw'll try for t' wed wi Vic.,
mon.

J. Harkness, Printer, 121, Church Street, Preston.

QUEEN VICTORIA'S BABY !

Tune—"Steam Arm."

OH, yes, I'll sing with all my heart,
    And tell you a very singular start
That lately occurred at Buckingham Palace,
That scene of waste, confusion, and malice,
    About the baby, the dear little baby,—
        Queen Victoria's baby !

About one in the morn, as I heard say,
The Queen she felt in a curious way—
She woke her husband, who said with great sorrow,
" Oh ! can't you, my love, put it off till to-morrow ?
    For I am so sleepy, and I don't want a baby !"
        " Ah !" says she, " but I will have a baby !"

So her husband got up and summoned them all,
The lords and the ladies, the short, fat, and tall ;
And they sent for the doctor, Sir Christopher Small,
Who said very soon they would hear the child squall,
    For he could feel the baby—the dear little baby—
        Queen Victoria's baby !

Then there was great bustle, confusion, and hurry,
The Queen was in labour—the Prince in a flurry ;
When the Princess was born the nurse loud did shout—
" Little girl, does your mother know you are out ?"
        Oh, oh ! little baby, &c.

Prince Albert, who before was considered a dawdle,
Gave the baby some pap—the mother some caudle.
With terror the ladies did all nearly drop
When a large German sausage for a lollypop
    He gave to the baby, the dear little baby—
        Queen Victoria's baby !

Now the Queen has recovered, and Albert 's the nurse,
He puts on the child's napkins, and don't care one curse ;
And ladies and gentlemen, your smiles give to me,
'Twas to gain your applause I sung, d' ye see,
   About the Queen's baby, the duck of a baby—
      Queen Victoria's baby !

Printed by J. Catnach, 2 & 3, Monmouth Court, 7 Dials.
Cards & Bills, Printed.   The Trade supplied Cheap.

Two days after the Princess was born, Mr. Selwyn, a gentleman with whom Prince Albert was reading English law and constitutional history, came to give his pupil his accustomed lesson.   The Prince said to him, "I fear I cannot read any law to-day, there are so many coming constantly to congratulate ; but you will like to see the little Princess."   He took his tutor into the nursery, as he found that the child was asleep.   Taking her hand he said, " The next time we read, it must be on the rights and duties of a Princess Royal."

On the 9th of November—Lord Mayor's Day—1841, the following bulletin, placed outside Buckingham Palace announced that " The Queen was safely delivered of a Prince this morning at 48 minutes past 10 o'clock. Her Majesty and the infant Prince are perfectly well."

A " London Gazette" extraordinary, which appeared on Tuesday evening, ran as follows :

Buckingham Palace, Nov. 9th.

This morning, at twelve minutes before eleven o'clock, the Queen was happily delivered of a Prince—His Royal Highness Prince Albert. Her Royal Highness the Duchess of Kent, several Lords of Her Majesty's Most Honourable Privy Council, and the Ladies of Her Majesty's Bedchamber, being present.

This great and important news was immediately made known to the town by the firing of the Tower and Park guns ; and the Privy Council being assembled as soon as possible thereupon, at the Council Chamber, Whitehall, it was ordered that a Form of Thanksgiving be prepared by His Grace the Archbishop of Canterbury, to be used in all churches and chapels throughout England and Wales and the town of Berwick-upon-Tweed, on Sunday, the 14th of November, or the Sunday after the respective ministers shall receive the same.

Her Majesty and the infant Prince are, God be praised, both doing well.

The joy of the nation at the succession to the Crown in the progeny of the Queen and Prince Albert being thus secured, was excessive. Upon the announcement of the happy accouchement, the nobility and gentry crowded to the Palace, to tender their dutiful inquiries as to the Sovereign's convalescence. Amongst others, came the Lord Mayor and civic dignitaries in great state. They felt peculiarly proud that the Prince should have been born on Lord Mayor's day—in fact, just at the very moment when the time-honoured procession was starting from the City for Westminster. In memory of the happy coincidence, the Lord Mayor of the year, Mr. Pirie, was created Sir John Pirie, Baronet. On the 4th of December, the Queen created her son, by Letters Patent, Prince of Wales and Earl of Chester :—"And him, our said and most dear son, the Prince of 'the United Kingdom of Great Britain and Ireland, as has been accustomed, we do ennoble and invest with the said Principality and Earldom, by girding him with a sword, by putting a coronet on his head, and a gold ring on his finger, and also by delivering a gold rod into his hand, that he may preside there, and direct and defend those parts." By the fact of his birth as Heir-Apparent, the Prince indefeasibly inherited, without the necessity of patent or creation, these dignities : the titles of Duke of Saxony, by right of his father ; and, by right of his mother, Duke of Cornwall, Duke of Rothsay, Earl of Carrick, Baron of Renfrew, Lord of the Isles, and Great Steward of Scotland.

THE BIRTH OF THE PRINCE OF WALES.

COME, all you bold Britons, and list for awhile,
And I will sing you a song that will make you all to smile.
A young Prince of Wales has come to town,
The pride of all the nation, and heir to the crown.
On the ninth of November, 'tis true, 'pon my life,
All Buckingham Palace was bustle and strife ;
The nurses stared at each other with joy,
Bawling, our Queen she has got a most beautiful boy.
    The bells they shall ring, and music shall play,
    The ninth of November, remember the day ;
    Through England, Ireland, Scotland and Wales,
    Shout long life to the Queen and the young Prince of Wales.

It was on the ninth, about eleven in the morn,
When the young Prince of Wales in the Palace was born ;
Little Vic. she was there, as you all may be sure,
Besides doctors, nurses, and gossips—a score.
Says Vic., " I declare he is the image of me,
And there 's my dear Albert's nose to a tee ; "
One and all declared, when he grew up a man,
He would drub all the foes that infested the land.
The bells they shall ring, &c.

From another street-ballad, entitled " A New Song on
the Birth of the Prince of Wales, who was born on Tuesday,
November 9th, 1841," we select, as follows :—

THERE 'S a pretty fuss and bother both in country and
town,
Since we have got a present and an heir unto the crown ;
A little Prince of Wales, so charming and so coy,
And all the ladies shout with wonder, what a pretty little boy.
Chorus—So let us be contented, and sing with mirth and joy,
Some things must be got ready for the pretty little
boy.

He must have a musket, a trumpet and a kite,
A little penny rattle, and a silver sword so bright,
A little cap and feather, with scarlet coat so smart,
And a pretty little hobby horse to ride about the park.

Prince Albert he will often take the young Prince on his lap,
And fondle him so loving, while he stirs about the pap ;
He will pin on his flannel before he takes his nap,
Then dress him out so stylish with his little clouts and cap.

He must have a dandy suit to strut about the town,
John Bull must rake together six or seven thousand pound ;
You 'd laugh to see his daddy, at night he homeward runs,
With some peppermint or lollypops, sweet cakes and sugar
plums.

We shall conclude our gathering of facts, scraps and street rare-bits in connection with the ascension to the throne, the marriage, &c., of our Most Gracious Majesty, Queen Victoria, by a brief description of the Queen's wedding-cake, which, fortunately for our enterprise, we have succeeded in disinterring from the contemporary records. It was described by an eye-witness as consisting of all the most exquisite compounds of all the rich things with which the most expensive cakes can be composed, mingled and mixed together with delightful harmony by the most elaborate science of the confectioner. It weighed 300 pounds, was three yards in circumference, and fourteen inches in depth. On the top was a device of Britannia blessing the bride and bridegroom, who were dressed, somewhat incongruously, in the costume of ancient Rome. At the foot of the bridegroom was the figure of a dog, intended to denote fidelity; at the feet of the Queen a pair of turtle-doves. A host of gamboling Cupids, one of them registering the marriage in a book, and bouquets of white flowers tied with true-lovers' knots, completed the decorations.

We will now attempt to deal a little in generalities, as regards the business which Catnach made for himself in London, and the first we would allude to are the "penny awfuls." From this particular line he must have realized a very snug thing. A fly-sheet, containing the latest particulars of some "'orrible" crime, at the low charge of one-penny, was something marvellous, and we can readily discern, even in these days, when the good, bad, and very indifferent pictorial newspapers are carried to such an extent, the interest and sensation which would be caused by the appearance of the embellished broadsides which emanated from the printing establishment in Seven Dials. Like the proprietors of the modern "Illustrateds," Catnach had in his day correspondents all over the kingdom. It was the duty of these persons to procure the latest information, especially that part which pertains to the awful and sensational. With regard to the "embellishments" we are not inclined to think for one moment that any of them were of a character likely to adorn the profession or elevate the masses—that will be judged by an examination of the various specimens we have given in the body of our work, but it would be a great injustice to the memory of the original proprietor to say they had no influence upon society. The large amount of patronage which the publications met with is conclusive proof that they found their way into the homes of many in the land.

There is a species of street-literature well known to the trade as "Cocks," and which are defined in "Hotton's Slang Dictionary" thus :—

"COCKS—fictitious narratives, in verse or prose, of murders, fires, and terrible accidents, sold in the streets as true accounts. The man who hawks them, a patterer, often changes the scene of the awful event to suit the taste of the neighbourhood he is trying to delude. Possibly a corruption of COOK, a cooked statement; or, as a correspondent suggests, the COCK LANE ghost may have given rise to the term. This had a great run, and was a rich harvest to the running stationers."

"Few of the residents in London—but chiefly those in the quieter streets," says Mr. Henry Mayhew, in his "London Labour and the London Poor," "have not been arouse'd, and most frequently in the evening, by a hurly-burly on each side of the street. An attentive listening will not lead any one to an accurate knowledge of what the clamour is about. It is from a 'mob' or 'school' of running patterers, and consists of two, three, or four men. All these men state that the greater the noise they make, the better is the chance of sale, and better still when the noise is on each side of the street, for it appears as if the vendors were proclaiming such interesting or important intelligence that they were vieing with one another who should supply the demand which must ensue. It is not possible to ascertain with any creditude *what* the patterers are so anxious to sell, for only a few leading words are audible, as 'Horrible,' 'Dreadful,' 'Murder,' 'One penny,' 'Love,' 'One penny,' 'Mysterious,' 'Seduction,' 'Former crimes,' 'Nine children,' 'Coal-cellar,' 'Pool of blood,' 'One penny,' and the like, can only be caught by the ear, and there is no announcement of anything like 'particulars.' The running paterers describe, or profess to describe, the contents of their papers as they go along, and they seldom or never stand still. They usually deal in murders, seductions, crim. cons., explosions, alarming accidents, assassinations, deaths of public characters, duels, and love-letters. But popular, or notorious murders are the 'great goes.' The running patterer cares less than any other street-sellers for bad weather, for if he 'work' on a wet and gloomy evening, and if the work be 'A COCK '—which is a fictitious statement—there is less chance of anyone detecting the *ruse*. Among the old stereotyped 'COCKS' are love-letters. One is well-known as a 'Married Man caught in a Trap.' And being in a dialogue and an epistolary form, subserves any purpose : as the 'Love-Letters,' that have passed between

Mr. Smith, the butcher, baker, grocer, draper, &c.—'the decoyer of female innocence'—and Mrs. Brown, Mrs. Jones, or Mrs. Robinson, or Miss A—, B—, or C—, not 100 yards off—'and the very image of his father,' &c., &c.--and can be fitted to any real or pretended local scandal.

"When the patterer visits the country, he is accompanied by a mate, and the 'copy of werses' is then announced as being written by an 'underpaid curate' within a day's walk. 'It tells mostly, sir,' said one man, 'for its a blessing to us that there always is a journeyman parson what the people knows, and what the patter fits.' Sometimes the poetry is attributed to a Sister of Mercy, or to a popular poetess; very frequently, by the patterers, who best understand the labouring classes, to Miss Eliza Cook. Sometimes the verses are written by a 'sympathising gent,' in that parish, 'but his name wasn't to be mentioned, or any nobleman or gentleman, whose name is before the public in connection with any recent event, or an assumed account of 'A Battle between Two Ladies of Fortune.' The patterers have only to stick a picture in their hat to attract attention, and to make all the noise they can.

"Occasionally, the running patterer transmigrates into a standing one, betaking himself to 'board work,' as it is termed in street technology, and stopping at the corners of thoroughfares with a large pictorial placard raised upon a pole, and glowing with highly-coloured exaggerations of the interesting terrors of the pamphlet he has for sale.

"When there are no 'popular murders' the standing patterer orders of the artist a new and startling 'cock-board,' and sells his books or pamphlets, the titles of some of which are fully set forth and well displayed; for example: 'Horrible murder and mutilation of Lucy Game, aged fifteen, by her cruel brother, William Game, aged ten, of Westmill, Hertfordshire. His committal and confession, with a copy of a letter sent to his affectionate parents.' 'Full particulars

of the poisonings in Essex—the whole family poisoned by
the female servant.   Confession of her guilt—Was seduced
by her master.—Revenged herself on the family.'   Another
is—' Founded on facts, The Whitby Tragedy ; or, the Gam-
bler's Fate, containing the lives of Joseph Carr, aged twenty-
one, and his sweetheart, Maria Leslie, aged eighteen, who
were found dead, lying by each other, on the morning of the
23rd of May.   Maria was on her road to town to buy some
ribbon and other things for her wedding-day, when her lover,
in a state of intoxication, fired at her, then run to rob his
prey, but finding it was his sweetheart, re-loaded his gun,
placed the muzzle to his mouth, and blew out his brains, all
through the cursed cards and drink.   With an affectionate
copy of verses.'

" A popular street-book for ' board-work' is entitled
' Horrible Rape and Murder ! ! !   The affecting case of
Mary Ashford, a beautiful young virgin, who was diaboli-
cally Ravished, Murdered, and thrown into a Pit, as she was
returning from a Dance, including the Trial of Abraham
Thornton for the Wilful Murder of the said Mary Ashford ?
with the whole of the Evidence, Charges to the Jury, &c.,
with a Correct Plan of the Spot where the Rape and Murder
were Committed.'

" The ' street-book' is founded on fact, and, in reality,
gives the salient points of a memorable circumstance which
took place in 1817, when Abraham Thornton was charged
at the Warwick Assizes, before Mr. Justice Holroyd, for the
murder and violation of Mary Ashford, at Erdington, near
Birmingham.   The prisoner was found—after a consultation
of the jury of five minutes—Not Guilty, to the utmost surprise and disappointment of all persons assembled.   The
second charge of committing a rape on the body of the said
Mary Ashford was abandoned by the prosecution.   The
case created the greatest possible sensation at the time, and,
the trial and subsequent appeal were printed and published

in a separate form, and occupies 120 pages in double
columns, 'with a correct plan of the spot where the rape
and murder were committed, and a portrait of Thornton
drawn and engraved by George Cruikshank.'

"The acquittal of Thornton in the atrocious rape and
murder of Mary Ashford excited the most undisguised
feelings of disappointment in all classes of persons throughout the kingdom, and various provincial newspapers began
to canvass the subject with vigour, freedom, and research.
This aroused most of the London papers, and the "Independent Whig," on Sunday, August 17th, after fully com-
menting on the case, -cited several instances where
individuals, who, after having been arraigned under the
charge of murder and acquitted, were tried a second time
for the same offence, in consequence of an appeal by the
next of kin of the' deceased against the verdict of the jury,
and wound up their remarks by saying that,—' If ever there
was a case of brutality, violation, and murder, that had greater
claims upon the sympathy of the world than another, and
demands a second trial, we think it is exhibited in that of
the unfortunate Mary Ashford.' This gave the 'key-note,'
a very large section of the press adopted the same view of
the case, and a subscription was immediately set on foot
—Mary's friends being in indigent circumstances—to defray
the necessary expenses. And Abraham Thornton was
apprehended a second time, on a Writ of Appeal, for the
murder of Mary Ashford, which excited an interest in the
public mind altogether unprecedented—an interest that was
heightened by the unusual recurrence of the obsolete
proceedings necessary in the case by the Saxon Writ of
Appeal, together with the staggering fact of Thornton
having challenged his appellant, William, the eldest
brother of the deceased, Mary Ashford, to a solemn
trial by battle, and avowing himself ready to defend his
innocence with his body.

" The challenge was formally given by throwing down a glove upon the floor of the Court of King's Bench, whence the case had been removed by ' Writ of Habeas Corpus,' to be heard before Lord Ellenborough.   But the combat did not take place, and the prisoner escaped.   An Act of Parliament was then passed abolishing the trial by battle in any suit, as a mode unfit to be used.

" Mary Ashford was buried in the Churchyard of Sutton Colefield, and over her remains is placed a stone with the following inscription, written by the Rev. Luke Booker :—

' As a warning to female virtue, and a humble
Monument to female chastity,
This stone marks the grave of
MARY ASHFORD,
Who, in the 20th year of her age,
Having incautiously repaired to a
Scene of amusement, without proper protection,
Was brutally violated and murdered
On the 27th of October, 1817.'

" The artist who paints the patterers' boards must address his art plainly to the eye of the spectator.   He must use the most striking colours, be profuse in the application of scarlet, light blue, orange—not yellow, that not being a good candle-light colour—and must leave nothing to the imagination.   Perspective and back-grounds are things but of minor consideration, everything must be sacrificed for effect.   These paintings are in water colours, and are rubbed over with a solution of gum-resin to protect them from the influence of rainy weather.

" The charge of the popular street-artist for the painting of a board is 2s. or 3s. 6d., according to the simplicity or elaborateness of the details ; the board itself is provided by the artist's employer.   The demand for this peculiar branch

ABRAHAM THORNTON.

Tried for the Murder of Mary Ashford.

of street-art is very irregular, depending entirely upon whether there has or has not been perpetrated any act of atrocity, which has rivetted, as it is called, the public attention. And so great is the uncertainty felt by the street-folk whether ' the most beautiful murder will take or not,' that it is rarely the patterer will order, or the artist will speculate, in anticipation of a demand, upon preparing the painting of any event, until satisfied that it has become 'popular.' A deed of more than usual daring, deceit, or mystery, may be at once hailed by those connected with murder-patter, as ' one that will do,' and some speculation may be ventured upon, as it was in such cases as Thurtell and Hunt, Corder, of the Red Barn notoriety, &c. ; or, in the later times, as Greenacre, Rush, Tawell, and the Mannings ; but these are merely exceptional, so uncertain, it appears, is all that depends, without intrinsic merit, on mere popular applause."*

But the gallows was not always a fruit-bearing tree, and a " stunning good murder " did not happen every day. Nevertheless, the patterer must live ; and lest the increase of public virtue should condemn him to starvation, the " Seven Dials Press " stepped forward to his aid, and considerately supplied him with—" cocks." With a good cock-crow, the patterer could do tolerably well; and with an assortment of them, to suit the several districts on his beat, he could do still better. The cock, like the ballad and the sorrowful lamentation, sells either at a penny or a half-penny ; but, in spite of all its crowing, not so readily ; partly because it is objectionable to the police, who will not allow it to remain long on its perch, and partly for want of faith on the side of the mob, whom, in these days of cheap newspapers, it is not so easy to delude in the article of news.

---

* Mayhew's " London Labour and the London Poor."

The late Mr. Albert Smith, the humourist and novelist, has very happily hit off this style of thing in "The Man in the Moon," one of the many rivals to "Punch," and edited by that very promising son of genius, the late Angus B. Reach, 1832—56. It is entitled—

A COPY OF VERSES

Found among the Papers of Mr. Catnach, the spirited Publisher of Seven Dials; originally intended to have been "printed and published at the Toy and Marble Warehouse, 2 and 3, Monmouth Court, Seven Dials."

DEDICATED TO THE LITERARY ORFILA, THE AUTHOR OF

"LUCRETIA."

I.

The Hero claims the attention of virtuous persons, and leads them to anticipate a painful disclosure.

DRAW hither now good people all
And let my story warn ;
For I will tell to you a tale,
What will wrend them breasts of yourn.

II.

He names the place and hour of the disgraceful penalty he is about to undergo.

I am condemn'd all for to die ·
A death of scorn and horror ;
In front of Horsemonger-lane Gaol,
At eight o'clock to-morrer.

III.

*He hints at his atrocity; and the ebullition produced by the mere recol-
lection of it.*

The crime of which I was found guilty,
Oh ! it was shocking vile ;
The very thoughts of the cruel deed
Now makes my blood to bile.

IV.

He speaks of the happy hours of Childhood, never more to return.

In Somersetshire I was born'd,
And little my sister dear
Didn't think then that my sad end
Would be like unto this here.

V.

The revelation of his name and profession; and subsequent avowal of his guilt.

James Guffin is my hated name,
And a footman I 'm by trade ;
And I do confess that I did slay
My poor fellow-servant maid.

VI.

He acknowledges the justice of his sentence.

And well I do deserve, I own,
My fate which is so bitter :
For 'twas most wicked for to kill
So innicent a critter.

VII.

And pictures what might have taken place but for the interference of Destiny.

Her maiden name was Sarcy Leigh,
And was to have been Guffin ;
For we was to have been marri-ed,
But Fate brought that to nuffin.

VIII.

He is particular as to the date of the occurrence.

All on a Wednesday afternoon,
 On the ninth of Janivary,
Eighteen hundred and forty-four,
 Oh ! I did kill my Sarey.

IX.

*And narrates the means employed, and the circumstances which led him
to destroy his betrothed.*

With arsenic her I did destroy,
 How could I be so vicious !
But of my young master I was jealous,
 And so was my old Missus.

X.

He is led away by bad passions.

I thought Sarcy Leigh warn't true to me,
 So all pity then despising,
Sure I was tempted by the Devil
 To give to her some p'ison.

XI.

His bosom is torn by conflicting resolutions ; but he is at last decided.

Long—long I brooded on the deed,
'Till one morning of a sudden,
I did determine for to put
It in a beef-steak puddin.

XII.

The victim falls into the snare.

Of the fatal pudding she did partake,
Most fearful for to see,
And an hour arter was to it a martyr,
Launch'd into eternity.

XIII.

He feels that his perception comes too late.

Ah ! had I then but viewed things in
The light that I now does 'em,
I never should have know'd the grief
As burns in this here buzum.

XIV.

He commits his secret to the earth.

So when I seed what I had done,
  In hopes of justice retarding,
I took and buried poor Sarey Leigh
  Out in the kitching garding.

XV.

But the earth refuses to keep it.

But it did haunt me, so I felt
  As of a load deliver'd,
When three weeks after the fatal deed,
  The body was diskiver'd.

XVI.

Remorse and self examination.

O ! why did I form of Sarcy Leigh
  Such cruel unjust opinions,
When my young master did her find
  Beneath the bed of inions.

XVII.

His countrymen form a just estimate of his delinquency.

Afore twelve jurymen I was tried,
  And condemned the perpetrator
Of this here awful Tragedy,
  As shocks one's human natur.

·XVIII.

He conjures up a painful image.

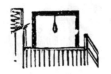

But the bell is tolling for my end ;
  How shocking for to see
A footman gay, in the prime of life,
  Die on the fatal tree.

XIX.

His last words convey a moral lesson.

Take warning, then, all ye as would
  Not die like malefactors ;
Never the company for to keep
  Of them with bad characters.

The following is the style of "gag" and "patter" of a man formerly well known in the "Dials" as "Tragedy Bill" —"Now, my kind friends and relations, here you have, just printed and published, a full, true, and pertickler account

of thē life, trial, character, confession, behaviour, condemnation, and hexecution of that unfortunate malefactor, Richard Wilbyforce, who was hexecuted on Monday last, *For the small charge of one ha'penny!* and for the most horrible, dreadful, and wicked murder of Samuel — I mean Sarah Spriggens, a lady's maid, young, tender, and handsome. You have here every pertickler, of that which he did and that which he didn't. It's the most foul and horrible murder that ever graced the annals of British history (?) Here, my customers, you may read his hexecution on the fatal scaffold. You may also read how he met his victim in a dark and lonesome wood, and what he did to her—*For the small charge of a ha'penny!* and further, you read how he brought her to London— after that comes the murder, which is worth all the money. And you read how the ghost appeared to him and then to her parents. Then comes the capture of the *willain;* also the trial, sentence, and hexecution, showing how the ghost was in the act of pulling his leg on one side, and the 'old gentleman' a pulling on the other, waiting for his victim (my good friends, fellow countrymen, and female women,

excuse my tears). But has Shakespeare says, ' Murder most
foul and unnatural,' but you 'll find this more foul and
unnatural than that ·or the t' other—*For the small charge of
a ha'penny !* Yes, my customers, to which is added a copy
of serene and beautiful werses, pious and immoral, as wot
he wrote with his own blood and a skewer the night after—I
mean the night before his hexecution, addressed to young
men and women of all sexes—I beg pardon, but I mean
classes (my friends its nothing to laugh at), for I can tell
you the werses is made three of the hard-heartedest things
cry as never was—to wit, that is to say, namely—a overseer,
a broker, and a policeman. Yes, my friends, I sold twenty
thousand copies of them this here morning, and could a'
sold twenty thousand more than that if I could of but kept
from crying—only a ha'penny !—but I'll read the werses :

' COME, all you blessed Christians dear,
 That's a-tender, kind, and free,
While I a story do relate
 Of a dreadful tragedy ˙
Which happened in London town,
 As you shall all be told ;
But when you hear the horrid deed
 ' 'Twill make your blood run cold.—
 For the small charge of a ha'penny !

'Twas in the merry month of May,
 When my true love I did meet ;
She look'd all like an angel bright,
 So beautiful and sweet.
I told her I loved her much,
 And she could not say nay ;
'Twas then I stung her tender heart,
 And led her all astray.—
 Only a ha'penny !

I brought her up to London town,
 To make her my dear wife,
But an evil spirit tempted me,
 And so I took her life !
I left the town all in the night,
 When her ghost in burning fire,
Saying, ' Richard, I am still with you,
 Wherever you retire.'—

      Only a ha'penny !

And justice follow'd every step,
 Though often I did cry ;
And the cruel judge and jury
 Condemned me for to die.
And in a cell, as cold as death,
 I always was afraid,
For Sarah she was with me,
 Although I killed her dead.—

    For the small charge of a ha'penny !

My tender-hearted Christians,
 Be warned by what I say,
And never prove unkind or false
 'To any sweet la'-dy.
Though some there, who wickedness
 Oft leads 'em to go astray ;
So pray attend to what you hear,
 And a warning take, I pray.

    All for the small charge of a ha'penny ! ' "

Subjoined is a " Murder Cock," and one which, in street phraseology, is said to " fight well." There is a great amount of ingenuity exercised in the composition—and, while it promises a great deal, it reveals nothing—and is suited for any time, or place—murder or no murder.

FULL PARTICULARS OF THIS DREADFUL MURDER.

A scene of bloodshed of the deepest dye has been committed in this neighbourhood, which has caused a painful and alarming sensation among all classes in this place, in consequence of its being committed by an individual that is well known to most of the inhabitants, who are going in great numbers to the fatal spot where the unfortunate and ill-fated victim has met with this melancholy and dreadful end.

On the news arriving at our office, we at once dispatched our reporter to the spot, and on his arrival he found the place surrounded by men, women, and children, gathered

around where the vital spark had fled, which was never to
be regained on the face of this earth. Deep was the conversation among the accumulated persons as to how a fellow
creature could be guilty of committing such a revolting and
diabolical act upon one, who, it appears, was much respected
in this neighbourhood.

ᵎ The reporter states that on the police authorities arriving
at the place, they had some difficulty in preserving order ;
but after a short lapse of time, this was accomplished. They
then proceeded to the house where the lifeless corpse laid,
and took possession of the same, and which presented one
of the most awful spectacles that has been witnessed for
many years.

What could have been the motive for such a cold-blooded
and wanton murder being committed we are at a loss to
conceive ; without it was in consequence of some disagree-
ment having taken place between the unfortunate victims
and their assailants, and then ending in depriving their
fellow-creatures of life, which we are forbidden, according
to the Commandments, to take away ; but this seems to be
entirely violated in many instances by our dissipated and
irregular habits which tends to the committal of such serious
things, and through disobeying the scriptural advice, brings
the degraded creatures to an untimely end. According to
the Scriptures, " He that sheddeth man's blood, by man
shall his blood be shed," which we entirely agree with in
these instances, and fully acknowledge the just sentence that
is often obliged to be carried into effect ; and certainly must
say that, were it not for the rigidness of those laws, many of
us would not be able to proceed on our journey at heart.
So, therefore, we are in duty bound to call upon those laws
being fully acted up to, for it is our opinion that those
crimes are very seldom committed without there is some
disregard or ill-feeling towards their unfortunate victims,
and thereby end their days in a dreadful manner.

The unfortunate persons being so well known and so much respected, everyone feels anxious to know all particulars, and it is the constant inquiry amongst them to know if there is anyone apprehended for the murder, or if there is anything more known as to lead to the suspicion who it has been committed by, all being very desirous to hear of the perpetrators of this diabolical and horrid deed. We feel much for the family, who are thrown into the greatest affliction through this dreadful circumstance, and which has cast a gloom over the circle of friends in which they moved.

As a member of society, there will be no one that we know of who will be more missed; one who was often known to relieve the wants of his fellow-creatures as far as his circumstances would permit, and whose society was courted by all. As a member of the family to which they belonged, none will be more deeply regretted, but those who are remaining will feel the loss and deplore the lamentable death of their respected and worthy friends. Just as we are going to press, we have received information from our reporter, that something has been elicited from a party that has thrown a light on the subject, and which has led to the apprehension of one of the principal offenders, and who, if proved guilty, will, we hope, meet with that punishment due to his fearful crime.

London : J. Lucksway, Printer & Publisher, High Street, Westminster.

THE LOVE LETTER,

MARRIED MAN CAUGHT IN A TRAP.

"Good morning, Sir."

"The same to you, Miss! Very happy to meet you here; how far are you going?"

"Not far, Sir, but I should be proud of your company for a short time."

"Thank you, Miss, I hope we shall be better acquainted ere long."

"I hope, Sir, you are unmarried?"

"Happy to say at present—I am!"

"Very well, Sir, I am at present without a sweetheart who has possession of my heart!"

"My dear, I will endeavour to try to gain you."

"Excuse me, Sir, I am poor."

"My dear, I am only a theatrical gentleman, but very fond of the fair sex."

"Do you think, my cherub, that you will be able to keep us when we are wed?"

"Yes, my dear, for I will feed you on oysters, beef-steaks, and all such fattening and strengthening things as are necessary for our conjugal happiness and comfort."

"But, Sir, can I really depend upon you?"

"Yes, my dear; shall we name the day for our marriage?"

"Suppose we say, my love, the day after to-morrow?"

"Agreed; until that, adieu."

On the morning appointed for the wedding, the young woman received the following epistle :—

"MY DEAREST FANNY,—I have thought on your proposal since last we met, but, from circumstances that have transpired, I beg leave to postpone our marriage to a future day. I thought on our conversation and your delightful company ever since, and have enclosed a copy for your perusal.

"I am,
"Yours for ever,
"HENRY J. N. S."

"Light of my soul! by night and day,
   I'll love thee ever;
Light of my soul! list to my lay,
   I'll leave thee never.
Light of my soul! where'er I go,
   My thoughts on thee are hov'ring;
Light of my soul! in weal or woe—
   Send by the bearer a sovereign."

The young woman read this letter with disdain, and wrote back the following answer :—

"SIR,—I return your note with disgust, having been informed that you are a married man, and I hope you will bestow the trash you offered me upon your wife. So pray trouble me no more with your foolery."

Poor H. took this so much to heart, that he went and drowned his senses in wine, and then returned home, undressing himself, the letter fell from his bosom, his wife picked it up, read it, and beat him about the head with a dish cloth.

There are two ways of reading this to discover the parties. Henry ——— lives in THIS STREET, and Fanny ——— at the Beer-shop round the corner, and is said to be no better than she should be.

———

Printed by J. Pitts, Wholesale Toy Warehouse, Great St. Andrew's Street, Seven Dials.

Following is "a cock," which, in the hands of a clever
patterer, can be made much of, and which is certainly
making "Much Ado About Nothing":—

ALL FOUND OUT AT LAST,

OR, THE SECRET DISCOVERED,

After having been carried on in a curious manner for a long time.

"Most Adorable Mary,—

"Why have you left me, and deprived me of those
pleasures of beholding the most charming face that nature
ever made? How shall I find words to express the passion
you have inspired me with? Since the day I first beheld
your form, I have felt the sharpest pangs of love, which have
worked me up to the utmost pitch of distraction. But alas!
such a shock I felt as is impossible to express. The dearest
object of my heart is locked in the embrace of Robert E——,
that vile monster and decoyer of female innocence. Oh!
never should I have thought that after so many pleasant
hours we have passed together, and promises pledged on
either side, that you would have slighted me in the manner

you have, and find your heart callous to one who adores you, and even the ground your angelic form walks upon. Oh, my adorable angel, do not forsake me and the welfare of yourself; drop all connection with that vile deceiver, R. E., and once more reinstate me to that pleasure which none but lovers know. My fluctuation of fortune shall never abate my attachment, and I hope the day is not far distant when I shall lead you to the altar of Hymen. Oh! soon may the time arrive when I may call thee, dearest Mary, my own. Oh! my dearest angel, consent to my request, and keep me no longer in suspense; nothing, on my part, shall ever be wanting to make you happy and comfortable. My engagement will expire in two months from hence, when I intend to open a shop in the small ware line, and your abilities as a seamstress and self-adjusting bustle maker, with the assistance of a few work girls shall be able to realise an independence; and, moreover, I will indulge you in all things needful in the marriage state, and show my regard for you by cleaning your shoes, lighting the fire every morning, buying crumpets, new butter, and so forth; besides, my dear Mary, we will live merrily upon beef-steak, oysters and other tasty articles necessary for our conjugal happiness, and upon my bended knees I pray for it, and may earthly friendship and confidence, with truest love, continue to the end.

> "You are the first, I freely own,
>   That raised love in my breast,
> Where now it reigns without control,
>   But yet a welcome guest.
> Ah! must I drive the cherub hence,
>   In sorrow to regret,
> And will you join to foster me,
>   And me no more neglect.

"Most adorable Mary,—I have to repeat my former request, that is, quit R. E.'s company, and place yourself under the protection of me only, in whom you will find all the comfort that wedded life can bestow.

" I remain, dear Mary,

" Yours till death,

" John S——.

" P.S.—Favour me, my angel, with an answer by return of post; if not, I shall start off directly for Liverpool, and embark for America."

J. Catnach, Printer, 2 & 3 ,Monmouth Court, 7 Dials.

One of the most favourite themes of the standing patterer was the " Annals of the White House in Soho Square." Although the house in question, which stood at the northern angle of Sutton Street, has long since been rebuilt, and its original character entirely altered, for some years the patterer did not scruple to represent it as still in existence —though he might change the venue as to the square at discretion, and attribute vile deeds to any nobleman or gentleman whose name was before the public, and to embellish his story by an allusion to a recent event.

The White House was a place of fashionable dissipation, to which only the titled and wealthy classes had the privilege of admission. Its character may be inferred from the fact that it was one of the haunts of the then Prince of Wales, the old Duke of Queensbury, and the Marquis of Hertford ; and the ruin of many a female heart may be dated from a visit within its walls. It is said by tradition that its apartments were known as the " Gold," " Silver," and " Bronze " Rooms, &c., each being called from the prevailing character of its fittings, and that the walls of nearly every room were inlaid with mirrored panels. Many of the rooms in this house, too, had a sensational name, as the " Commons," the " Painted Chamber," the " Grotto," the " Coal Hole," and the " Skeleton Room "—the latter so styled on account of a closet out of which a skeleton was made to step forth by the aid of machinery. The " White House," as a scene of profligacy, lived on into the present century, and having been empty for some years, was largely altered, and to some extent rebuilt, by the founders of the extensive business of Messrs. Crosse and Blackwell, the well known pickle manufacturers.

" The authors and poets who give this peculiar literature, alike in prose or rhyme to the streets, are all in some capacity or another connected with street patter or song ; and the way in which a narrative or a ' copy of werses ' is prepared for the press is usually this :—The leading members of the ' schools '—some of whom refer regularly to the evening papers—when they hear of any out-of-the-way occurrence, resort to the printer and desire its publication in a style proper for the streets. This is usually done very speedily, the school—or a majority of them—and the printer agreeing with the author. Sometimes an author will voluntarily prepare a piece of street-literature and submit it to a publisher, who, as in case of other publishers, accepts or declines, as he believes the production will or will not prove remunerative. Sometimes the school carry the manuscript with them to the printer, and undertake to buy a certain quantity to insure publication. The payment to the author is the same in all cases—a shilling; but sometimes if the printer and publisher like the verses he 'throws a penny or two over.' And sometimes, also, in case of a great sale, there is the same 'over-sum.' The 'Dials' and its immediate neighbourhood is the chief residence of these parties, as being nearest to the long-established printer, they have made it the 'head meet' of the fraternity.

It must be borne in mind that the street-author is closely restricted in the quality of his effusions. It must be such as the pátterers approve, as the chanters can chant, the ballad singers sing, and, above all, such as the street buyers will buy." *

When trade was quiet in the "sensationals," Jemmy would commence to get-up some of the small histories, several of which had almost become stereotyped on his memory. Some of these little books he considered eminently suited for certain localities. An anecdote is related of him : "Early one Monday morning, an Alnwick friend called to see him. They were in the act of conversing together when the principal pressman came to inquire what work should next be proceeded with. He was told to go on with some of the old traders, and that on a certain shelf in the workshop he would find 'Jack, the Giant Killer,' and 'The Babes in the Wood,' and not far from these were 'Blue Beard' and 'Tom Hickathrift,' and lying between them was 'Crazy Jane,' 'The Scarlet Whore of Babylon,' 'Nancy Dawson,' and 'Jane Shore.' 'These,' added Jemmy, slily, 'will do for the Bristol trade.'"

---

* Mayhew's " London Labour and the London Poor."

Most of Catnach's customers paid all coppers, and he used to take them to the Bank of England, in large bags, in a hackney coach, because most of his neighbours, knowing from whom he received them, dreaded to take them of him in exchange for silver, because of a fever which was reported to have been propagated by the filthy money he used to take from the cadgers and hawkers. After this he used to boil all his coppers in a strong decoction of potash and vinegar before exchanging them, which used to make them look as bright as when they were first coined. The journeymen and boys in his employ were obliged to take their wages in coppers; and on Saturday night they had to get their wives or mothers to call for them to help carry home ten, twenty, thirty, or forty shillings, all in coppers, for the penny pieces in those days were much larger and heavier than they are now; some of them were of George the Second's time, and would outweigh two of the present genteel-looking bronze coins of the same value. In spite of all his pains to detect them Catnach used to take so many bad pennies that he at length paved his small back kitchen, which was used as a wetting-room, with them, by having them embedded in plaster of Paris.

"Songs! Songs! Songs! Beautiful songs! Love songs! Newest songs! Old songs! Popular songs! Songs, *Three Yards a Penny!*" was a " standing dish " at the " Catnach Press," and Catnach was the Leo X. of street publishers. And it is said that he at one time kept a fiddler on the premises, and that he used to sit receiving ballad-writers and singers, and judging of the merits of any production which was brought to him, by having it sung then and there to some popular air played by his own fiddler, and so that the ballad-singer should be enabled to start at once, not only with the new song, but also the tune to which it was adopted. His broad-sheets contain all sorts of songs and ballads, for he had a most catholic taste, and introduced the custom of taking from any writer, living or dead, whatever he fancied, and printing it side by side with the productions of his own clients.

Catnach, towards the latter part of his time and in his threefold capacity of publisher, compositor, and poet, was in the habit of taking things very easy, and always appeared to the best advantage when in his printing office, or stationed behind the ricketty counter which for a number of years had done good service in the shop in Monmouth Court. In this incongenial atmosphere, where the rays of the sun are seldom or never seen, Jemmy was as happy as a prince. "A poor man's home is his castle," so says an old proverb, and no one could have been prouder than he was when despatching to almost every town in the kingdom some speciality in the printing department. He naturally had a bit of a taste for old ballads, music, and song writing ; and in this respect he was far in advance of many of his contemporaries. To bring within the reach of all the standard and popular works of the day, had been the ambition of the elder Catnach; whilst the son was, *nolens volens*, incessant in his endeavours in trying to promulgate and advance, not the beauty, elegance, and harmony which pervades many of our national airs and ballad poetry, but very often the worst and vilest of each and every description—in other words, those most suitable for street-sale. His stock of songs was very like his customers, diversified. There were all kinds, to suit all classes. Love, sentimental, and comic songs were so interwoven as to form a trio of no ordinary amount of novelty. At ordinary times, when the Awfuls and Sensationals were flat, Jemmy did a large stroke of business in this line.

It is said that when the "Songs—*Three-yards-a-penny*" —first came out and had all the attractions of novelty, some men sold twelve or fourteen dozen on fine days during three or four of the summer months, so clearing between 6s.

and 7s. a day, but on the average about 25s. a week profit. The "long songs," however, have been quite superseded by the "Monster" and "Giant Penny Song Books." Still there are a vast number of half-penny ballad-sheets worked off, and in proportion to their size, far more than the "Monsters" or "Giants."

There are invariably but two songs printed on the half-penny ballad-sheets—generally a new and popular song with another older ditty, or a comic and sentimental, and "adorned" with two woodcuts. These are selected without any regard as to their fitness to the subject, and in most cases have not the slightest reference to the ballad of which they form the head-piece. For instance :—" The Heart that can feel for another" is illustrated by a gaunt and savage-looking lion ; "When I was first Breeched," by an engraving of a Highlander *sans culotte ;* " The Poacher " comes under the cut of a youth with a large watering-pot, tending flowers; " Ben Block" is heralded by the rising sun ; The London Oyster Girl," by Sir Walter Raleigh ; " The Sailor's Grave," by the figure of Justice ; " Alice Grey " comes under the very dilapidated figure of a sailor, or "Jolly Young Waterman ;" " Bright Hours are in store for us yet " is *headed* with a *tail-piece* of an urn, on which is inscribed FINIS ! " Watercresses," with the portrait of a Silly Billy ; " The Wild Boar Hunt," by two wolves chasing a deer ; " The Dying Child to its Mother," by an Angel appearing to an old man; " Crazy Jane," by the Royal Arms of England ; " Autumn Leaves lie strew'd around," by a ship in full sail ; " Cherry Ripe," by Death's Head and Cross Bones ; " Jack at the Windlass," falls under a Roadside Inn ; while " William Tell " is presented to the British public in form and style of an old woman nursing an infant of squally nature. Here are a few examples :—

Fair Phœbe and her Dark-Eyed Sailor.   My Pretty Jane.

· The Thorn.   The Saucy Arethusa.

The Gipsy King.   Hearts of Oak.

Harry Bluff.   Death of Nelson.

John Anderson, my Joe.

Old English Gentleman.

The Bleeding Heart.

Wapping Old Stairs.

Poor Bessy was a Sailor's Bride.

Poor Mary Anne.

The Muleteer.

Tom Bowling.

Ye Banks an' Braes.

The Mistletoe Bough.

The Woodpecker.

The Soldier's Tear.

Besides the chanters, who sing the songs through the
streets of every city, town, village, and hamlet in the kingdom—the long-song seller, who shouts their titles on the
kerb-stone, and the countless small shop-keepers, who, in
swag-shops, toy-shops, sweetstuff-shops, tobacco-shops, and
general shops, keep them as part of their stock for the
supply of the street boys and the servant girls—there is
another important functionary engaged in their distribution,
and who is well known to the inhabitants of large towns, .
this is the pinner-up, who takes his stand against a dead
wall or a long range of iron railing, and first festooning it
liberally with twine, pins up one or two hundred ballads for
public perusal and selection.   Time was when this was a
thriving trade : and we are old enough to remember the
day when a good half-mile of wall fluttered with the minstrelsy of war and love, under the guardianship of a scattered
file of pinners-up, along the south side of Oxford Street
alone.   Thirty years ago the dead walls gave place to shop
fronts, and the pinners-up departed to their long homes.
As they died out no one succeeded to their honours and
emoluments ; and in place of the four or five score of them
who flourished in London at the commencement of this
century, it is probable that the most rigid search would
hardly reveal a dozen in the present day.   In the provincial
towns, the diminution is not so marked ; and there, from
causes not difficult to explain, the pinner-up has been better
able to hold his ground.   This functionary, wherever he is
found, is generally a superannuated artisan or discarded
servant ; and as he is necessarily exposed to all weathers,
his costume usually consists of everything he can contrive
to hang about him.

We will now briefly allude to the wood-blocks which Catnach had in his possession, and which served for the purpose of illustrating during the time that he had been in business. He had a large collection, such as they were; but as works of art they had little or no pretension, being, upon the whole, of the oddest and most ludicrous character. Those that were intended for the small books were very quaint—as we have shown by the fac-similed specimens we have given—whilst the larger portion, which were chiefly intended for the "awfuls," were grotesque and hideous in their design and execution. No more ghastly sight could be imagined than one of Jemmy's embellishments of an execution. It would appear that for the last discharge of the law he had a large collection of blocks which would suit any number of victims who were about to undergo the dread penalty. It mattered little how many Jack Ketch was going to operate upon, wood-blocks to the exact number were always adopted, in this particular the great "Dying-Speech Merchant" would seem to have thought that his honour and reputation were at stake, for he had his network so formed as to be able to secure almost every information of news that was passing between the friends of the culprits and the prerogative óf the Crown. But we are informed that upon one occasion he was nearly entrapped. Three victims were upon the eve of being executed, and in those days—and in later times—it was not an uncommon thing to see the confession and dying speech printed one or two days previous to the event. This we are told by those in the trade was almost necessary, in order that the sheets might be ready for the provinces almost as soon as the sentence of the law had been carried out. It so happened that on the night previouś to an execution, one of the culprits was reprieved. It was solely by a piece of good luck that Catnach heard of it. Several sheets had been struck off; and Jemmy was often chaffed about hanging three men instead of two; but our informant assures us that the error was corrected before any of the impressions were dispatched from the office. Had they gone before the public in their original state, the *locus standi* of the great publisher in Monmouth Court would have been greatly imperilled. To those who are fond of the fine arts, *in usum vulgi*, Catnach's embellishments will afford a fund of amusement. Amongst the lot were several well known places, the scenes of horrible and awful crimes, engravings of debauchery and ill-fame, together with an endless number of different kinds, suitable at the shortest possible notice, to illustrate every conceivable and inconceivable subject.

The Seven Dials in general, and "The Catnach Press" in particular, had no dread of copyright law—the principal Librarian of the British Museum, Stationer's, or any other Hall in those days—and as wood engravings were not to be had then so quickly or cheap as now-a-day's, Jemmy used at times to be his own engraver, and while the compositors were setting up the types, he would carve out the illustration on the back of an old pewter music plate, and by nailing it on to a piece of wood make it into an improvised stereo-plate off-hand, for he was very handy at this sort of work, at which also his sister, with his instruction, could assist; so they soon managed to rough out a figure or two, and when things were dull and slack they generally got one or two subjects ready in stock, such as a highwayman with crape over his face, shooting a traveller, who is falling from his horse near a wide-spreading old elm tree, through which the moon was to be seen peeping; not forgetting to put the highwayman in top boots and making him a regular dandy. This was something after the plan of the artists of the cheap illustrated papers of the present day, who generally antici-pate events sometime beforehand to be ready with their blocks. As a proof of this, the editor of the "London,

Provincial, and Colonial Press News," says "I happened to call one day on an artist for the 'Illustrated Press,' and found him busily engaged in sketching a funeral procession with some twenty coffins borne on the shoulders of men who were winding their way through an immense crowd. Upon inquiry, I was told that it was intended for the next week's issue, and was to represent the funeral of the victims of the late dreadful colliery explosion, for although the inquest was only just then sitting, and all the bodies had not yet been found, there was sure to be a funeral of that kind when it was all over, and as they did not know how many bodies were to be buried at one time, it was very cleverly arranged to commence the procession from the *corner of the block*, and so leave it to the imagination as to how many more coffins were coming in the rear; something after the plan of a small country theatre, when representing Richard the Third, and in the battle scene, after the first two or three of the army had made their appearance, to cry 'halt!' very loudly to all those behind who were not seen, and leave the spectators to guess how many hundreds there were to come."

For the illustrating of catchpennies, broadsides, and street-literature in general, particular kinds of wood-cuts were required. In most cases one block was called upon to perform many parts; and the majority of metropolitan printers, who went in for this work, had only a very limited number of them. Very often the same cuts were repeated over and over again, and made to change sides with one another, and that simply to make a little variation from a ballad or broadside that had been printed at the same office on the day, week, or month previous. It mattered little what the subject was, it required some adornment, in the shape of illustration, to give effect to it. The catchpennies, especially those connected with the awfuls, were in general very rough productions. A lover strangling his sweetheart with a long piece of rope. A heartless woman murdering an innocent man. Vice punished and virtue rewarded, and similar subjects, were always handled in such a manner as to create a degree of excitement, sympathy, and alarm. The broadsides, generally adorned with some rough outline of the royal arms of England, a crowned king or queen, as the subject might be, received their full share of consideration at the hands of the artist. Scions of royal blood, and those connected with the court, were often painted in colours glaring and attractive, whilst the matter set forth in the letterpress was not always the most flattering or encouraging.

In course of time, what with wood-cuts getting cheaper, and opportunities for purchasing them presenting themselves, Catnach's stock gradually improved in quantity, if not always in quality; and he had in his miscellaneous collection many designed and cut by Thomas Bewick, the man who took the greatest part in raising the art of wood-engraving as it is now practised, and whose pictures in the "History of Quadrupeds" and the "Book of Birds," are still unrivalled as specimens of exquisite truthfulness and finish. Bewick was born at Cherryburn, in Northumberland, in 1753, and as he had shown some taste in drawing, was apprenticed to a copper-plate engraver at Newcastle-on-Tyne. His master, Mr. Beilby, engraved door-plates, clock-faces, and occasionally copper-plates for illustrating books, and with his brother, Thomas Beilby, also taught drawing. They never gave Bewick a lesson, however, for they undertook such a variety of work that the lad was always employed, and had no time to study. Etching sword blades, making bookbinders' stamps and dies, engraving seals, rings, jewellery, and silver plate, and, in fact, all the business that could be supposed to belong to their trade, and never refusing an order, the workshop of the Beilbys was always full. It happened, however, that this brought about the very event which afterwards made Bewick famous; for, among other orders, there occasionally came some from printers, asking the Beilbys to execute some wood-cuts for their books and handbills. Mr. Beilby was such a bad hand at wood-engraving, and disliked it so much, that he soon left that branch of the work to his apprentice, who then began to design and make drawings on the wood—an occupation in which he delighted—and to engrave the designs that he had made. One of these was a picture of St. George and the Dragon, for the top of a bill, and it was so well executed, and attracted so much attention, that more orders were sent than he could easily undertake, and his whole time was devoted to designing and cutting wood-blocks. Some pictures which he engraved for "Gay's Fables" were so good that his master sent a few impressions of them to the Society for the Encouragement of Arts, who sent to ask him whether he would have a gold medal or seven guineas in money. He chose the money, and said that he never felt greater pleasure in his life than in presenting it to his mother. When he was out of his apprenticeship Bewick found himself constantly employed; and some of his works will remain as exquisite specimens of the art as long as wood-engraving is practised. A series of his designs may be seen at the South Kensington Museum, along with many other pictures illustrative of the progress of drawing and engraving on wood.

Since the death of Bewick, in 1828, the establishment of so many illustrated magazines and newspapers, the immense increase in the number of picture books for children, and the substitution of wood-cuts for copper and steel-plate engravings, have all made the trade of the wood engraver of greater importance; and most of our great artists have devoted their attention to drawing pictures on wood blocks, that they might be cut afterwards by those who make engraving only their particular business. In this respect the

modern differs very materially from the ancient practice.
The old masters not only made the design of the picture on
the wood, but very often engraved it afterwards. This is
not very often the case in our own day, and though to be a
skilful wood engraver it is necessary also to be a tolerably
good artist—the two professions are in most instances quite
distinct.

It is remarkable how great the demand has become within
the last few years to secure copies or early impressions of
the works of our great wood engravers. The large sums of
money which are given for, and the eagerness in which the
works of many of our north country artists are sought after,
is really marvellous. One of the most curious and interesting books published of late years is that which was brought
out a few years ago by Mr. William Dodd, of Newcastle.*
He succeeded to the business of the late Mr. Emerson
Charnley. The latter through life had been a diligent
student and collector of the old books, rarities, and such
like, and the result of his enterprise was that, at the time of
his death, he possessed a valuable collection of wood blocks,
extending over a period of upwards of 200 years. These
had been principally intended for the illustration of books
of history, poetry, adventure, &c. From the pages of the
work we catch at a glimpse the progressive stages which the
art has made in this country during the last two centuries,
and this is the more noticeable when we compare the state
of things that existed prior to the time of Thomas Bewick.†
It was towards the close of the last century when this great
artist set himself to improve, adorn, and shed an
additional lustre over a profession which hitherto it had not
known. How he succeeded will be best shown by a careful

---

* A copy in Hugo's sale, August, 1877, brought £1 12s. od.
† Hugo's copy of the catalogue sold for £1 14s., od.

examination of the many beautiful productions which emanated from his hands. By his great abilities, energy, and perseverance, he gained for himself a niche in the temple of fame. No works of the present day are more eagerly sought after than those of this great north country artist.

On this subject Mr. Hugo, in his " Bewick Collector," says :—" The most extraordinary sums are asked for and paid for what would appear to the unlearned the most valueless and uninteresting articles. From the present state of the market, and the still increasing avidity of collectors, it may be fairly augured that the prices will progressively and largely increase ; and it would appear, to quote the words of an eminent bookseller, lately used to myself, that ' anything may be asked and anything may be had.' All, therefore," continues Mr. Hugo, " that I can advise the collector is, not so much to be cautious against paying too dearly for what he gets, as to be sure that what he gets is genuine."

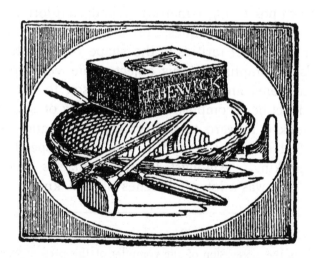

One of the best private collections of wood-blocks in the north part ·of the kingdom was held by the late Mr. William Davison. Independent of his own, he had also those that formerly belonged to Mr. John Catnach. They were chiefly the productions. of Bewick, Clennel, Harvey, Reaveley, &c. During the lifetime of Mr. Davison the principal portion of his stock of engravings was published in the form of a catalogue, and they make an attractive volume.* After his· death, the whole of the blocks, together with his other effects, were sold at Newcastle-on-Tyne. The illustrations that were used for the " Hermit of Warkworth,"† the poems of Burns and Ferguson, "Beattie's Minstrel," " Crazy Jane," and " Shepherd Lubin," were· purchased by Mr. Robert Robinson,' of ´Pilgrim Street, Newcastle, who afterwards sold them to Mr. Hugo, several of which appear in his book entitled, the " Bewick Collector." It was rather unfortunate that Mr. Davison's valuable collection did not find a resting place in the town of his adoption.‡

In late years there has been a growing desire on the part of many to possess specimens, in a collected form, of some of the best catchpennies, broadsides, and fly-sheets, together with other rarities in the shape of street-literature. Towards accomplishing this object some very good work has been done, and there is every reason to believe that more will yet be accomplished. The issuing of such a work will be looked forward to with great interest and curiosity, and we feel sure that many will wish a God-speed to such an undertaking. Amongst Jemmy Catnach's treasures in the fine arts, was a lot of sketches of well known Alnwick

---

* Hugo's copy sold for £1 18s. 0d.

† Now in the possession of the compiler of the present work : purchased at Mr. Hugo's Sale, August, 1877.

‡ Mr. George Skelly, Alnwick.

characters, including those of Dicky Greenhead, Ralphy
Docus, Billy Cleghorn, Derick Ormond, Forster Rattray,
Jemmy Bamforth, &c. A portion of these was exhibited
at the Jubilee Exhibition of the Alnwick Mechanics'
Institution, held in 1873. They were executed by Mr.
Percy Foster, and are the property of Mr. William Thew of
London.

A POLITICAL ALPHABET,

FOR

THE RISE AND INSTRUCTION

OF

JUVENILE POLITICIANS.

A is Prince Albert, once buxom and keen,
Who from Germany came and got spliced to the Queen ;
His time passes happily—I wish him good joy,
Now he has one little maiden and one little boy.

B stands for Bright, such a chap we are told,
For puddings and muffins, hot crumpets and rolls :
He hollows and raves, till his sides they do ache,
And he wants for to feed all the world on plumb cake.

C is brave Cobden, who one night it is said,
Threw a large quartern loaf at poor Buckingham's head ;
Concerning the Corn Laws he laid it down strong,
And he spun out a yarn seventeen hours long.

D is Tom Duncombe, a real ladies' man,
And greatly respected all over the land ;
He strives day and night, like a jolly M.P.,
To procure old women a strong cup of tea.

E is General Evans, a member again,
Who beat forty thousand old women in Spain ;
He wanted to sit in Parliament House,
So he kicked up a rumpus and turned out poor Rouse.

F stands for Ferrand, a Protectionist tool,
He spoke seven hours and talked like a fool ;
He represents Knaresborough just for a joke,
Where there's nothing but porage pots, mouse-traps, and
  smoke.

G is for Graham, who early and late,
Attends to the post office, church, and the state ;
He once turned his jacket, but that never mind ;
He's a good servant now, and employment ·does find.

H is old Hume, who is clever we see
At addition, substraction, and the rule of three ;
He's acquainted with practice, I've heard so at least,
And he jumps round the house like a fourpenny piece.

I is Bob Inglis, a chap for to pray,
Who'd not suffer one on the great Sabbath day
To eat, drink, or sleep, talk, whistle, or sing,
The cat say moll-row, or the ladies lay-in.

J stands for Jersey, who governs the horse,
And a short time ago his fair daughter he lost ;
She was fond of soldiers, and off she went slap,
With a gun and a knapsack slung over her back.

D D

K is Fitz. Kelly, such a chap for to jaw,
And can tell you about L A W law ;
To get into Cambridge he strove very hard,
Where they sell out fresh butter at 9d. a yard.

L. is for Lincoln, who none can rebuke,
He offended his daddy, old Nottingham's Duke,
'Cause manly he acted, Newcastle mad run,
He elected a stranger and turned out his son.

M is Lord Morpeth, who nothing could baulk,
To be elected so free for the county of York ;
He vows if a Protectionist does him come nigh,.
He 'll give him a terrible slap in the eye.

N is old Nosey, a soldier so true,
Who frightened old Boney at great Waterloo.
Although he is old, he is able to run,
With the musket and bayonet to follow the drum.

O is O'Connell, a Repealer so big,
With a stick in his hand, like the mast of a brig ;
He calls himself Daniel, the pride of the law,
The King of old Ireland, Erin go Bragh !

P stands for Peel, who is acting upright,
And between you and me, he has got a long sight ;
If he don't beat his opponents all very slap,
He will bolt off to Tamworth and swallow his trap.

Q is the Queen, who to John Bull did say,.
" You must recollect, Johnny, in April, or May
A blooming young Albert I shall then bring to town,
So move along, Johnny, and gather the browns."

R is Lord Russell, how hard was his case,
When he ran down to Windsor to look for a place ;
'Cause they wouldn't employ him he held down his nob,
And vented some curses on Arthur and Bob.

S is Lord Stanley, who scampered with fear,
Afraid that old Derby, his father, oh, dear !
Should take away from him his trousers and coat,
And drown him in vinegar, barley, and oats.

T is for Thesiger, Abinger's man,
The Attorney-General for old England's land ;
For the life of the Corn Bill he swears he won't plead,
Although he 's a counseller able, indeed.

U is for Uxbridge, who wonders have done,
He was born in the barracks, old Anglesey's son ;
His father 's a marquis, none can him degrade,
He lives in Burlington Gardens, near to the Arcade.

V stands for Villiers, whom the farmers detest,
For to slaughter the Corn Laws he will do his best ;
For Free Trade he struggles by day and by night,
He is next in command to Dick Cobden and Bright.

W is Wakley, a doctor so bold,
Who declares on the Corn Bill an inquest he 'll hold ;
When the jury he 'll charge, but England shall see
A verdict returned of *Felo-de-se.*

X is a letter which puts me in mind
Of a ship load of landlords sailing against wind,
Right over the ocean from England away,
To spend their last hours in Botany Bay.

Y is for York, the Archbishop so big,
Who loves for to dine on a little tythe pig ;
Free Trade on last Sunday so did him perplex,
That he sung Rule Britannia, and thought 'twas the text.

Z is for Zetland, an English peer
Who likes to see bread ánd potatoes sold dear ;
He is very kind to a stranger in need—
This Political Alphabet take home and reàd.

Birt, Printer, 39, Great St. Andrew Street, Seven Dials, London.

LOOK at me : Then comes answer like A B C.

We gather from a paper which was written by an old pressman, who died, a few years ago, in the Clerkenwell Workhouse, a good deal of matter relative to Catnach. The paper is illustrative of many of the eccentricities of Jemmy Catnach, but there is very little in it as to the mode in which he spent his life, whilst his early career is never spoken of. This may have arisen from the fact that very few, save his more intimate friends were cognizant with his youthful adventures.

The preliminary remarks to the article are perhaps a little too severe. The writer stigmatizes Jemmy as having been a "plodding, ignorant, dirty, successful individual," this, to say the least, is rather a harsh assertion. To say that he was ignorant and dirty is a base calumny, to which many of his old friends can testify. The peculiar place where he pitched his tent, and where he spent the best years of his life, together with the queer and mysterious customers that he was in the habit of doing business with, most certainly did not add many charms to the man, or to the locality; but as to dirtiness, we never heard the least suspicion laid to his charge. He was, we must admit, extremely singular both in dress and manners.

In dress he was very indifferent—almost eccentric. He seldom wore a coat, and he never appeared so much at ease than when in his shirt-sleeves and a white apron, with a bib coming close up to his neck. When business matters compelled him to go abroad, it was invariably his custom to put over his shoulders a loose cloth tippet, and to this must be added a paper cap, common to printers, at other times a low-crowned or cut-down hat. In the eyes of the Londoner's this mode of apparel would now appear ludicrously strange; but north-country people are very familiar with the "shirt-sleeve costume," and fifty years ago it was nearly as common in the northern counties as the "shepherd's plaid," which, even at the present day, in

some of the border villages, is worn by a few of the oldest
male inhabitants

Behind Catnach's shop in Monmouth Court was a small
parlour, and this place was converted into a printing-office.
It presented an odd appearance, and to the nervous and
timid mind the ceiling of this room was anything but assur-
ing; but it never troubled the mind of the principal occupant.
The "Old Pressman" thus describes the place, and the
appliances in it : " The printing-office was in a little back
parlour.   In it was an old wooden demy two-pull press,
which, when in full work, would raise the floor above it, to
which the steadying-beams were attached, several inches,
and would rock the old four-poled bedstead, which stood
immediately overhead, like a cradle every time the bar-
handle was pulled home."   It was in this apartment where
many of the north-country lads, of whom we have previously
spoken, met at night and talked over the affairs of the day.

There can be little doubt that Catnach justly earned the
distinction of being one of the great pioneers in the cause
of promoting cheap literature—he was for a long time the
great Mæcenas and Elzévir of the Seven Dials district. We
do not pretend to say that the productions which emanated
from his establishment contained much that was likely to
enlighten the intellect, or sharpen the taste of the ordinary
reader ; but, to a great extent, they served well in creating
an impetus in the minds of many to soar after things of a
higher and more ennobling character.   Whilst for the little
folk his store was like the conjuror's bag—inexhaustible.
He could cater to the taste and fancies of all, and it is
marvellous, even in these days of a cheap press, to look
back upon the time when this enterprising man was, by a
steady course of action, so paving the way for that bright
day in the annals of Britain's history, when every child in
the land should be educated.

JAMES CATNACH

TO HIS

JUVENILE READERS.

LITTLE Boys and Girls will find
At CATNACH'S something to their mind ;
From great variety may choose,
What will instruct them and amuse.
The prettiest plates that you can find,
To please at once the eye and mind,
In all his little books appear,
In natural beauty, shining clear ;
Instruction unto youth when given,
Points the path from earth to heaven.

He sells by Wholesale and Retail,
To suit all moral tastes can't fail.

Catnach, to the day of his retirement from business in 1838, when he purchased the freehold of a disused public-house, which had been known as the Lion Inn, together with the grounds attached at Dancer's Hill, South Mimms, near Barnet, in the county of Middlesex, worked and toiled in the office of the "Seven Dials Press," in which he had moved as the pivot, or directing mind, for upwards of a quarter of a century. He lived and died a bachelor. His only idea of all earthly happiness and mental enjoyment was now to get away in retirement to a convenient distance from his old place of business, so to give him an opportunity occasionally to go up to town and have a chat and a friendly glass with one or two old paper-workers and ballad-writers, and a few others connected with his peculiar trade who had shown any disposition to work when work was to be done. To them he was always willing to give or advance a few pence or shillings, in money or stock, and a glass—

" Affliction's sons are brothers in distress ;
   A brother to relieve, how exquisite the bliss ! "   •

But Jemmy knew the men that were "skulkers," as he termed them, and there was no coin, stock, or a glass for them. He invariably drank whiskey, a spirit not in general demand in England in those days. Gin was then, as now, the reigning favourite with the street folks. When the question was put to him in reference to his partiality to whiskey, he always replied—the Scotch blood proudly rising in his veins, and with a strong Northumberland burr, which never wholly forsook him, particularly when warmed by argument or drink—that, " He disdained to tipple with ' stuff,' by means of which all the women of the town got drunk. I am of Catnach. Yes ! there 's Catnach blood in me. Catnach—King Catnach—Catnach, King of the Picts. We descend in a right straight line from the Picts. That 's the sort of blood-of-blood that flows in the veins of all the true-bred Catnach's." Jemmy would be for continually arguing when in his cups, and the old and the more artful of the street-folk would let him have all the say and grandeur that he then felt within him on the subject, well knowing that they would be much more likely to have their glasses replenished by agreeing with him than by contradicting him. Even in his sober moments Jemmy always persisted, right or wrong, that the Catnach's, or Catternach's, were descended direct from a King of the Picts. Yet, what is somewhat anomalous, he was of himself a rigid churchman and a staunch old Tory, "one of the olden time," and "as full of the glorious Constitution as the first volume of Blackstone."

An anecdote is told of him, which goes a long way to establish his claim to be ranked amongst the true Constitutionists. "He, having invited a few Alnwick friends to spend a day with him in London, resolved, after dinner, to take a walk with them into the suburbs. Upon the road various subjects were introduced, and amongst the lot was politics. Jemmy, and one of the party, who, by-the-bye, was a Radical of the extreme caste, got to very high words. Suddenly Catnach turned upon his heels and bade the company good-day, exclaiming with the next breath that he would not associate with one who was little better than the 'scum of the country.'"

On Catnach's retirement from the business, he left it to Mrs. Anne Ryle, his sister, charged, nevertheless, to the amount of £1,000, payable at his death to the estate of his niece, Marion Martha Ryle. In the meanwhile Mr. James Paul acted as managing man for Mrs. Ryle. This Mr. Paul—of whom Jemmy was very fond, and rumour saith, had no great dislike to the mother—had grown from a boy to a man in the office of the "Catnach Press." He was, therefore, well acquainted with the customers, by whom he was much respected; and it was by his tact and judgment that the business was kept so well together. He married a

Miss Crisp, the daughter of a publican in the immediate
neighbourhood.   At Catnach's death he entered into partnership with Mrs. Ryle, and the business was carried on
under the title and style of Paul & Co.   At the end of one
of the farthing series of children's books, entitled "The
Tragical Death of an Apple Pie, who was cut to pieces and
eaten by twenty-five Gentlemen, with whom All Little
People ought to be acquainted," we find the following
ingenious trade announcement, " If my little readers are
pleased with what they have found in this book they have
nothing to do but to run to J. Paul & Co's., 2 and 3, Monmouth Court, 7 Dials, where they may have a great variety
of books not less entertaining than this of the same size and
price."   In 1845 the partnership existing between Mrs.
Ryle and Paul was dissolved, Mr. Paul receiving £800 in
settlement.   He then entered into the public line, taking
the Spencer's Arms, at the corner of Monmouth Court.   A
son that was born to him in 1847, he had christened James
Catnach Paul.   He died in the year 1870, just six weeks
after Mrs. Ryle, and lies buried in the next grave but one
to Catnach and his sister.

　　After Mr. Paul had left the business it was carried on as
A. Ryle & Co., and ultimately became to be the property
of Mr. W. S. Fortey, who still carries on the old business in
the same premises.   A copy of whose trade announcement
runs thus :—

"THE CATNACH PRESS."   (Established 1813.)

"William S. Fortey, (late A. Ryle, successor to the late J. Catnach)
Printer, Publisher, and Wholesale Stationer, 2 and 3, Monmouth Court,
Seven Dials, London, W.C.
　　"The cheapest and greatest variety in the trade of large coloured
penny books ; half-penny coloured books ; farthing books ; penny and
half-penny panoramas ; school books ; penny and half-penny song
books ; memorandum books ; poetry cards ; lotteries ; ballads (4,000
sorts) and hymns ; valentines ; scripture sheets ; Christmas pieces ;

Twelfth-night characters; carols; book and sheet almanacks; envelopes, note paper, &c., &c.

"W. S. Fortey begs to inform his friends and the public generally, that after 19 years' service, he has succeeded to the business of his late employers, (A. Ryle and Co.), and intends carrying on the same, trusting that his long experience will be a recommendation, and that no exertion shall be wanting on his part to merit a continuance of those favours that have been so liberally bestowed on that establishment during the last 56 years."

Catnach did not long enjoy or survive his retirement. After the novelty of looking, as the poet Cowper puts it, and no doubt in his case found it, "Through the loop-holes of retreat, to see the stir of the Great Babel, and not feel the crowd," had worn itself out, "James Catnach, Gentleman, formerly of Monmouth Court, Monmouth Street, Printer," grew dull in his "Old Bachelor's Box;" he was troubled with hypochondriasis, and a liver overloaded with bile, and was further off than ever from being a happy man. He had managed to rake and scrape together—as far as we can get any knowledge—some £5,000 or £6,000, although £10,000 and upwards is mostly put down to him. However, he had grabbed for and caught a fair amount of "siller and gold," but it failed to realize to him—

> An elegant sufficiency, content,
> Retirement, rural quiet, friendship, books,
> Ease and alternate labour, useful life,
> Progressive virtue, and approving Heaven!

No! all he had realized was that unenviable position so popularly known as of a man not knowing what to do with himself. His visits to town were now much more frequent and of longer duration, and for hours he would sit and loiter about the shops and houses of his old neighbours, so that he might catch a glimpse, or enjoy a friendly chat with his old friends and customers. At length he got sick at heart, "wearied to the bone," and sighed for the bustle of London life.

From the following letter written to his sister, Mrs. Ryle, in 1840, and now before us, we glean something of his state of mind and bodily health :—

July 4th, '40·

Dear Sister,—

I have been very ill for these last three weeks. I was obliged to send for Dr. Morris to Cup me, which did some good for a few days, since then the pains have gone into my breast and ribs, and for the last three days I have kept my bed, and could take nothing but a little tea and water-gruel. I wish you to procure me 6 Bills to stick on my window shutters, outside and in, "This House to be Let," and send them with ½ lb. Tea as soon as possible—but do not send them by Salmon's Coach, for he will not leave them at Jackson's as Wild does, but sends a boy with it, which costs me double porterage. I feel the loss of my jelly now I am so ill, and can eat little or nothing, it would have done my throat good. I have a great crop of black and red berries [currants] if you choose I will send them up, and you can make some jelly for us both ; let me know as soon as you can, say Wednesday morning and I will make the Postwoman call for the parcel at Jackson's. I also wish you to enquire of Carr what is the lowest he will take for the rooms over Mrs. Morgan, by the ½ year.

I have nothing more to say but to be remembered to Mary and Paul, and remain

Yours truly

James Catnach

Pray send a Paper of the Execution of the Valet, and the trial of Oxford—Mrs. Westly has not sent me 1 paper since I was last in town —neither has Thornton.

Mrs. Ryle,
    2 & 3, Monmouth Court,
        Compton Street,
            London.

Ultimately Catnach hired the rooms he speaks about in the body of his letter to his sister, which were on the first floor of No. 6, Monmouth Court. All the vacant space in his old premises being now fully occupied by Mrs. Ryle and her assistants, now "the humble cottage fenc'd with osiers round," which to his leisure afforded no pleasure, was entirely deserted, and in London he fretted out the remaining portion of his life. He soon grew peevish, and his brain got a little out of balance, then he listlessly wandered in and out of the streets, courts, and alleys, "infirm of purpose." On stormy days and nights to stand and view the lightning from Waterloo Bridge was his special delight and wonder. His temper and liver were now continually out of order, and which whiskey, even "potations pottle deep," failed to relieve. At length he died of jaundice, in the very London court in which he had mucked and grubbed for the best part of his life, on the first day of February, 1841. Like other great men of history he 'has several *locales* mentioned as his final resting-place—Hornsey, Barnet, South Mimms, &c.

> *Urbes, certarunt septem de patria Homeri,*
> *Nulla domus vivo patria fuit.*

Seven cities strove, whence Homer first should come,
When living, he no country had nor home :—*Tom Nash*, 1599.

SEVEN Grecian cities vied for Homer dead,
Through which the living Homer begged his bread.

Seven cities vied for Homer's birth, with emulation pious,—
Salamis, Samos, Colophon, Rhodes, Argos, Athens, Chios.
                                    —*From the Greek.*

But Catnach lies buried in Highgate Cemetery, in one of the two plots that Mrs. Ryle purchased sometime previous to her brother's death. The official number of the grave is 256, SQUARE 29, over which is placed a flat stone, inscribed :—

IN MEMORY OF

JAMES CATNACH,
Of Dancer's Hill.
DIED 1st FEBRUARY, 1841,
Aged 49.

ANNE RYLE,

Sister to the above, and widow of Joseph Ryle, who died in India, 10th October, 1823. She died 20th April, 1870, Aged 75.

Blessed are the dead which die in the Lord.

The freehold in the other plot of ground, after Catnach's death, was transferred to Mr. Robert Palmer Harding, the accountant of London, who married Catnach's niece. The stone records the death of ELIZABETH CORNELIA, third daughter of Robert Palmer Harding and Marion Martha Harding, born 9 June, 1848, died 8 November, 1848 ; and GREVILLE, second son of the above, born 29 May, 1856, died 3 September, 1856. This grave is now numbered 5179. We have been thus minute in respect to Catnach's grave, from the circumstance of our having received so many contradictory statements as to its whereabouts. But, however, we have removed all doubt from our mind by a personal visit to the Highgate Cemetery, where, under the guidance of the very civil and obliging superintendent of the grounds, Mr. W. F. Tabois, we were conducted to the spot we required, then introduced to Mr. Marks, the sexton, "here man and boy thirty years," and whom we found very intelligent and communicative on various *subjects*—

"From *grave* to gay, from lively to severe."

The murder of Lord William Russell by his Swiss valet Francois Benjamin Courvoisier, in the year 1840, excited immense interest at the time of its occurrence, not only from the position in society of its ill-fated victim, but from the strange combination of circumstances that led to the conviction of the culprit. The trial of the prisoner commenced at the Central Criminal Court, Old Bailey, on the morning of Thursday, the 17th of June, and terminated on Saturday evening following.

The counsel for the prosecution were Mr. Adolphus, Mr. Bodkin, and Mr. Chambers, and for the prisoner, Mr. Charles Phillips and Mr. Clarkson. The attorney for the prosecution was Mr. Hobler, and for the prisoner Mr. Flower. Lord Chief Justice Tindal, Mr. Baron Parke and the Common Sergeant presided.

On the prisoner being placed in the dock, the Clerk of the Arraigns then proceeded to read over the indictment, and told him, that as he was an alien, he had the privilege of being tried by a jury composed half of foreigners and half of Englishmen, and asked him whether he wished to have six of the jurors foreigners, or whether he was content with a jury consisting entirely of Englishmen. The prisoner replied that he was content to be tried by Englishmen. Lord Chief Justice Tindal then directed the foreign jury to be discharged. The prisoner having pleaded *Not Guilty*, Mr. Adolphus rose to address the jury for the prosecution.

The case for the prosecution closed at twenty minutes to eight on Friday night. On the next day, the jury having been re-sworn, Mr Charles Phillips, commonly known as "Charley Phillips," and the greatest "Thieves Counsel" and blustering, bullying, blackguard Old Bailey' barrister of the day, commenced his memorable address on behalf of the prisoner. The effect of the learned gentleman's address was very visible on almost every person in the court ; it was not only admirable for its eloquence, but a remarkable illustration of the ease with which an ingenious advocate may pervert the best developed train of evidence, and out of his own subtilty make the worse appear the better argument. The effect it had on the jury was to make them hesitate on their verdict for full an hour and a half; and considering that the confession of the culprit has set at rest all questions of his guilt, it is painful to reflect how the accorded permission to prisoners to address juries by counsel, may be made the means of violating the stern demands of justice. There is now no doubt that on the extraordinary and unexpected discovery of the missing plate during the progress of the trial, and the fact that Madame Piolani had identified the prisoner as the man who had left that plate in her charge, that he became dreadfully agitated and sent for Mr. Charles Phillips, to whom he at once confessed his guilt, and that before Mr. Phillips had delivered the speech in his defence, in which, among other things, he unblushingly said, "The God above *alone* knows who is guilty of the terrible act of which the prisoner stands accused," the whole speech afterwards became the subject of much comment and public discussion as to whether such a speech, under such circumstances, was or was not an abuse of the privilege of counsel—some contending that counsel are bound by all means within their power to save their clients from the consequences even of admitted crimes, others contending that the privilege of counsel is accorded to prisoners for the due and just administration of the laws—to protect the innocent from wrongful conviction, not to pervert the ends of justice, and the whole object of the existence of criminal courts ; and that, therefore, no sophistry—no professional practice or compact—can justify a man retained for one known to be guilty in doing more than protecting his client from illegal conviction.

Following are the two concluding paragraphs, which we give as a fair specimen of the whole :—

E E

"And now, gentlemen, having travelled through this case of mystery and darkness, my anxious and painful task is ended. But, gentlemen, your's is about to commence, and I can only say, may Almighty God guide you to a just conclusion! The issues of life and death are in your hands. To you it gives to consign that man once more to the enjoyments of existence and the dignity of freedom ; or to send him to an ignominious death, and to brand upon his grave the awful epithet of a murderer. Gentlemen, mine has been a painful and awful task ; but still more awful is the responsibility attached to the decision upon the general facts or circumstances of the case. To violate the living temple which the Lord hath made—to quench the fire within a man's breast, is an awful and a terrible responsibility, and the decision of ' Guilty,' once pronounced, let me remind you, is irrevocable. Speak not that word lightly—speak it not on suspicion, however strong —upon moral conviction, however apparently well-grounded—upon inference—upon doubt—or upon anything but the broad, clear, irresistible noon-day conviction of the truth of what is alleged.

"I speak to you thus in no hostile feeling : I speak to you as a brother and a fellow Christian. I thus remind you of your awful responsibility. I tell you that, if you condemn that man lightly, or upon mere suspicion consign him to an ignominious death, the recollection of the deed will never die within you. If you should pronounce your awful verdict without a deep and irresistible conviction of his guilt, your crime will be present to you during the rest of your lives—it will pursue you with remorse, like a shadow, in your crowded walks—it will render your death-bed one of horror—and, taking the form of that man's spirit, it will condemn and sink you before the judgment-seat of your God ! So beware, I say, beware what you do ! "

The result of the discussions that arose out of Mr. Charles Phillip's speech, was that that gentleman never appeared again in a criminal court of justice ; he received an appointment, and accepted it, as a commissioner in the Court of Bankruptcy, which he retained until his death.

The following is a fac-simile of the " Execution Paper,"
from the press of Paul and Co.

TRIAL, SENTENCE, CONFESSION, & EXECUTION

OF

F. B. COURVOISIER,

FOR THE

Murder of Lord Wm. Russell.

THE VERDICT.

OLD BAILEY, SATURDAY EVENING,
June 20th, 1840.

After the jury had been absent for an hour and twenty minutes, they returned into court, and the prisoner was again placed at the bar

The names of the jury were then called over, and the clerk of the court said—"How say you, gentlemen, have you agreed on your verdict? Do you find the prisoner Guilty or Not Guilty of the felony of murder with which he stands charged?"

The foreman of the jury, in a low voice, said—"We find him GUILTY!"

The Clerk of the Court then said Francois Benjamin Courvoisier, you have been found Guilty of the wilful murder of William Russell, Esq, commonly called Lord William Russell; what have you to say why the court should not give you sentence to die according to law?

The prisoner made no reply The usual proclamation for silence was then made.

SENTENCE.

The LORD CHIEF JUSTICE TINDAL, having put on the black cap, said Francois Benjamin Courvoisier, you have been found guilty by an intelligent, patient, and impartial jury of the crime of wilol murder That crime has been established against you, not indeed by the testimony of eye-witnesses as to the fact, but by a chain of circumstances no less unerring, which have left no doubt of your guilt in the minds of the jury, and all those who heard the trial. It is ordained by divine authority that the murderer shall not escape justice, and this ordination has been exemplified in your case, in the course of this trial, by the disclosure of evidence which has brought the facts to bear against you in a conclusive manner The murder, although committed in the dark and silent hour of night, has nevertheless been brought clearly to light by Divine interposition The precise motive which induced you to commit this guilty act can only be known to your own conscience; but it now only remains for me to recommend you most earnestly to employ the short time you have to live in prayer and repentance, and in endeavouring to make your peace with that Almighty Being whose law you have broken, and before whom you must shortly appear. The Learned Judge then passed sentence on the prisoner in the usual form.

The court was very much crowded to the last.

THE CONFESSION OF THE CONVICT.

After the Learned Judge had passed sentence on the convict, he was removed from the bar, and immediately made a full confession of his guilt.

THE EXECUTION.

At eight o'clock this morning, Courvoisier descended the steps leading to the gallows, and advanced, without looking round him, to the centre of the platform, followed by the executioner and the ordinary of the prison, the Rev Mr Carver. On his appearance a few yells of execration escaped from a portion of the crowd, but the general body of the people, great as must have been their abhorrence of his atrocious crime, remained silent spectators of the scene which was passing before their eyes. The prisoner's manner was marked by an extraordinary appearance of firmness. His step was steady and collected, and his movements free from the slightest agitation or indecision. His countenance indeed was pale, and bore the trace of much dejection, but it was at the same time calm and

unmoved. While the executioner was placing him on the drop he slightly moved his hands (which were tied in front of him, and strongly clasped one within the other) up and down two or three times, and this was the only visible symptom of any emotion or mental anguish which the wretched man endured. His face was then covered with the cap, fitting so closely as not to conceal the outlines of his countenance, the noose was then adjusted. During this operation he lifted up his head and raised his hands to his breast as if in the action of fervent prayer In a moment the fatal bolt was withdrawn, the drop fell, and in this attitude the murderer perished. He died without any violent struggle In two minutes after he had fallen his legs were twice slightly convulsed, but no farther motion was observable, excepting that his raised arms gradually losing their vitality, sank down from their own weight.

After hanging one hour, the body was cut down and removed within the prison.

AFFECTING COPY OF VERSES

Attention give, both old and young,
Of high and low degree,
. Think while this mournful tale is sung,
Of my sad misery

I've slain a master good and kind,
To me has been a friend,
For which I must my life resign,
My time is near an end.

Oh hark ! what means that dreadful sound !
It sinks deep in my soul,
It is the bell that sounds my knell,
How solemn is the toll.

See thousands are assembled
Around the fatal place,
To gaze on my approaching,
And witness my disgrace.

There many sympathising hearts,
Who feel another's woe,
Even now appears in sorrow,
For my sad overthrew.

Think of the aged man I slew,
Then pity's at an end,
I robb'd him of property and life,
And the poor man of a friend.

Let pilfering passions not intrude,
For to had you prepare,
From step to step it will delude,
And bring you to despair,
Think of the wretched Courvoisier,
Who thus dies on a tree,
A death of shame, I've sought to blame,
But my own dishonest.

Mercy on earth I'll not implore,
To crave it would be vain,
My hands are dyed with human gore,
None can wash it from thence,
But the merits of a Saviour,
Whose mercy alone I crave,
Good Christians pray, as thus I die,
I may his pardon have.

PAUL & Co., Printers, 2, 3, Monmouth Court Seven Dials.

The duel between the Earl of Cardigan and Captain Tuckett—"Two military cads, Sir, who met on Wimbledon Common, September 12, 1840, and had a couple of shots at each other with rifle pistols, when on the second firing my Earl hit the Captain very near to that part he used to sit upon, then a signal was given and up went the medical chap, Sir James Edward Anderson, especially engaged for the part at an enormous expense, and said the Capt'n had better be taken home to his mother and put to bed. Yes, Sir, that job made a bit of a blaize for three or four months, that is up to the time the Earl played the principal part in the farce of being tried in the House of Lords before his Peers, when they—Earl being a pal of their'n—pronounced him 'Not Guilty, upon their Honour and Glory, Hallelujah Amen.' You see, Sir, my Earl of Cardigan was no favourite of the people, and all us street-patterer's made the most we could out of that fact ; we let him have it to-rights, I can tell you, and song after song, and 'cock,' or catchpenny after catchpenny, was printed in quick sticks. Yes, and they all sold well, I can tell you."

We have shown that one of Catnach's sisters, Mrs. Anne —baptized Nancy, married a soldier—a Waterloo man, named Joseph Ryle, with whom she went to India, where she had one daughter, Marion Martha, who afterwards inherited Catnach's property, and is now the wife of Mr. Robert Palmer Harding, a London accountant. Mary Catnach became the wife of a sailor named Haines, who was a mate in one of the training ships stationed at Portsmouth, and they kept a shop in Gosport for the sale of small wares and ballads, acting as a sort of wholesale agent for the surrounding district for Catnach. Elizabeth married Mr. Benton, who was for many years a confidential servant, assistant treasurer, and box-book keeper to Mr. Alfred Bunn, of Covent Garden and Drury Lane Theatres. At one period Benton and his wife lived with Mr. Bunn in St. James' Place, St. James' Street, Mrs. Benton acting in the capacity of housekeeper. During several seasons Mr. Benton was also treasurer for the proprietors of Vauxhall Gardens, afterwards he filled the same office for E. T. Smith —*Dazzle Smith !* at Cremorne Gardens. He died abroad in 1856. At the present time of writing, his widow is living in the London district. Julia, the youngest sister, was a little loose in her intellect and morals—" She loved not wisely, but too well ! " but ultimately married and settled in Sydney, N. S. W. Of all the sisters, Mrs. Ryle was the only one that could manage her brother best. She was of a motherly turn of mind, and was particularly shrewd and modest in her manners and conversation, and of active business habits.

For the purpose of clearing up, if possible, some contradictory statements, a few years ago we made personal search through the musty-fusty and red-tapeism of Doctors' Commons for the Will and Testament—or " LAST DYING SPEECH " of " James Catnach, of Dancer's Hill, South Mimms, in the county of Middlesex, Gentleman, formerly of Monmouth Court, Monmouth Street, Printer," an office copy of which, together with Probate and Administration Act, we give below, by which it will be seen that the Personal Effects are sworn to as under three hundred pounds. But this gives us no idea of the value of his " Freehold, Copyhold, or Leasehold Estate " mentioned in the body of the Will.

" Extracted from the principal Registry of Her Majesty's Court of Probate.

" In the Prerogative Court of Canterbury—

· "**This is the last Will and Testament** of me JAMES CATNACH of Dancers Hill South Mimms in the County of Middlesex Gentleman formerly of Monmouth Court Monmouth Street Printer I direct that my just debts funeral and testamentary expences be paid as soon as conveniently may be after my decease and subject thereto I give devise and bequeath all my real and personal Estate whatever and wheresoever and of, what nature or kind soever to my Sister Anne the Widow of Joseph Ryle now residing in Monmouth Court aforesaid her heirs executors and administrators according to the nature and· qualities thereof respectively   In trust nevertheless for her Daughter Marion Martha Ryle her heirs executors administrators and assigns respectively when she shall attain the age of twenty one years absolutely with power in the meantime to apply the rents interest dividends or proceeds thereof for and towards the maintenance education and advancement of the said Marion Martha Ryle and notwithstanding the private means of my said Sister may be adequate to such purpose but if the said Marion·Martha Ryle shall depart this life before she shall attain the age of twenty one years then I give devise and bequeath all my said real and personal Estate to my said Sister her heirs executors administrators and assigns absolutely I hereby direct that during the minority of the

said Marion Martha Ryle it shall be lawful for the said Anne
Ryle her heirs executors administrators to demise or lease
all or any part of my freehold copyhold or leasehold Estate
for any term consistent with the tenure thereof not
exceeding twenty one years so that on every such demise
the best yearly rent be reserved that can be obtained for the
property which shall be therein comprised without taking
any fine or premium and so that the tenant or lessee be not
made dispunishable for waste I hereby nominate constitute
and appoint my said Sister sole Executrix of this my Will
and hereby revoking all former and other Wills by me at
any time heretofore made I declare this to be my last Will
and Testament In witness whereof I have hereunto set my
hand the twenty second day of January one thousand
eight hundred and thirty nine—JAMES CATNACH—
Signed and acknowledged by the above named James
Catnach as and for his last Will and Testament in the
presence of us present at the same time who in his presence
and the presence of each other have hereunto set our names
as Witnesses—William Kinsey 13 Suffolk St. Pall Mall
Solr.—Wm. Tookey his Clerk."

[THE PROBATE AND ADMINISTRATION ACT.]

" EXTRACTED from the principal Registry
of Her Majesty's Court of Probate
" In the Prerogative Court of Canterbury—
April, 1842.

" JAMES CATNACH—Ou the second day of April
administration (with the Will annexed) of the Goods
Chattels and Credits of James Catnach formerly of
Monmouth Court Monmouth Street Printer but late of
Dancers Hill South Mimms both in the county of Middle-
sex Gentleman deceased was granted to William Kinsey
Esquire the Curator or Guardian lawfully assigned to Marion
Martha Ryle Spinster a Minor the Niece and usufructuary

Universal Legatee until she shall attain the age of twenty one years and the absolute Universal Legatee on attaining that age named in the said Will for the use and benefit of the said Minor and until she shall attain the age of twenty one years having been first sworn duly to administer Anne Ryle Widow the Sister sole Executrix Universal Legatee In trust and the contingent universal Legatee named in the said Will and also the natural and lawful Mother and next of kin of the said minor having first renounced the probate and execution of the said Will and the Letters of administration (with the said Will annexed) of the Goods of the said deceased and also the Curation or Guardianship of the said Minor and consented (as by Acts of Court appear).— *EFFECTS UNDER THREE HUNDRED POUNDS.*

It is gratifying to be able to record that what the late Mr. Catnach was to the masses in the way of news provider some forty years ago, the penny papers are now, with this exception, that the former tended to lower and degrade their pursuit after knowledge, the latter, on the contrary, improve and elevate them, while they amuse and instruct all who peruse their contents. With the march of intellect, and the thirst for knowledge blended with the desire for truth, out went, to a great extent, the penny broad-sheet. Several persons made the attempt to revive it long after the death of the great original Jemmy Catnach, but without success.

INDEX.

Brighton: A. G. LEE, Printer, 45, Market Street.

ghtning Source UK Ltd.
ton Keynes UK
W05f1910300517
339UK00017B/648/P